One Man,
One Voice

One Man, One Voice

CHARLES MORGAN, JR.

HOLT, RINEHART and WINSTON   New York

Published by Holt, Rinehart and Winston,
383 Madison Avenue, New York, New York 10017.

Published simultaneously in Canada by Holt, Rinehart
and Winston of Canada, Limited.

Library of Congress Cataloging in Publication Data

Morgan, Charles Jr., 1930–
  One man, one voice.

    1. Morgan, Charles Jr., 1930– 2. Lawyer—United
States—Biography. I. Title.
KF373.M567A34   342′.73′0850924 [B] 78-12590
ISBN 0-03-013961-9

Designer: A. Christopher Simon
Printed in the United States of America
10 9 8 7 6 5 4 3 2 1

If a man were permitted to make all the ballads, he need
not care who should make the laws of a nation.

—ANDREW FLETCHER, an eighteenth-century
Scottish political writer

The author deeply appreciates the assistance of the world's best editor, Burroughs Mitchell, and of Donald Hutter, who rivals him. In an early stage of this book, two Mississippians, Patricia M. Derian and Jane Watkins, read the part then completed and made suggestions, all of which were appreciated and some of which were followed. And, as far as appreciation is concerned, my agent, Gerard F. McCauley, deserves much. He obtained for me a fine contract and what was, for an ACLU lawyer, a whopping advance.

CHARLES MORGAN, JR.
Washington Lawyer

Preface

Almost forty years ago, a law professor named J. Ed ("Judge Ed") Livingston won his first nomination to be chief justice of Alabama's highest court. That was May 7, 1940, and on that night, as they counted ballots in Alabama (and no doubt stole a few), the American Civil Liberties Union's board of directors was meeting in New York City to try, judge, and expel a founder of the organization, Elizabeth Gurley Flynn, because she was a real-live Communist. They tried her on charges which I believe set the pattern for cold-war liberalism. The expulsion of Elizabeth Gurley Flynn was a major event in American history which hardly anybody knows about.

I was ten years old in 1940, but the reality of conservative law professors like Judge Ed and "liberals" like those who judged Miss Flynn was to affect much of my life. I am less than reverent about lawyers and liberals. I know us.

For a quarter-century Judge Ed presided in Alabama. He signed my certificate to practice law. As the pillar of the state's legal community, he taught the people—especially lawyers and judges—by his example to be "practical." And that was exactly the lesson preached by pragmatic liberalism. The tolerance of great fortunes in a democratic society requires "practicality" of the liberals. But liberalism's "Is it right?" directly conflicts with pragmatism's "Does it work?" Liberalism assumes that if you do right, good will follow, even when the ultimate outcome cannot be rationally foreseen. Liberalism requires faith. The running mate of pragmatism, cynicism, undercuts faith, and when liberals describe themselves as "pragmatic," they tout their weakness as their strength. I still believe that in a democracy, idealism is realism. The ideal is the *only* reality.

In the Birmingham church bombing on September 15, 1963, four black girls were killed. The next day, in a speech, I condemned Birmingham's silence. That message propelled me north. It also gave me the title of my first book—*A Time to Speak*—and minor status in the culture called "liberal."

Some of my friends have tried their best to rescue me from the "liberal" labeling. One night during the 1972 Democratic convention, I was sighted by Ruby Folsom Ellis Austin, "Big Jim" Folsom's sister. Clutching her drink in one hand, she threw her other arm around me in a half nelson.

"Chuck! Chuck Morgan!" she cried. "You and George are just going to have to kiss and make up."

Ruby's daughter, Cornelia, had married George Wallace. I like both mother and daughter.

Big Ruby's conversational tones carry thirty feet. "You know, Chuck, you and George have a lot in common."

As a crowd gathered, I found myself counting the things we had in common. Ruby grabbed for one.

"George just hates Comminists and so do you, don't you, Chuck?"

I demurred.

"I just knew you hated Comminists." Ruby paused. "You know, I've been defending you for twenty years, Chuck. You taught my boy, Charles, economics at the university and gave him a passing grade."

~~~~~~~~~

During the civil rights movement, the Vietnam War, the Watergate case, and the impeachment campaign, my clients uncompromisingly relied upon truth to free us from history's fictions. To them, to the hundreds of clients whose cases are not recounted here, and to the underpaid lawyers, secretaries, and other employees of the ACLU whom I overworked, this book is dedicated. They have understood what Tom Paine meant when he said, "A long habit of not thinking a thing *wrong*, gives it a superficial appearance of being *right*, and raises at first a formidable outcry in defense of custom. But the tumult soon subsides. Time makes more converts than reason. . . ."

In *A Time to Speak* I wrote of Birmingham: "The decent burghers looked back at the bunkers and trench graves . . . and said, 'We didn't know.' What they meant was, 'We didn't care enough to know.' " My wife, Camille, has always cared enough. The late Edward King, black, worked for her father for forty years. Most folks thought his name was Ed *Porter*. With blacks, what they did was who they were. But Camille knew Ed's last name. As he helped us pack for one of our several moves, Ed summed up my dependence by saying: "That Miss Camille can lift the other end of anything."

And has.

So this book is, most of all, for Camille.

PART
ONE

1

"Oh, yes," Roger N. Baldwin said to me, "you're the young man who's going south. We sent a man south in the 1930s. He lasted about six weeks, as I recall."

I had just met the spry, leathery, eighty-year-old at a 1964 fall board meeting of the American Civil Liberties Union in New York City. They wanted to expand and had hired me to open their southern regional office in Atlanta.

Baldwin, a Harvard graduate and social worker, had served a stint in jail as a comfortable, if conscientious, objector to World War I. In 1920, with an amalgam of liberals and a sprinkling of Socialists, conservatives, and Communists, he had founded the ACLU and become its first executive director.

I suppose it is an attribute of my insularity that before I went to work for the ACLU I had never heard his name.

The ACLU board was dominated by members from the Manhattan Stockade, with a few from the Far West (eastern New Jersey) and the Deep South (Washington, D.C.). Some had served for decades. Their meetings were frequent and friendly, like Lions Club luncheons in small southern towns.

3

Apparently Baldwin did not expect me to last in the South. I had a different perspective. I had graduated from high school in Birmingham and from the University of Alabama. I had practiced law in Birmingham for eight years, leaving when I could no longer live there and work for equal civil rights. For twelve months we had made our home in northern Virginia. But when the ACLU's executive director, John de J. Pemberton, Jr., offered me a ticket south, I grabbed it. They were willing to pay me to do what I wanted to do, and even if the budget wasn't much, I've always believed that if you can't go first-class, go second-class, or even steerage—but go.

∾∾∾∾∾∾∾

On March 11, 1930, I was born kicking and screaming into the Episcopal Church, the Democratic party, the Great Depression, and Our Southern Way of Life.

My mother had the southern accent of western Kentucky (Paducah), which had been slave country. My father grew up near Prestonsburg in the eastern Kentucky mountains. He had a near-reverence for "education" and for "The Company" (the National Life and Accident Insurance Company). He recounted his experiences from boyhood to me and my brother, John. They included ten cents pay a day for shoving logs away from the banks of Beaver Creek and back into the current so they would pass downstream to the sawmill. He told us how he had worked his way out of those mountains selling photographs. He understood the hard world of one pair of shoes a year, of mountainside farmland and coal mines and railroad section gangs. He remembered the differences between his boyhood and the middle-class life into which he carried us. Love caused him to reject the fundamentalist Baptist Church and a basic tenet of the Christian faith: he couldn't understand, let alone worship, a Father who had the power to stop the mob but stood by and let them kill His Son.

His sense of fairness helped lead me into civil rights practice. But he feared for me.

The blacks I knew as a child were maids and yardmen. I grew up knowing not to mistreat them and not to take advantage even of whites who were poor and unlearned. My father told me never to work for a company that lied and refused to pay its claims. I remember one night during the Depression when he came home heartsick. He had finally fired an agent who wouldn't refrain from calling policyholders "niggers."

He felt sorry for the white man. "I've told him time and time again," my father said. "But we take the poor devils' money and we have to treat them like human beings."

One of my earliest lessons was "Never say 'nigger.'" When I was eight and he was five, my brother, John, got into a debate with a five-year-old neighbor who looked up at Irene Logan, our maid, and who, as Irene stared stony-faced, shouted: "You're a nigger!"

"She is not a nigger!" John shouted back.

"She is too a nigger!"

That was the way the lore and language of the South came to us. Casually.

In 1944 I was fourteen. We were at war with the Nazis. That fall my parents sent me to Kentucky Military Institute. An hour after I arrived on campus, upperclassmen confronted me with "Repeat the rules of conduct for a new cadet."

I didn't know what they were talking about. "Assume the position!" one of them ordered. He removed his saber, intending to apply its flat side to my backside.

This initial encounter with the military ended in a rough-and-tumble stalemate, but that night—my first away from home—as I lay awake in the top tier of a three-bunk bed listening to taps and the long, low diesel honk of a nearby train, I cried myself to sleep.

A year later I slipped from my room at midnight, dashed across the golf course in a cold and blinding rain, hiked up my thumb, and hitched a ride with a trucker. Later, when I was discovered in a Cincinnati suburb, "laying low" with friends, KMI requested that the local police return me to campus. That

done, KMI promptly expelled me. From then on I had no difficulty understanding the military mind: I had run away to get
away and they had brought me back to kick me out.

During the summer of 1945 my parents had moved from Fort
Thomas, Kentucky, to Birmingham, Alabama, so it was to a new
hometown that I was kicked. After a long and lonely train ride I
was greeted with open arms and "another chance." My parents
filled my life with other chances, always insisting that there
would be no forgiveness for lying. "Tell the truth," they said.
"Tell the truth even when it hurts." In Birmingham it began to
hurt, as I began to understand the politics of race.

Public officials there spoke of progress, but I could see sprawl-
ing shantytowns. While they spoke of happiness among "our
colored people," I learned that white folks' happiness too often
came at the expense of blacks and sometimes in their pursuit.

One night my friend Bill Conway told of hitchhiking into
Birmingham from "over the mountain." Picked up by friends on
their way to "egg niggers," Conway watched in horror as the
front-seat passenger thrust out the window the aerial he had torn
from a parked automobile. As they sped past a bus stop where a
black soldier stood waiting, the aerial snaked through the darkness and cut across that soldier's face.

I never went "eggin' niggers," but *many* of my upper-
middle-class contemporaries did. Later, nice white people
blamed racial violence on "poor white trash." Later still, black
children randomly lashed out at whites who walked big-city
streets. And I remembered those nights at Birmingham's
Pickwick Club when "stags" ("nice" white boys without dates)
returned to our high school dances after intermission, sometimes with a swagger, sometimes with an exaggerated air of
unconcern, and told us that they had been out "eggin' "!

Even though truth was the ultimate threat to Our Southern
Way of Life, our parents insisted that we tell it. Most of us
desperately tried. Even when we drank beer we did so where
they asked no questions, for it never occurred to us to forge
identity cards.

College and law school educated us into "sweet reason" and

"understanding." As we learned the truth about The Issue, "two-sides-to-everything," "matters-of-degree," "shades-of-gray," and "fine-lines" reasoning were required to make "tolerance" of Our Southern Way of Life possible, and to immobilize most of us.

During the years of college and McCarthyism I learned that the Fifth Amendment was basic to truth telling. If the answer to "Are you now or have you ever been . . ." or "Did you . . .?" required a lie, you didn't have to answer. Many liberals seemed to agree with that, but . . . They always seemed able to find "buts," for simple answers such as "yes," "no," and "I refuse" required great sacrifice.

Years later, at Mike Palm's restaurant on Capitol Hill, Senator Sam J. Ervin explained to me why southerners' values are different. The Watergate hearings were under way. I listened carefully. The honest, straightforward old man with the dancing eyebrows seemed to peer into the past. He slowly said, "Our heroes were men of honor. Lee and Stonewall Jackson and J. E. B. Stuart were men of honor. Since our heroes lost, winning never was as important to us as telling the truth and personal honor."

Sam Ervin was right, but he was also wrong: since the docking of the first slave ship and the introduction of that kind of "property" into American life, "that race question" had made liars out of almost all of us—even Ervin and Jackson, Lee, and J. E. B. Stuart.

Liberal corporate lawyers devised our nation's "containment policy." There was nothing novel about it. After the 1831 Nat Turner rebellion, the Old Confederacy lowered a cotton curtain to keep out hostile ideas and people. After the war and Reconstruction, the North and South termed their détente "Reconciliation." But the ideological wall, like the iron and bamboo curtains, extended as a "strategic crescent" along rivers and state lines from Maryland to Texas. The "border states"—Kentucky, Maryland, and West Virginia—were satellite or demilitarized zones.

On the Deep South side of the cotton curtain there were

recurrent rumors of invasions. One Easter Sunday in the early 1960s, at our Episcopal church, the rector stationed me in the parking lot. I was to let him know if blacks came and were turned away by the ushers. He would have halted the services unless the intruders were seated, but as on every other Easter Sunday, rumors came, but blacks didn't.

During my childhood, peacetime soldiers were victims of discrimination, thought of as bums and ne'er-do-wells. I remember hearing that judges offered troublesome young men an option—the army or jail.

In 1940, when I was ten, Congress enacted the first peacetime draft. The attack on Pearl Harbor came a year later. After that, draftees (mostly young men) would never be able to forget their war. They won against racism in Europe. At home their government locked up Americans of Japanese descent. Besides victory, that Wonderful War provided many of them with their first paycheck, their first drink, their first woman, even their first chance to drive an automobile. After the war their investment of time paid financial dividends. They received mustering-out pay. Some states provided them with bonuses. They joined the "52–20 club" and received fifty-two twenty-dollar paychecks to help them readjust to "civilian" life. They attended college under the GI Bill of Rights. "Veterans' preference" moved them ahead of equally qualified competitors for government jobs.* They kept their military life insurance and even received low-interest GI loans with which to purchase their first homes.

If they were neither wounded nor maimed, and lost neither

---

*Race and sex sometimes are used to provide applicants with bonus points for acquiring jobs or admission into educational institutions. Because veterans lost from their careers the years which they spent in the service, "veterans' preference" was universally praised. Similar aid to dark-skinned applicants whose careers have been set back by national discrimination is termed "affirmative action," "quotas," "preferential treatment," and "discrimination in reverse."

family nor friends, the World War II years *were* wonderful years—the best of their lives.

Many pragmatic liberals said peacetime conscription would democratize the military. Instead, the draft made soldiering respectable and that militarized the democracy. Within the electorate there are 30 million veterans—our presidents, cabinet members, judges, senators, representatives, columnists, editors, commentators, corporate, foundation, and labor executives, and university teachers. Their common experience shaped their character and—as they turned Athens into Sparta—our lives.

I was sixteen, in 1946, when Big Jim Folsom, the six-feet-eight-inch-tall man in the white suit, spoke of democracy as a natural equalizer. He even sought to abolish the poll tax and reapportion the state legislature.

The pamphlets said he was a "Communist" and a "CIO puppet." To rich whites, near whom we lived, he was "foolish," "trashy," and "ordinary." They *all* seemed to despise and fear James E. Folsom and the string-band-gathered crowds of illiterate farmers he drew in his quest for the governorship.

Birmingham's rich—Folsom called them "Big Mules"—were in-state representatives of the absentee-owned coal, iron, and steel industry, and we learned while young the truth of the phrase "At United States Steel, we're involved." Steel's allies were textile mill owners and Black Belt farmers whose primary concern was the maintenance of a cheap, docile, unskilled labor force.*

By the time I studied law and instructed in American economic history at the University of Alabama, I understood that

---

*"Black Belt" refers to a geographic area. The descriptive phrase grew from the color of the section's rich soil, not the skin color of the inhabitants. But cotton required black labor, and the Black Belt is where the bulk of the South's black population lived. Because of outdated legislative apportionment laws and shifts in population, the Alabama legislature was controlled by the few white voters of this conservative, overrepresented rural area of the state.

Folsom's "simplistic" dreams were no more "Marxist" in origin than were those of Jefferson, Jackson, and Lincoln. Each believed in the people's birthright claim to the nation's land and its resources. Folsom also knew that even though the Constitution requires government to pay for what it takes, it doesn't mention capitalism, communism, socialism, free enterprise, or any other economic system. That knowledge, Folsom's 1944 Democratic national convention delegate vote for Henry A. Wallace for Vice President, and his appeals to illiterate whites and blacks really did frighten "the better class" who lived Our Southern Way of Life.

Few blacks could vote. Many of those who could seemed to "scratch where it don't itch and laugh when it ain't funny." But they, like poor whites, knew they had been done wrong. And like poor whites, they expressed their hopes in pie-in-the-sky hymns, bitter humor, and votes for Big Jim.

When I was twenty-one (that was in 1951) I worked with George C. Hawkins, Folsom's legal adviser during his first term (1947–51), in the successful statewide campaign to repeal the cumulative cost-of-voting feature of the poll tax. Under Alabama's constitution the state charged its twenty-one-to-forty-five-year-old citizens $1.50 per annum for the right to vote. Missed payments became debts against the vote. At age forty-five a first-time registrant automatically owed the state the cumulated total of $36.00. As an additional deterrent to voting, the poll-tax-payer had to remember to make on-time annual payments. This required a fall visit to the white man's courthouse.

Hawkins was elected to the state house of representatives as an anti-industrialist, anti-Black Belt, pro-poor folks legislator. Immediately, he proposed a constitutional amendment to repeal the poll tax. His fellow representative and former law school classmate, George C. Wallace, cosigned it, but Wallace was from the Black Belt. When he felt pressure from the home folks, he asked Hawkins to remove his name from the bill.

The people ratified a compromise proposal. That cut the maximum time for which back tax could be charged to two years and thereby lowered the cost of the vote to three dollars.

Since veterans were exempt from the tax, its discrimination fell upon the nonveteran poor and women. When my wife, Camille, turned twenty-one, she faced Jefferson County's (Birmingham's) registrar, the late Gus Thompson. He was then so old that he might once have played dominoes with Robert E. Lee. Ol' Gus asked, so Camille explained her opposition to the poll tax. He lectured her on the need to keep the "nigger vote" down and public education, to which the poll tax went, up. But as a white southern gentleman Ol' Gus couldn't flunk a poll-tax-paying white lady. Muttering at Camille's lack of ancestral reverence, he entered her name on the voter roll.

George Hawkins, unlike his law school classmate, George Wallace, was first a trial lawyer and second a politician. After law school Wallace lived on one government check or another or on campaign funds, but Hawkins, who represented industrialized Etowah County's (Gadsden's) CIO unions when others dared not, built a law practice despite the county's blue-ribbon jury roster, which resembled the membership roll of the local country club. Jurors were "well educated," affluent, white, middle-aged, and middle-minded men, so the only patronage Hawkins asked for during Folsom's first term was the right to name the members of the County Jury Commission. Usually these minor posts were filled by courthouse hangers-on.

Big Jim assented. Hawkins's jury commissioners set up temporary tables at plant gates to make it easy for steel and rubber workers to sign up. Overnight, juries became cross-sectional and the quality of justice for average and poor whites changed. Anti-labor violence subsided and the political power of personal injury lawyers, of whom Hawkins was number one, grew in direct proportion to the monetary judgments awarded their clients—and the fees awarded them.

As with George Hawkins I got to know George Wallace while I was still an undergraduate student at the University of Alabama. In our first conversation he put down our two senators, Lister Hill and John Sparkman, by telling me that they were not "real liberals."

Two years later, I was national committeeman of the state's

Young Democrats. Wallace, an aging if perpetual Young Democrat, was chairman of our delegation to the 1953 national convention in St. Paul, Minnesota.

He expressed no concern at my Credentials Committee vote which unseated Texas Governor Allan Shivers's oil-rich Dixiecrat delegation. They arrived in an airplane. I favored the Loyalists. They came in a chartered Greyhound bus. And without my Alabama vote on the committee the Dixiecrats had too few supporters to bring a minority report to the floor.

Confused as to which candidate for president of the national organization stood on the "right" side of "that race question," Wallace, to be on the safe side, made a speech nominating Jack Smith of Slocomb, Alabama. I watched Wallace as he shook hands and smiled and listened to our Yankee colleagues voluntarily confess that they "understood" the South's peculiar problem. On that foray north, none of us sensed any liberal commitment to racial equality. The young on-the-way-up pragmatists we met spent so much of their time "understanding" us, that we came to understand that they had few beliefs of their own.

In 1954 Folsom sought a second term. The two Georges went to work. Wallace was Folsom's south Alabama campaign manager; Hawkins managed north Alabama. Folsom won again. Two weeks later the Supreme Court announced its school desegregation decision.

Hawkins remained basically "liberal," but Wallace was a Black Belter and his liberalism ran skin-color deep.

Sandy-haired with fair skin, Hawkins was thoughtful and deliberate; the short, black-haired, campaign-tanned Wallace was fast-talking and instinctive.

Hawkins trusted almost everyone. He drank warm beer.

Wallace trusted no one. He drank Coca-Cola.

Hawkins liked the good life. Wallace, his life a perpetual campaign, hardly paused long enough to read a menu, let alone a lawbook. He lived out of an automobile trunk. To him a twenty-five-cent hamburger steak was more quickly eaten and, therefore, better than a New York strip, so he differed from mortal politicians. He was running, running, running. His physical movement attracted crowds and lent force to his words. On a flatbed truck or in a hotel lobby he bobbed and weaved in rhythm as he talked, feinting, jabbing here and there, searching for an opening, always moving, rocking backward and forward on his feet, his life lived to the beat of the Deep South's ancient political tune. To me he appeared to be the Sammy Glick of American politics. If I had asked, "Why do you run, George?" he might have considered power with introspection and responded, "Because it is there."

~~~~~~~~

On January 2, 1958, I opened my own law office in Birmingham with law school friend George V. Eyrand, Jr., as my partner. Approximately twenty-four hours later I hit the campaign trail.

Folsom couldn't succeed himself. Hawkins, Wallace, and Attorney General John Patterson were running for governor, and I was running Hawkins's campaign.

I was twenty-seven, in my third year out of law school and fresh out of the law firm of Dumas, O'Neal, and Hayes. I had left their antiseptic, respectable world of corporate and municipal-bond law with the concurrence of Camille, whom I'd known since high school, dated, and married at the University of Alabama.

"Country Boy" Eddie Burns tried to sing the Hawkins message across. After the first few hundred recorded renditions of the campaign lyrics which my University of Alabama roommate, friend, and now conservative writer, Victor Gold, wrote to the tune of "Movin' On," all of us were ready to move someplace.

"Fourteen men in the governor's race, watch George Hawkins, he'll set the pace, he's movin' on, he's amovin' on. . . ." sang Country Boy from the loudspeaker truck which preceded us into every town. But Hawkins was "soft" on The Issue so he was not to become governor. He did become president *pro tempore* of the state senate, where he remained independent of Wallace. In 1958 not even Wallace and his high-priced Grand Ole Opry stars could keep the pace set by our "fighting, effective" segregationist attorney general, John Patterson.

In state campaigns at that time, to have been "caught" in unsegregated secret meetings with Alabama's black leaders would have been akin to behind-the-lines capture, but their secret influence could swing 30,000 to 50,000 black votes. In a close election they could provide a front-runner a majority, or could move a back-runner up and into a runoff.

Arthur D. Shores, whose home held the state's record for being the most bombed, is the dean of Alabama's black lawyers. I had met him and his young cousin Orzell Billingsley, Jr., at the courthouse, where black lawyers could not even enter the coffee shop. Upstairs, in the county law library, they were restricted to one room into which the elderly white law librarian brought the books they requested; so the courthouse was a place to meet, but it was no place to talk.

Orzell and I were to become good friends. A morning visit to his office in the black Masonic Temple building was lucid but relatively uneventful. A late-afternoon get-together was a thigh-slapping, tornadic event. A handsome man and a consummate actor, Orzell moves his face from rage to a broad smile with a looseness which belies his intelligence. I have met no brighter man—let alone lawyer.

We did our drinking "across the tracks," usually at Orzell's house, which stood beside the railroad tracks, so near to them that it literally shook when trains approached. In Birmingham the lines were so clearly drawn that it was against the law even to fish or to play checkers with blacks, let alone to "socialize" or plot with them. But plot we did, and one night after a few drinks, Orzell even christened me his daughter Shawn's Great White Godfather.

Orzell and his lawyer friends were black, so their clients were black. The justice system was white, so, when automobile accident and other civil jury cases came to them, black lawyers shared fees with the across-town white trial lawyers to whom they sent their injured clients.*

Orzell Billingsley, Sr., was the first black promoted to mine foreman by Birmingham's United States Steel subsidiary, so there wasn't much he didn't know about coal mines or life in general. He couldn't read or write, but he made it possible for his son to graduate from college and law school at a time when the economics of family survival required that millions of white as well as black southern children leave classrooms to enter cotton fields.

To supplement his income, Mr. Billingsley, Sr., sold a little bootleg whiskey. One night, as he walked beside the road near his home, he was struck and seriously injured by an automobile. The intoxicated black driver claimed he'd purchased the whiskey that made him drunk from Mr. Billingsley and, consequently, the injured victim was the real culprit.

Mr. Billingsley's medical bills were substantial. When the driver said no to reimbursement, Orzell, Jr., filed suit in state court. But he knew that an all-white jury would buy the driver's story. Most whites were anxious to believe any story one black man told about another if it was humorous or ironic or had a moral to it.

Besides, whites would consider Mr. Billingsley's injuries less serious than would blacks. That was one effect of white man's justice. Another was different standards of punishment for crimes: crimes by blacks against whites called for the harshest penalties; whites against whites, lighter sentences; whites against blacks, lighter still; and since, to whites, black lives were

---

*Gunnar Myrdal, in *An American Dilemma*, put it harshly: "Negro clients know that a Negro lawyer is not much use in a southern courtroom. Lower-class Negroes sometimes believe that Negro lawyers are not permitted in courtrooms even where they are permitted."

Most injured blacks avoided black lawyers. They went directly to white lawyers to settle their claims or to plead their cases before white judges and juries.

worthless, for crimes by blacks against blacks the penalties were wrist slaps.

As early as 1950, Supreme Court Justice Robert H. Jackson "supposed" that blacks systematically excluded from juries could obtain a federal court order requiring their inclusion on state-court jury rolls. That would have resulted in integrated juries for all cases tried in the area, but since Reconstruction only one such suit had been reported, and even then no injunction had been issued.

To combat a death-penalty sentence, a black would occasionally challenge the exclusion of blacks from the grand and trial juries that considered his case, but even if the Supreme Court reversed the conviction, the racially exclusive jury system continued.

So, rusty and unused, a statutory remedy slumbered in the lawbooks while tens of thousands of white grand and trial jurors interrupted, judged, and often ended the lives of blacks.

Real change in the justice system was as likely to arise from the illicit sale of liquor as from Supreme Court suppositions, so Orzell and I supposed our way into a lawsuit to protect Mr. Billingsley from irony. Orzell filed in federal court seeking an injunction against the state court's jury officials. If they were forced by a federal judge to include a cross-section of the population on the jury roll, all of Jefferson County's state-court civil and criminal cases, not merely Mr. Billingsley's, would be tried before juries selected from that roll.

I would carry *Billingsley* v. *Clayton* with me to the ACLU. The court of appeals would use it to authorize jury desegregation cases. But it would rule against Mr. Billingsley on the merits. Orzell and I would count it a loss—until a few years later when the factual record in that lost case unexpectedly saved the life of another client, Caliph Washington, who helped us desegregate the prisons from his solitary cell on death row.

∽∽∽∽∽∽∽

In the spring of 1962 I entered a case in Talladega, Alabama, that grew out of the sit-ins. I defended the Reverend Norman C.

Jimerson and the Alabama Council on Human Relations. With local Ku Klux Klansmen as daily observers, the town, population 17,742, provided a *Bad Day at Black Rock* setting. The court-house drinking fountains had been turned off to keep blacks from drinking. Even the rest rooms were locked up to keep blacks from resting.

After students from the local black college, well mannered and dressed fit to be killed, "trespassed" at local drugstores, the local court judge enjoined them from "sittin'-in." My client Jimerson, a white American Baptist minister, had tried to establish local détente. He had commenced negotiations between students and store owners. He was enjoined along with the students. Before the outgoing Alabama attorney general, Mac-Donald Gallion, went out, the state tried to prove that the desire to purchase a Coca-Cola and to sit while drinking it was subversive and, according to some, "Communist inspired." I tried the case for two weeks and won it, but only because Alabama's incoming attorney general, Richmond M. Flowers, came in and dismissed the charges.

I don't believe I had met a Communist. (One never knows. My father-in-law insisted that they all wore horn-rimmed glasses.) So "Communists" were less bothersome to me than were people who wanted to lock them up. Them, I had met.

That trial led to my personal, unilateral disarmament. Court had adjourned. Early one evening I was driving the twenty miles from Talladega to Oxford, Alabama, where for a week the Holiday Inn had accepted us as tenants—until they discovered a defendant-tenant was black. I glanced into the rear-view mirror and thought of black baseball pitcher Satchel Paige's advice: "Don't look back. Someone might be gaining on you."

In my briefcase, under books and papers, I carred a .32-caliber revolver. If a Klucker had been gaining on me, I would have had to remove two law books to find the pistol. After shuffling through papers and legal pads I might have found the clip. With my right hand, I might have gotten the clip in—backward. Even if everything went perfectly, if the clip was correctly in and the safety off, I might have shot myself in the foot.

Worse than that, I might have shot my stalking adversary. Then the all-white Southern Justice System would have taken over, and it had been designed to convict all blacks and white folks who thought like me.

There was one satisfying episode in that period when racial bombings seemed no less natural than thunderstorms. One Saturday afternoon I answered the office telephone.

"Chuck, this is Carl. Meet me down front on the corner of Twenty-first and Second Avenue in twenty minutes sharp."

"Sure, Carl; want to tell me what the problem is?"

"No, no problem. Just be there."

Twenty minutes later, Carl ("Bear") Statum, the white, bald young labor leader, pulled up in front of the old Comer Building. In his early thirties, he weighed well over 200 pounds and stood about five feet ten inches tall, with his upper arms and size-eighteen neck bulging beyond the T-shirt which trapped them.

Friendly and jovial, Carl Statum liked to hunt and drink. He also liked working people, labor unions, poor white folks, politics, and me. He was not smiling.

A stranger, also unsmiling, sat in the front seat, staring straight ahead.

"Chuck, meet ———," Carl said, introducing us. I stuck out my hand. He grasped it limply, then quickly let it go.

"You know those bad threats you've been getting lately?" Carl barked. "This son of a bitch is the Kleagle and it's his Kluckers that've been doing the calling."

The silent man in the front seat stared straight ahead. Carl turned to him. "Tell him what I told you."

"He said if anything happened to you he'd kill me."

"How'd I say I'd do it?"

"You said you'd put your hands around my neck and squeeze my head off."

"Do you believe I'd do that?" Statum asked.

"Yes, sir. I do."

"Is he going to have any more trouble out of your people?"

"No, sir."

"Tell him!"

"Mr. Morgan,"—the frightened man shuddered as percepti-
bly as did Orzell's house when the freight trains passed by—
"you won't have a bit more trouble out of us."

〜〜〜〜〜〜〜

In Birmingham, real trouble came without warning. On September 16, 1963, the day after four little girls were killed in the
bombing of Birmingham's Sixteenth Street Baptist Church, in a
speech to the Young Men's Business Club, I accurately placed
the blame where it really belonged—with the community's "not
me!" leaders who professed loyalty to Our Southern Way of Life.

The theme of that speech was Who Threw That Bomb? An
Anxious Community Asks. The answer should have been, "We
all did it."

The speech ended: "Birmingham is not a dying city, it is
dead."

The national newspapers reported that speech. Victor Gold
telephoned from Falls Church, Virginia. "You've got to get out
of there! We've already talked with the principal of the children's school. Charles [our son] can be enrolled immediately."

We moved to Alexandria, where I finished writing *A Time to
Speak.* Aside from the advance from Evan Thomas at Harper
and Row, and the check from William B. Arthur at *Look* for an
article on Birmingham I co-authored with journalist Thomas B.
Morgan, we had no income. Hundreds of people had written,
cheering me on. Two had offered me jobs—Attorney General
Robert F. Kennedy and William P. Fidler, the general secretary
of the American Association of University Professors. Later
some of my liberal friends had a hard time understanding my
support of Bob Kennedy for President.*

---

*Even my secretary, Jane Gunthorpe, was a casualty of that speech. Her
courage and sense of humor enabled her to answer telephone bomb threats
courteously. But after we moved, even the Alabama state employment service
told her that since she had worked for me, she would be unable to find work in
Birmingham. One of my former clients gave her a job. On the night of

In January 1964, I went to work for the American Association of University Professors (AAUP), where I discovered that academic bureaucrats are addicted to writing memoranda "for the files"; that Washington lawyers, as an article of faith, never tried a case; and that Washington's well-educated liberals feared the ghost of Senator Joseph R. McCarthy.

Fidler wasn't afraid of much of anything and my work with him was enjoyable. But when Jack Greenberg, director-counsel of the NAACP Legal Defense Fund (LDF) telephoned one evening in the late spring of 1964 and asked if I wanted to help them out in the South, I said yes. I did ask him to wait while I asked Camille. She said she expected me to say yes. So, due to the admonitions of dinner guest Harry N. Cook, an Alabama friend who understood the intensity of my unpopularity and figured I'd soon get killed, and who wanted dinner served before I left, I ate before saying yes.

Jack Greenberg was one of the few northerners who understood or cared that the few white southern lawyers who accepted civil rights cases lost money on them and lost other practice as well. One hot July night, after the Civil Rights Act of 1964 had passed, Charles Jones, a black lawyer who worked for Greenberg, and I were eating in the coffee shop of Birmingham's Parliament House Hotel. My friend George Harduvel raced across from the lobby to greet me. He had discovered that I was in town when he overheard two white couples who had come into Michael's Restaurant across the street, having just stormed out of the Parliament House. "They said they didn't mind eating with 'niggers,' " George told me, laughing uproariously. "But eating with Chuck Morgan was more than they could stand."

President Kennedy's assassination, Jane telephoned us in tears from a Birmingham restaurant. The laughter and ribald jokes which ricocheted from the assassination were too much for her. I got her a job in Washington with the American Association of University Professors.

Northern liberal lawyers in major firms berated white southern lawyers for their refusal to take civil rights cases. Simultaneously, these liberals sent their paying clients' law business to Ivy League law school classmates who had joined the South's leading segregationist firms. The closet liberal members of those large Deep South law firms were locally identifiable by acts of minor rebellion, such as support for the arts and fluoridated drinking water and rejection of the Episcopal Church in favor of Unitarianism. But not one of them took a civil rights case. Ever.

As "moderates," they were busy "preserving their effectiveness." They saw themselves as tomorrow's senior partners. Then, they rationalized, they would be able to effect great change. More often than not, Ivy League–educated white southern lawyers simply became effectively respectable spokesmen for The Order.

They reminded me of an incident at a Birmingham party during a year when state legislators were stumbling over each other in the race to record their vote against blacks. The party was hosted by Hobart A. McWhorter, Jr., a conservative Birmingham friend whose Exeter, Yale, and Virginia law schooling failed to dull his sense of humor. I encountered a fellow guest, the moderate Ivy League–student son of an Ivy League–graduate state bar leader. The father, deferentially described as a "South-wide authority on the School Placement Act," had extolled its virtues in a lengthy paper delivered that afternoon to an Alabama State Bar Association meeting. The son knew my views. Despite my anger, I preferred moderate friends to outright enemies. And do-gooders to do-badders. Besides, I liked him. So in one of many nonconfrontational moments I told him that his father's message was "well written." Hobart half turned and laughed. "Yeah, but he could have said, 'I hate niggers' and sat down. He wouldn't have had to cite a case."

In mid-June, 1964, northern liberal parents had begun to end their rationalizations. At the Western College for Women in Oxford, Ohio, I cited reality to the first wave of 650 Mississippi Freedom Summer Volunteers. Sponsored by the National

Council of Churches and allied civil rights groups, my task was to introduce these mostly young people to the Deep South's harshest reality—the risk of death—for it was likely that some of them would be killed.

In her *Letters from Mississippi,* Elizabeth Sutherland quoted a message home from a young man named Mike: "Tuesday evening was a talk by Charles Morgan. . . . He warned us gravely about the dangers of Mississippi. . . . He ended by solemnly stating that he admired our courage. From a guy like that who has seen a lot of fire, this was really frightening. We have all lived under the increasing weight of fear, and the struggle to come to terms with the possibility of death consumes much of our emotional energy. . . ." *

And their parents' emotional energy, too.

On Father's Day, June 21, 1964, Andrew Goodman, twenty, Michael Schwerner, twenty-four, both white New Yorkers, and James Chaney, twenty-one, black, of Meridian, Mississippi, drove from Meridian to Philadelphia, Mississippi, to investigate the burning of a black church. As they changed a flat tire, Chief Deputy Cecil Price of Neshoba County arrested them for speeding. Held at the county jail for several hours, they were released at about 10:30 P.M. Waiting Klansmen followed them for several miles. Then the law, in the person of Chief Deputy Price, red light flashing, ordered their Ford station wagon to the roadside.

At noon the next day, reports that the young men were missing came to the FBI. On Tuesday their burned-up station wagon

---

*After I spoke, others taught those who still wanted to spend their summer in Mississippi how to stay alive. As Mike went on to write: "Just the security precautions are scary: beware of cars without tags—they are always danger; never go out alone; never go out after dark; never be the last out of a mass meeting; watch out for cops without their badge; listen for an accelerating car outside; if you wake up at night thinking there is danger, wake everybody up. There seems to be a very good type instinct for preservation. Some of the Negro field secretaries I was talking to informally told how they played like real Uncle Toms to the cops when in danger. . . ."

was found thirteen miles northeast of Philadelphia on a dirt road off State Highway 21.

As soon as the search got under way, Colonel Al Lingo, director of the Alabama Highway Patrol, said that the three young men had been spotted in his state. "They've gone to Cuba" became a common refrain.

On Monday, June 22, I was back in Oxford, Ohio, to speak to the second group of volunteers. During the previous week, Andrew Goodman had sat in the front row. But that night at the Cincinnati airport a former Alabama client, Student Non-Violent Coordinating Committee (SNCC) worker Bob Zellner, black Mississippian Fannie Lou Hamer, and I stood by as Mickey Schwerner's wife began her sad journey to Mississippi.

The urgency of black civil rights worker Jimmy Travis's words shouted in the auditorium earlier that day, "We've got to change the system! To change the system!," echoed in my mind as we stood there watching one more national tragedy unfold.

Seven weeks later, after an unsuccessful search by hundreds of Marines, FBI agents proved that the three young men were not in Cuba or Alabama. They did that by digging their bodies out of a newly built dirt dam six miles south of Philadelphia.

≈≈≈≈≈≈≈

Later that summer, still working for the NAACP Legal Defense Fund and living in northern Virginia, I received the call from Jack Pemberton, the ACLU's executive director, to ask why I had not applied to be director of the southern regional office. He had hired Aryeh Neier to be development director. Neier visualized the southern office as a way to enter the civil rights movement. The idea was not new. According to the January 16, 1957, minutes of the organization's Public Relations Committee, the ACLU had decided "to concentrate more of its efforts in the South . . . [and] review . . . aspects of our public relations position [including] . . . attacks based on . . . alleged sympathy for Communist causes . . . [and] the physical safety of lawyers. . . ." Seven years passed. The ACLU was organized in only two Old Confederacy states and the road South still was paved with mixed intentions.* The civil rights movement was the major concern of northern liberals, and in liberal organizations money tends to follow right. If the ACLU moved into the faraway South, the patronage and interest of northern liberals would follow and ACLU membership rolls *in the north* would grow.

Members mean money, and money means power. Coming of age in Alabama had taught me that power is *never* neutral. The justice and electoral systems were not textbook abstractions or law school exercises. Like money, they were instruments of power—weapons used by the rich against the poor.

Pemberton said that I could bring some of my private-practice cases with me. Included were *Billingsley* v. *Clayton,* the ongoing struggle to desegregate the jury system, and *Reynolds* v. *Sims,* in which the Supreme Court had already established the one-person, one-vote rule for legislative apportionment. Later, we might be able to produce on the American-birthright promise—"Forty acres and a mule."

But I had no birthright, no acres, not even a mule. I told Pemberton I couldn't afford the job. We had left Birmingham more than $30,000 in debt. Our mortgaged house had not been sold. Jack asked me how much we would need to live on and pay debts. I told him $16,000. He hired me, I received Roger Baldwin's benediction in New York, and we packed and moved south, back home.

---

*In the eleven-state region, the ACLU had only 2,988 memberships in 1964. Ten years later there were 24,764 members in the South and 1,965 in Georgia alone. Alabama grew from 72 to 700 and Mississippi from 21 to 591. Today, each of the eleven southern states is organized, all with full-time paid staff directors and most with paid staff counsel as well as volunteer attorneys.

2

"If I die and go to hell, I'll have to lay over in Atlanta," said those of us from Birmingham. In envy. Atlanta was the ideal purgatory. We moved there in the fall of 1964. Our layover was to last for eight great years.

Atlanta was also a Deep South decompression chamber. Its leaders faced their problems, showed the rest of the South the way, and kept rising black and white people from getting the bends.

It took us weeks to find the perfect apartment. Then I discovered the For Clean White Gentiles Only sign over the swimming pool. I told the landlord that was quite a compliment to Jews and blacks whom he assumed "clean." He clarified his assumption and we found a different apartment at a rent of fifty dollars more per month.

In November our son, Charles, entered his all-white neighborhood school. A teacher, in preparation for the coming tide of integration (which turned out to be one black boy), told the class that when blacks came they should be sure to put paper on the school toilet seats to avoid disease. She also said that she had seen a black person drop an ice cream cone on the floor, pick it up and serve it to someone. And that Martin King was a Communist.

So Charles learned that an otherwise excellent teacher was sometimes wrong. We encouraged him in believing that she had a right to be wrong—even very, very wrong. A few years later, another teacher told us of that first black student's (Herman Jeter's) reminiscent essay about his best friend. That was how we discovered that on Herman's first day in school Charles had invited him to play baseball with his friends. Herman starred that day, as he did on many others during the next seven years.

The return address of the new ACLU office—Five Forsyth Street, Atlanta, Georgia—reminded southern mailmen that the envelopes they delivered came from "nigger-lovers." Five Forsyth Street contained the offices of the Southern Regional Council's Leslie W. Dunbar, white, Paul Anthony, white, the Voter Education Project's Wiley Branton, black, and Vernon Jordan, black.

Numerous biracial agencies were located in other crannies. They included the Episcopal Society for Cultural and Racial Unity (ESCRU), the National Sharecroppers Fund, the ACLU of Georgia, and the Law Student Civil Rights Research Council. Similar organizations came and went. But when I sought space for the ACLU's southern regional office, Vernon Jordan told me the building management wanted an FBI statement that the ACLU was not on a "list" as a "Communist organization." We laughed. Later I discovered that some old-boy ACLUers had such a cordial relationship with J. Edgar Hoover that had they asked him, he might have cosigned our lease.

I telephoned New York. They provided me with a stack of ready-made, prepackaged quotations from Presidents Johnson, Kennedy, Eisenhower, and Truman endorsing the ACLU. The accolade from General Douglas MacArthur probably convinced the management.

After finding places to live and work, Atlanta was a pleasure. The city had known crinoline and lace, magnolias, mocking-birds, and black education. Under the county-unit system of voting, Atlanta's votes hadn't counted much in statewide elections, so there was less opposition to black registration than there otherwise might have been. When former Mayor Willie B. Hartsfield termed the city "too busy to hate," he had known he could count on black voters who wished that were so.

The legendary Ralph McGill and his protégé Eugene Patterson presided over the *Atlanta Constitution*'s editorials. Under constant attack from white politicians, they shrugged, returned to their typewriters, and drummed out a succession of messages to call forth the better traditions of the Deep South.

In addition to the city's black voters and progressive newspaper, Atlanta's wealth was home-owned. Much of it came from sales of consumer goods. Those who manufactured the miraculous Coca-Cola realized that racial trouble in Atlanta meant diminished sales to the world's black, brown, and yellow peoples. So Coca-Cola provided more than a dime's worth of the difference between Atlanta and Birmingham. Ten-cent drinks could be boycotted, but a Birmingham black man couldn't turn to his wife and seriously say, "Marge, don't buy any U.S. Steel today."

Rich's, Atlanta's locally owned department store, is a social institution. No matter what you buy there or when you buy it, they'll take it back. Rich's did lag behind its Macy's-owned competitor, Davisons, in accepting racial change, and when Martin King sat-in at Rich's he was arrested. During the ensuing years, Rich's took that back, too.

Birmingham's powerful men met in Pittsburgh and New York. Their view of Alabama was like their view of Venezuela, which also had iron-ore mines. Atlanta's powerful men lived in Atlanta, where they sold consumer goods, always with the understanding that in a free marketplace consumers vote with their nickels and dimes. Even so, one leading member of Atlanta's "progressive" banking community had written Yale University to express disgust at its award of an honorary degree to Martin King. Others joined the FBI's attempt to kill off an Atlanta dinner planned to honor the Nobel Peace Prize winner. Three white leaders countered them. Ralph McGill and Eugene Patterson of the *Atlanta Constitution* were intensely patriotic. Ex-Marine McGill respected the FBI as an institution and the government of the United States as divinely inspired. Patterson was once described to me as "even when wrong, the most totally educable man in America." They and Mayor Ivan W. Allen, Jr., the millionaire who regularly led or shoved Atlanta's power-structure to its own salvation, again triumphed.

At that dinner in the Dinkler-Plaza Hotel on January 27, 1965, Martin King thanked the assembly for honoring him and reminded them that it was not the length of life which mattered; what mattered was how you used what you had.

Two days before that, his wife, Coretta, and I had spoken at the fashionable suburban home of a member of the National Council of Jewish Women. I was asked what my wife, Camille, thought about my constant travel; what effect my repeated absences had on our home life; what it was like for our son. The question could have been interpreted "How's your marriage?" I answered it briefly with slightly more than "Just fine" and slightly less than "How's yours?" Sensing that the question had been intended for Coretta and asked of me in classic southern indirection, I turned to her. I asked, "What have these years with Martin been like, Coretta?"

She smiled and spoke softly.

"Well," she began haltingly, "when I was a little girl I wanted to be a singer, a concert singer." She told of her childhood in Marion, Alabama, of her graduation from college and attendance at the New England Conservatory.

"In Boston I met Martin," she continued. "And I fell in love with him. When he asked me to marry him I didn't want to. You see, I knew that marriage would mean the end of my career."

She spoke with total assurance. The room was hushed. She told of their first church in Montgomery, their children, and their lives in Atlanta. She told of her work with women's and peace groups.

"I do concert singing now," she said, "at benefits for the Southern Christian Leadership Conference."

Then she spoke of Martin.

She had heard him lied about, had seen him in despair, had laughed with him when laughter and faith were all they had.

"He's away a lot," she said slowly, without a trace of bitterness. "And the children do miss him, and so do I."

Then she said, ever so softly, "You see, our children know what their father believes in, what he's working for, what he wants for them, and all other children.

"He's not at home as much as most fathers are, but our children have a father they're proud of and that counts for an awful lot."

There was a long silence.

～～～～～～

Two weeks before the dinner for Martin King, eighteen white Mississippians had been charged with violating the civil rights of the late Andrew Goodman, Michael Schwerner, and James Chaney. The defendants faced four misdemeanor charges and one felony; five years in prison for the misdemeanors, ten for the felony.

Federal Judge William Harold Cox presided over Mississippi's southern district. Cox was a roommate of United States Senator James O. Eastland, and that qualified him for the federal bench. In court he distinguished himself by commenting that blacks in a voter registration line were "acting like a bunch of chimpanzees." Since the Kluckers were to be tried there, Cox's court was as bad a place as any to begin the attack on racially exclusive *federal* court juries.

Assisted by Alvin J. Bronstein, I filed *Bailey* v. *Wharton*. That boxed the Justice Department into one of history's traps, for it *always* defended federal officials sued for official acts. But the defense of Cox's racially exclusive jury system would be politically embarrassing and, if the jury rolls included the proper proportion of blacks, prosecutor John Doar could select twelve people willing to convict Klansmen-killers.

On February 1, 1965, Cox confidently wrote his former law partner, Charles Clark, of Jackson (presently a judge on the

Court of Appeals for the Fifth Circuit), and asked him to help the local United States attorney defend the jury officials. His letter described his juries as "a fair cross-section." He termed my lawsuit "unwarranted meddling by outsiders." He intended to answer "this infamous attack."

But unanswered it went, for the Kluckers, grasping at any defense, claimed the indictment was invalid due to the exclusion of blacks from the grand jury. Doar called their bluff. He agreed with them—and us. With blacks, Klansmen, and their prosecutors in agreement about Cox's jury system, Cox had no choice.

A new jury list was selected and the defendants were reindicted. In December 1966, almost two years after I filed suit, Doar reported that federal court juries were being selected without regard to race or sex.

A year later, when Chief Deputy Price and six co-defendants were convicted by an all-white jury, I was in New York City. Of the fifty prospective jurors called, eighteen were black. The government was allowed six peremptory (without cause) challenges; the defendants, twenty-eight. The defendants used eighteen of their challenges on blacks, so only ten remained for whites. The jury finally selected included seven women, and the backgrounds of all twelve jurors were different than they would have been if the defense hadn't had to waste their challenges on blacks.

The twelve who served knew, as white southern jurors in civil rights cases always knew, that their verdict would ratify or reject race killings. They voted no to Southern Justice.

But even at times like that I found myself humming Bob Dylan's song: "And how many deaths will it take 'til they learn that too many people have died." Soon Mickey Schwerner's father and I would march side by side at the funeral of Dr. Martin Luther King, Jr.

≈≈≈≈≈≈

As the hearts and minds of northern white parents followed their children into democracy's Deep South underbrush in 1964 and 1965, their concern, naturally, centered on their children's safety. I had that concern too, but I was most interested in the hometown black and white folks who would remain after civil rights workers went home. I knew, as did almost all southerners, black and white, that sooner or later northern liberals would lose interest in the South. If the state courts weren't straightened out before the federal courts reverted to their traditionally conservative role, the states would lock up hometown civil rights workers until they finally disappeared with a sigh, a shrug, and the phrase used by Harriet Beecher Stowe in *Uncle Tom's Cabin*: "What a fuss for a dead nigger." And, true to history, it was the killing in 1965 of three whites, not blacks, which turned Lowndes County, Alabama, into the be-all and end-all of segregated justice.

There was to be a march from Selma to Montgomery, but between the two there was "Bloody Lowndes," where the heat shimmered from tin-roofed, ten-by-ten shacks that dotted the countryside. Blacks toiled in white-owned fields and Spanish moss stirred in live oak trees.

In college when I drove a beer truck along a regular Black Belt route, I came to love the place. And to hate it. The clawing lush green, the rich black soil, and the pleasant lives of rich whites contrasted with the lives of heads-down black folks who walked the roadsides wearing faded bib overalls or cotton, often floursack, dresses. On Sundays "pickaninnies," as some whites referred to black children, "dressed out." The little girls usually wore white, stiffly starched dresses, their short hair braided into tight corn rows. The boys wore well-ironed, often too-short black suits to the tiny churches which were the social, spiritual, and soon-to-be political centers of their lives.

Between 1865 and 1965 not much had changed in Lowndes County. The Supreme Court was light-years from Hayneville's courthouse square and the local folks knew that it was in the local courthouse that power really mattered. Whites owned the land and the blacks worked it. Whites owned the government and blacks were "kept in line" by it. Eighty-one percent of the population was black but not one black was registered to vote. No black had served on a jury—ever.

Young people from SNCC worked in the toughest areas of the Deep South and, at age twenty-five, John Lewis led them. In 1961, as a preministerial student at Nashville's American Baptist Theological Seminary, he joined the Freedom Rides. After that he led the sit-ins.

His soft-spoken, deeply Southern speech distinguished his Pike County, Alabama, upbringing from that of his companions Stokely Carmichael, Bob Moses, Jim Forman, and even his best friend and fellow southerner, Julian Bond, who had been educated at the Quakers' George School in Pennsylvania.

Arrested forty times, John had been beaten often. He understood, as few men can, what James Oppenheim meant when he wrote that "Free men set themselves free."

On March 7, 1965, John Lewis paused at Selma's Edmund Pettus Bridge. Although he was headed for Montgomery, he was more likely to meet his Maker than he was his governor, for George Wallace's bullyboys had drawn one more line across which they dared blacks to walk. At the bridge John Lewis heard The Man with the bullhorn order him and those who followed him to turn back.

The state troopers, accompanied by Dallas County Sheriff Jim Clark's posse of volunteer mounted horsemen, anxiously awaited their unarmed fellow citizens. The horses stirred. The beefy bullnecked Clark, a symbol of white man's authority in the Black Belt world, scanned the crowd. His riders donned their gas masks and prepared for a cavalry charge into our never-ended civil war.

John Lewis and his companions marched. The men on horseback charged through clouds of tear gas. Their swinging clubs thudded off the heads and backs of the Movement's advance brigade. John Lewis crumpled to the ground. For a second time his skull was fractured. But as the gas lifted from the beaten, trampled marchers and as their screams died away, the sights and sounds, recorded on film, were whisked to the news department of Alabama's network television outlets, where they were processed into national news.

Birmingham Police Commissioner T. Eugene ("Bull") Connor and his police dogs had prepared Americans for the message they received from Selma that Sunday night. On ABC they were watching the first televised showing of the film *Judgment at Nuremberg.** When the motion picture ended they saw and heard the march, the charge, the clubs, followed by screams of terror and pain. The impact was personal; the message was clear; and the reaction was immediate.

As out of step as Lowndes County was with the nation, the marchers laughed, sang, and clapped their hands and straggled in apparent disorganization. They wore beads, beards, blue jeans, and bib overalls, cassocks and clerical collars. One man hobbled along on crutches. They were a bedraggled lot, constantly joined by newcomers, surrounded by cameramen, visited by physicians and food trucks. They were footsore and weary, but tough. They had freedom in their hearts and Montgomery on their minds.

On March 25, 1965, twenty-six months after Wallace called for "segregation now, segregation tomorrow, and segregation forever," John Lewis stood with Martin King on Alabama's state capitol steps in Montgomery, where Jefferson Davis had taken the oath of office to serve as president of the Confederacy. A block down the street, in the Dexter Avenue Baptist Church,

---

*During the next few days I was to hear, over and over again, "I was watching *Judgment at Nuremberg* when . . ."

At the conclusion of that film there was a dialogue between the American war crimes tribunal judge and the German judge-defendant who, in his cell, gave the American judge "a record. A record of the cases I remember."

"This," he said, "is a record of what can happen."

As the film ended, he spoke of Nazi killings: "Those people. All those people. I never knew it would come to that. You must believe it."

There was a pause. The camera closed in on the American.

"Herr Janning," he said. "It came to that the first time you sentenced a man to death you knew to be innocent."

Martin King had begun his ministry to the world. Now these two black men spoke for the future "of all God's children," and again thousands of Americans learned that truly rational men do not have to see to the end of the highway to take first steps.

But for some, first steps were final. Two days after John Lewis's skull had been cracked, the Reverend James Reeb's skull was splintered. On Tuesday, March 9, the thirty-eight-year-old father of four, a white Unitarian minister, was clubbed to death by white men on Selma's Washington Street.*

Again, on March 25, four members of the United Klans of America, Bessemer klavern, had driven to Montgomery in the red and white 1962 Super Sports Impala of Eugene Thomas. At forty-two, Thomas was about to cap his career as a Klan enforcer. He parked two blocks from the capitol. At a nearby service station he and his three companions mingled with the covey of whites who watched as civil rights workers prepared for the marchers from Selma.

Occasionally the service station's pay telephone was used by demonstrators and federal agents. A white man came out and cut the telephone wires.

A black man carrying a walkie-talkie entered the service station. He left when a white man slammed a fist in his face.

An FBI agent came in. He purchased two Coca-Colas, a package of fig bars, and cigarettes. He left.

In midafternoon the four men drove to the outskirts of Montgomery and made arrangements for bail—if they happened to need it. Then they drove out U.S. Highway 80. At Tyler's Cross Roads, eleven miles from Selma, the Alabama Highway

---

*Camille served on the board of the fund created as a memorial to Reeb. Constance Curry and Winifred Green of the American Friends Service Committee patrolled Deep South small towns to learn of blacks fired from their jobs or forced off the land when their children desegregated local schools. They and the board members met to underwrite the courage of those blacks with small loans for seed in the springtime and, if their often tiny land holdings failed to yield sufficient crops, rent loans and food money in the fall.

Patrol stopped them. Thomas had been designated a special police officer of the city of Bessemer and a Special Constable of Law Enforcement. He flashed his credentials, received a warning ticket, and drove on.

As they approached the Negro housing project near Selma's African Methodist Episcopal Church, one of the four white men, Collie Leroy Wilkins, saw several blacks crossing the street.

Thomas saw an army truck parked nearby, so they drove on.

At the intersection of Broad Street and Jeff Davis Avenue, Thomas turned the red and white Chevrolet left onto Broad Street. He stopped for the light at approximately 7:30 P.M. He looked to his left: A white woman was driving a 1963 blue Oldsmobile Dynamic 88 two-door hardtop with a Michigan license plate. A black man sat beside her. Thomas edged his automobile in behind those two total strangers and followed them out U.S. Highway 80 back toward Montgomery.

The four lanes narrowed to two. Near Lowndes County's Big Bear Swamp, 25.5 miles from the center of the Edmund Pettus Bridge, Thomas pulled to the left as if to pass. Wilkins lowered the right front window. Directly opposite the white woman, they fired.

One of them shouted: "She's following us!" Then the lights of the blue Oldsmobile veered from the road.

The next day President Johnson went on television to announce that FBI agents had arrested the four white men for conspiring to deprive Viola Gregg Liuzzo—forty, white, blonde hair, gray eyes, five feet two and one-half inches tall, 127 pounds, wife of a Michigan Teamsters Union business agent, and the mother of four children—of her civil rights to go upon a United States highway "to peacefully assemble, publicly protest, and petition the governor of Alabama for a redress of grievances."

When I heard that four whites from Bessemer had killed Mrs. Liuzzo, I knew that they were as much products of Bessemer's mines and mills as were the Pullman-Standard products which clanked down the Deep South's railroad tracks. They bore the invisible, but indelible, stamp, MADE IN JEFFERSON COUNTY, ALABAMA. So did Angela Davis and thousands of other black and white radicals.

Eugene Thomas, Collie Leroy Wilkins, and Orville Eaton would be convicted on federal civil rights charges. (Those charged with the killing of the Reverend James Reeb would be acquitted by an all-white jury.) They were bona fide Ku Klux Klansmen, but Gary Thomas Rowe was more—and less—than he appeared to be.

Rowe said he had only simulated firing his pistol as they passed Mrs. Liuzzo's automobile. But, if seated behind Thomas and Wilkins, he had done nothing to prevent their killing Mrs. Liuzzo, even though for five years Rowe had worked for the FBI. Since May 26, 1960, FBI "informer" Rowe had drawn ninety-two federal payments totaling $12,375.77.

The prospective jurors said sure, they could convict the murderer of Mrs. Liuzzo, even on circumstantial evidence. They also said yes, they "believe[d] that the white race is superior to the Negro race; [that] the white man . . . [is] superior to the Negro man; and a white civil rights worker closely associated with Negroes in demonstrations and efforts to integrate our schools and churches, and who lives with Negroes and rides around with them in the furtherance of civil rights movements, is an inferior person."

Wilkins's lawyer, Matt H. Murphy of Birmingham, convinced ten of the twelve white jurors that, even on manslaughter charges, Wilkins ought to go scot-free. On May 7, 1965, the jury deadlocked. The judge declared a mistrial. Murphy had told them, and through them the nation: "I thought I'd never see the day when Communists and niggers and white niggers and Jews were flying under the banner of the United Nations flag, not the American flag we fought for. . . . I'm proud to be a white man and I'm proud that I stand up on my feet for white supremacy." The "mixing and mongrelization of races" was at issue. "The Zionists run that bunch of niggers. The white people are not gonna run before them.

"Noah's son was Ham . . . no white woman can ever marry a descent [sic] of Ham . . . that's God's law.

"Do you know those big black niggers were driven by the woman? . . . Niggers! One white woman and these niggers. Right there. Riding right through your county. Communists dominate them niggers. . . ."

〰〰〰〰〰〰〰

In the Deep South those who enforced the law were more important than those who made it. As far as Martin King was concerned, FBI Director J. Edgar Hoover agreed with Klan lawyer Murphy's cry: "Communists dominate them niggers. . . ." King's marching forces were treading on Hoover's carefully planted southern political relationships. But it had to be ideology that made King numbers one through ten on Hoover's personal-enemies list.

Martin King was critical of the FBI. He knew of the all-white bureau's legendary facility for remembering facts, tapping wires, recovering stolen cars, and incarcerating bank robbers; yet, when agents were *eyewitnesses* to civil rights violence, they made no arrests. They had arrest jurisdiction under Reconstruction civil rights acts. As witnesses to crimes, under state law they could make citizens' arrests like other citizens, let alone other cops. Instead, they took notes.

Stung by Martin King's accurate criticism, Hoover, the consummate public relations bureaucrat, moved to destroy him. For years the FBI had served as a national clearinghouse for lies about those with whom Hoover disagreed. His strictly disciplined, well-educated agents were the nation's primary "informed sources." They were the information lifelines of reporters who, without them, would have found day-to-day work difficult. Up the journalistic ladders there were editors and publishers for whom Hoover or his aides had done countless favors. Years before those miserable, ignorant white men killed Mrs. Liuzzo, FBI agents surreptitiously peddled the lies which those killers believed and which lawyer Matt Murphy openly argued: there was Communist influence over King; he pilfered funds; he had secret Swiss bank accounts; he caroused around.

Much of what became "common knowledge" never occurred. Martin's assistants, Andrew Young, Ralph Abernathy, and Walter Fauntroy, did meet with Hoover's associate director, Cartha D. ("Deke") DeLoach and confronted him with the FBI-planted rumors. DeLoach denied FBI culpability. He suggested they talk to the American Legion or the House Committee on Un-American Activities. That is "like sending us to the Ku Klux Klan," said Andy Young.

༄༄༄༄༄

Jonathan M. Daniels, twenty-five, a white seminarian from Keene, New Hampshire, was in charge of the Selma-based work of ESCRU. On Saturday, August 14, 1965, Daniels joined Catholic Father Richard Morrisroe, twenty-six, and a group of blacks in tiny Fort Deposit, Lowndes County, Alabama.

For carrying signs which read EQUAL JUSTICE FOR ALL and NO MORE BACK DOORS, eighteen of them, including Daniels and Morrisroe, were held incommunicado in nearby Hayneville. On Friday, August 20, they were unexpectedly released *without bail,* and were ordered to leave the courthouse. After the 1964 killing of Chaney, Goodman, and Schwerner in Neshoba County, Mississippi, all civil rights workers knew that it was important to flee the jail area when released. One of Daniels and Morrisroe's companions hurried to a pay telephone to ask friends to pick them up.

Tom L. Coleman, fifty-four, white, had lived in Lowndes County almost all of his life. For twenty-five years he'd worked for the State Highway Department, and he served the county as a quasi-deputy sheriff who helped out when there was "trouble." Earlier in the day he'd driven to Montgomery to obtain some riot equipment to help "maintain peace and order." Back home, he played a game of dominoes at the courthouse and then, carrying his twelve-gauge shotgun, he sauntered across the street and into the Cash Store. He was there as Jonathan Daniels, two black women, and Father Morrisroe approached the small, unpainted building seeking a cold soft drink.

Daniels opened the door for SNCC Field Secretary Ruby Sales.

A survivor would testify that Coleman shouted: "Get out! The store is closed! I'll blow your goddamned heads off, you sons of bitches!"

According to Father Morrisroe, Daniels asked Coleman if he was threatening them.

"You damn right I am!" Coleman replied.

There was a shot. Daniels's hand flew up. He "caught his stomach, and then he fell backwards."

"Run, you niggers!" Coleman shouted. "I'll kill all you niggers!"

Daniels lay dead on the porch. The others ran. The shotgun roared. The white priest, Morrisroe, lay in the dust quite still, wounded in the lower spine.

When abolitionist blood flowed on Black Belt soil, the question was not "Who done it?" The question was "Who cares?"

The Reverend John B. Morris cared. The soft-spoken, pink-cheeked Episcopal priest served as ESCRU's executive director. He had grown up in Brunswick on the Georgia coast. We had met in Birmingham. Now his office was down the hall in Five Forsyth Street. We were the same age and our mutual tendency to good food and almost any quality whiskey provided us with common ground beyond Episcopalianism.

Morris had offended many white southern Episcopalians, including the bishops whom ESCRU sought to embarrass into doing the right thing. Now he wanted the Justice Department to do something. Anything. They wouldn't, so we did.

Five days after the murder of Jonathan Daniels, I joined five brave black people, Gardenia White, Lillian S. McGill, Jesse W. Favor, Willie May Strickland, and John Hulett, with ESCRU, John Morris, and Daniels's bereaved mother, in a lawsuit against Bruce Crook, his fellow white jury commissioners, and other

Lowndes County officials. That case, *White* v. *Crook*, brought the federal government into the struggle against the all-white, all-male juries of the Southern Justice System. It also brought the Justice Department into the struggle for equal women's rights.

∿∿∿∿∿∿∿

Of the Deep South states, Alabama can be simultaneously the best and the worst on the same subject. Women had been elected to statewide office. They practiced law and presented cases to juries. Judge Annie Lola Price, who presided over the Alabama Court of Appeals, could reverse a jury's verdict. Lurleen Wallace was about to succeed her husband as governor and appoint every jury commissioner in the state. Hulda Coleman was Lowndes County's superintendent of education, and Kelly D. Coleman (both women said to be kin of Tom) was clerk of the circuit court and the jury commission, but there was an absolute bar against women jurors in Alabama.*

In cotton country, the male members of families of "substance" (also termed "old" families, as though the families of poor whites were "new") took care of those kinds of tasks. Tom Coleman himself had been called for jury duty twelve times in the preceding twelve years. He would be summoned to serve on the jury which would try him for killing Jonathan Daniels. The judge would excuse him.

In *An American Dilemma*, Gunnar Myrdal described the South's "parallel" discrimination against women and blacks, and pointed out that the abolitionist movement once flourished in the South, which he described as a "stronghold of liberal thinking." But in 1793 the patron devil of the southern system, the white genius Eli Whitney, invented the cotton gin, which made

---

*And in Mississippi and South Carolina. If the white males of the South had been successful, women wouldn't have been able to vote, either. All of the states which opposed the Nineteenth (women's suffrage) Amendment, were located below Mason's and Dixon's line except for Delaware, a border state.

cotton King and slaves valuable, enslaved the section and, through it, the United States.

By the mid-1950s the cotton man's parallel discrimination (which was never the same for women and blacks) had produced contradictions. In Montgomery, for instance, poor black women and reasonably rich white women made the bus boycott work. Black maids liberated their mistresses from housework and made them "queens for a day." The mass refusals of maids to ride buses to work were essential for boycott success. Some walked. Others rode in the carpools the black community organized. Many white housewives were willing to do anything to keep their maids. To transport them to and from work they enlisted in a fifth column of secret chauffeurs.

White southern women were less fearful of blacks than were their northern counterparts, let alone white southern men. Their relationship with blacks, even if paternalistic and master-servant, was better than no relationship at all. Besides, middle-class white male southerners were fearful for their jobs. Some of their "ladies" (for whom they were "preserving their effective-ness") sympathized with the civil rights movement. Since they had no jobs, they were free to say so.

〰〰〰〰〰

While I was preparing *White* v. *Crook*, Richmond Flowers, the state attorney general, took control of the Coleman case away from the local prosecution. That breached the tight solidar-ity of Hayneville's white community. "Should have stayed in Montgomery and let the local folks handle it," said the kindest of the local white folks. To them, the tall, handsome, red-headed state attorney general was "soft on the race question." To others the son of a south Alabama Bourbon banking family was a "turncoat," a "puppet" of "the centralized forces in Wash-ington."

Flowers's life was threatened. He found a bug in his tele-phone. He was spat upon while running for office. He was slugged at a high school football game. Later he would be convicted of extortion, disbarred, and imprisoned.

Ten days before Daniels and Morrisroe were gunned down, according to Flowers, who was watching federal officials register Lowndes County blacks as voters, Coleman snarled at him:

"You and Katzenbach ought to get off the Ku Klux Klan and get on these outfits down here trying to get these niggers to register! If you don't get off the Klan investigation, we'll get you off!"

Flowers's principal assistant, Joe Breck Gantt, was to try the Coleman case. At thirty-six, the prematurely balding, well-tanned lawyer from Florala *really* intended to prosecute. "Sincerity" added to his problems, just as it burdened Atticus Finch in *To Kill a Mockingbird.* "The Court appointed Atticus to defend him," Harper Lee wrote in her modern classic. "Atticus aimed to defend him. That's what they didn't like about it. It was confusing."

I had learned in Birmingham that in civil rights cases you were safest when you were believed to be "insincere," for if those in law enforcement assumed you took cases for "big fat fees," they "understood." I once let them believe their jovial fantasy that I was collecting a $60,000 fee in a civil rights case rather than the actual $100 the client scraped up.

Gantt rose from his seat at the counsel table in the slave-built Hayneville courthouse. He calmly told Circuit Court Judge T. Werth Thagard that it was "impossible for the State to obtain a fair trial."

Simultaneously, in the adjoining Montgomery County federal courthouse, I urged the federal judges to enjoin all Lowndes County jury trials until they had disposed of the jury discrimination question raised in *White* v. *Crook.*

I argued that "all white juries drawn from all white lists give killers a license to murder!"

I lost.

It was September 27, 1965. Only thirty-eight days had passed since Daniels's killing, and Gantt's problem extended beyond the jury selection. His primary witness, Father Richard Morrisroe, was confined to a Chicago hospital "medically and physically unable to testify." He "looked pathetic and could barely talk."

"I can't prosecute this case without Morrisroe," Gantt insisted. "The only reason he is not here now is because he is in danger of losing his life."

Besides that, Wallace's director of public safety, Colonel Al Lingo, who had once threatened federal marshals ("If they want a police state, we will have one too") and whose men had beaten John Lewis and the marchers at Selma's Edmund Pettus Bridge, refused to provide Gantt with the results of the state's "investigation."

None of that mattered. Judge Thagard ordered that the prosecution go forward. Gantt looked up quizzically. Then with all the respect he could muster, he sighed, resigned himself to his fate, and said: "The State has no alternative than to ask that this case be *nolle prosequi*." Gantt was seeking to dismiss the manslaughter indictment in a way that would not prevent his later prosecution of Coleman for murder.

The judge glowered down. He accused Gantt of "trifling" with the court. He ordered him "here and now to proceed with the prosecution of this case!"

"I don't want to be a part of putting perjured testimony on that witness stand," Gantt protested. "I can't proceed any further, I can't prosecute this case. I have no case whatsoever."

Thagard threatened to cite the white prosecutor-politician, a third-generation south Alabama lawman, for contempt if he did not proceed.

The crowd, blacks on one side, whites on the other, was hushed. The early-fall sun burned through ceiling-tall windows. Gantt stood, stared at the judge, and paused. Then he said, "No."

With the world watching, Thagard did not cite Gantt for contempt. He removed him from the case and immediately opened the trial. The watching world was of no concern to Tom Coleman's longtime friend—chunky, red-faced Deputy Sheriff Joe Jackson—who the reinstated local prosecutor put on the stand. Deputy Jackson chuckled as a defense lawyer cross-examined.

> Q.   What, if anything, did Jonathan Daniels do that attracted your attention, Mr. Jackson?
> A.   One thing, he kissed that nigger girl.
> Q.   Did he kiss her on the cheek or did he kiss her in the mouth?. . .
> A.   He kissed her right in the mouth.

The white spectators roared with laughter. Some jurors joined in.

The basic question was, Did Coleman act in self-defense?

Coleman's witnesses testified that the Episcopal seminarian, Daniels, just released from jail, had had a switchblade knife in his hand, and the Catholic priest, Morrisroe, had had a pistol in his. Neither a knife nor a pistol was offered in evidence. Blacks testified that Daniels and Morrisroe had held books. The Bible, *The Fanatics, The Church in the New Latin America, Life and Times of Frederick Douglass*, and *Native Son* had been found

According to Morrisroe (whose written statement was read to the jury), they sought to purchase cold soft drinks: "When Daniels was shot, I turned to leave. I did not want to play hero. Another shot was fired, and I was struck by that shot in my lower spine, and I fell to the ground. To my knowledge, at the time of the threat and the first shot, Daniels did not have a knife, gun, stick, or other weapon in his hand. The only thing I had in mine was a dime."

During recesses, the paunchy, black-suited Coleman, his hands jammed deep in his pants pockets, stood staring out the courtroom window across nearby Coleman Field, where games were played. He did not testify.

The judge told the jury that it was proper to "consider the acts of the deceased and the circumstances of their being jailed, their release from jail, and their activities" between their release and the shooting. Also relevant was "the tension or lack of tension existing in Hayneville, Alabama, on August 20, 1965."

Court adjourned. As the jurors filed past, one of them turned toward Coleman and winked. The next morning, after one hour and twenty-nine minutes of deliberation, they filed back. Judge Thagard asked, "Gentlemen, have you reached a verdict?"

A JUROR: We have, your honor.
THE COURT: Do you have it prepared?
A JUROR: Certainly.
THE COURT: Give it to Mrs. Coleman, please.
CLERK [*Mrs. Coleman*]: We the jury find the Defendant Tom Coleman, not guilty.

"That's the price you have to pay for the jury system," said Attorney General Nicholas deB. Katzenbach in an offhand comment on the acquittal.

"I'm all for the jury system," I snapped to the reporter who told me that. "I certainly think we ought to try it sometime."

That jury operated as had hundreds of others, but this time the Southern Justice System was on trial. No civil rights workers did more to confront the American people, the democracy's ultimate jury, than did the national correspondents who covered the South.

Gene Roberts and Roy Reed of *The New York Times,* like their predecessor, Claude Sitton, filed the daily reports which each morning told New York and Washington's network television newsmen where the revolution was. Reed and Roberts, white southerners who love the South and hate injustice, wrote the report *Racial Discrimination in Southern Federal Courts,* which the ACLU and the Southern Regional Council published.

There was a finely honed cold fury in the crisp reports filed by Jack Nelson of the *Los Angeles Times.* He still can't forget the elderly white man who, for no good reason, kicked black spectator Stokely Carmichael before the deputies and bailiffs removed Carmichael from the courtroom. From Lowndes County,

Alabama, through Meridian, Mississippi, to the Orangeburg, South Carolina, massacre, Nelson went, saw, heard, and wrote, filing his words by telephone to Los Angeles and from there across the country. His newspaper reprinted his "Jim Crow Justice" series and it was widely distributed.

Time correspondent Arlie Schardt covered the Coleman trial, despite orders from New York that he not do so. When he filed his first story, he expected to be fired. His editors wanted more. He expected worse than firing when a white man's hands tightened around his throat and bent him backward over a courtroom table during a trial recess. The judge ordered him turned loose and he was.

Back in Atlanta I met with the Southern Christian Leadership Conference's (SCLC's) Andrew Young, Ralph Abernathy, Hosea Williams, and Martin King, who proposed marches on courthouses and sit-ins in jury boxes, for the courts had "forfeited their right to administer justice."

That they had. In the preceding fifteen years, the Justice Department three times had asked its ninety-two United States attorneys to report instances of jury discrimination by *federal* courts. Not one response had been received. And when we urged the Justice Department to prosecute civil rights cases, they asked: "Why prosecute?" Then answered themselves: "All-white juries will turn the killers loose."

In eighty-five years there had been not one federal criminal prosecution of a state official for excluding blacks from juries. Burke Marshall, assistant attorney general in charge of civil rights under Robert Kennedy, summed up the problem to Jack Nelson of the *Los Angeles Times*: "The restructuring of juries is very important. But the issue is much like reapportionment: not very sexy and hard to get people interested."

But the black people of Lowndes County were interested. The Justice Department entered *White* v. *Crook* on our side and the federal judges ordered the inclusion of blacks on the jury rolls. They also applied the equal protection clause of the Fourteenth Amendment to sex as well as race discrimination. In a ruling which was to grow in importance, they struck down Alabama's statute which excluded all women from jury service.

White folks killed more than white folks during that march to acquire the vote.

They killed Southern Justice.

3

I was ten when my father told me "why black folks steal." As we drove beside cane and cotton fields in the Mississippi Delta he said: "They're brought up that way. They fill their cotton sacks and set aside a little bit for themselves. They pick almost all of it for the farmer but they hold back a little bit. As children they are told to hold some back. They hide it in their mother's dress or over in the woods. They can't get money any other way—poor devils."

Once he took me to the police station to see if a bicycle which had turned up was mine. When he showed me the barred jail cell where those who broke the law went, he shook his head and muttered, "Poor devils." Whenever we saw poor blacks, I'd heard him mutter softly, "Poor devils"; and, along the highway all prisoners were "poor devils."

We learned young that the prisoners who worked outdoors, no matter the weather, were the lucky ones. It was after I began to practice law that I came to hate even the sounds of penitentiaries—the clanging of metal doors, the jangle of five-inch-long door keys, the grating sound of scraping metal chairs and cups and trays, the filtered voices over speaker systems and through slits in metal doors, and the clanging of bells.

On February 18, 1966, eleven days after we won *White* v. *Crook*, we moved to desegregate the prisons. Orzell Billingsley, Jr., came up with two of the clients: Caliph Washington, convicted of murdering a Bessemer, Alabama, policeman; and Greene County's Johnnie Coleman, also black, also convicted of murdering a white man. They awaited execution on Kilby Prison's death row. Orzell believed them innocent. But in the Southern Justice System, when their testimony was contradicted by a white person, blacks were hard put to prove their innocence.

Awaiting trial in the Birmingham city jail at that time were Hosea L. Williams, black, and Thomas E. Houck, Jr., white. Both were SCLC staffers who knew that white folks listened to the truth only during demonstrations. To Hosea Williams, jail bunks were merely resting places along the road to equal rights and the seat he finally won in Georgia's House of Representatives. To Tom Houck, prison was preferable to freedom in a racially segregated outside world. I joined Williams and Houck with Washington and Coleman in a single lawsuit to desegregate all Alabama state, county, city, and town prisons and jails.*

The state's commissioner of corrections, Frank Lee, was the principal defendant, so the case name was, appropriately, *Washington* v. *Lee*.

≈≈≈≈≈≈≈

All prisons are bad. In the Deep South they are worse. In Georgia, they had been studied, and that was what made that state's system appear to be the worst of all.

---

*In federal-court civil "class actions," citizens joined together share expenses and achieve a common remedy in a single lawsuit. Individual lawsuits by individually affected prisoners are not required. Since the law allows named defendants as well as plaintiffs to represent a "class," Alabama's state prisoners could be desegregated as a single entity, as could its sixty-seven county jails and hundreds of city and town facilities.

The white men who designed that prison system wanted cheap labor. When Emancipation struck them an almost fatal economic blow, wealthy planters found salvation in the criminal laws. In pre—Civil War Georgia, for example, no blacks were in a prison. The total locked-up population consisted of 200 white males. Immediately after the slaves were freed, the prison population jumped tenfold, with the male ratio nine-to-one black and the female ratio forty-to-one black.

Complex sets of vagrancy statutes called "Black Codes" regulated labor and apprenticeships and kept "free" black sharecroppers and tenant farmers in line. As John L. Spivak wrote in *Georgia Nigger,* "The proclamation to free niggers had really only reduced prices for niggers. White trash who never had a thousand dollars or fifteen hundred dollars to pay for a slave could get niggers now for a few dollars a head by giving them an advance against wages."

Reconstruction failed to include the redistribution of Black Belt land. For almost all blacks, there were no forty acres, no ten acres; not even a mule.

The moneyless, bankless black farmer received, instead, a small cash advance, seed, and some food against the crop he was to raise on the white man's land. In the fall, when picking-time came, the price the black man received for his share of the cotton crop rarely met the debt he owed.

With the black man thus trapped, if he tried to flee, The Law retroactively presumed that at the time he accepted the advance he had had a criminal intent to defraud the white landowner. The burden of proof rested upon the "freed" black man.

Even though the Thirteenth Amendment forbade slavery, it did not apply to convicted criminals. Justices of the peace (known as "JPs") collected their fees as part of the court costs which were charged to defendants. Naturally JP came to mean "Judgment for the Prosecution" and "Judgment for the Plaintiff." Often they farmed out the convicted black man to the very landowner from whom he had fled. To satisfy his sentence he was required to work out the fine and costs and his original debt, which, of course, at "reasonable interest," grew and grew and grew.

Penitentiaries became plantations; wardens, managers, and guards were overseers. At Mississippi's 21,000-acre Parchman cotton plantation, blacks worked under the watchful eyes of their armed fellow prisoners, designated "trusties." Docile prisoners were allowed conjugal rights, not as a prison reform, but as a work reward.

In Louisiana, blacks were confined to the 20,000-acre prison farm named for the Portuguese African colony Angola. Located twenty-two miles from the nearest highway, accessible only through snake-infested swamps, it is almost as remote from New Orleans and the state capital at Baton Rouge as is its African namesake.

At the top of the system was the governor's mansion. In the Deep South, black trusties sometimes served as valets while "field niggers" slaved on the cotton farms. In the Alabama governor's mansion I discovered that the chefs, chauffeurs, butlers, and baby-sitters were often black "lifers," usually convicted murderers, who took good care of the state's number-one white man while they served their terms. Black trusties were trusted because the folks they had killed were "nonwhites."

By the time I began law practice, the balls, chains, and spiked ankle manacles even of South Carolina's work gangs had been removed, but in Alabama and elsewhere, groups of blacks still were brought manacled together from county jails. A single chain ran from each of them to each of the others. Their families and friends watched intently as they shuffled into racially separated courtrooms.

In the Jefferson County, Alabama, courthouse I watched as the bailiffs and deputy sheriffs kept back the mothers, daughters, wives, and friends of chained-together prison-garbed black men. Faltering and crying, their loved ones asked me or some other white lawyer, "Please tell him that . . ."

By then I knew that we would have annihilated blacks had they been more literate and less useful. In Hitler's Germany armbands identified Jews. Those with black skin could have been annihilated more easily. But they were the labor pool with which to break strikes. They served as the pickers of cotton, the diggers of ditches. They emptied the bedpans and cleaned the outhouses of our lives. Uneducated, propertyless, disfranchised, and excluded from justice, except as defendants, they were no threat to whites. While they remained useful and didn't get "out of line," their lives were assured, for no matter how worthless lower-class white folks said blacks were, the rich, well-born, and able upper-class whites knew that they and black folks were really the only people indispensably required by Our Southern Way of Life.

Assigned to try *Washington* v. *Lee* were Montgomery's District Judge Frank M. Johnson, Jr., and Court of Appeals Judge Richard T. Rives. Unlike many—perhaps most—judges, south and north, they really believed in the Constitution. Besides, they had defended and prosecuted scores of Alabama blacks and whites in their private law practices, so they knew to ignore the state's allusion to "violent, dangerous criminals."

Some liberals expressed a similar fear. Camille provided me with the phrase I used to counter their concern about the safety of civil rights workers: "Integrated prisons should be a great deterrent to white crime."* Governor Lester G. Maddox unintentionally said the same thing in a different way. He contended that there would be no penal reform "until we have a higher class of prisoners in Georgia."

The third judge assigned to our case, Birmingham's Chief District Judge Seybourn H. Lynne, had designated himself a

---

*Several years after we initiated the Southern Justice litigation, national and Alabama Klan leader, Robert Shelton, was convicted of contempt of Congress. He'd refused to answer questions asked him by the House Committee on Un-American Activities.

Shelton lost his appeals but refused to surrender to Washington, D.C., federal authorities. He feared imprisonment in the nearby overwhelmingly black penitentiary at Lorton. He did agree to surrender if sent to the more genteel, and therefore overwhelmingly white, facility at Montgomery's Maxwell Air Force Base. They compromised and the Klan leader went to prison at Texarkana.

great deterrent to desegregation. He was bright, competent, and consistently wrong. When he sat with Johnson and Rives in Montgomery's bus boycott case, Lynne had written, "Only a profound, philosophical disagreement . . . that the separate but equal doctrine can no longer be safely followed as . . . the law would prompt this, my first dissent." A loyalist Southern Democrat from Decatur in north Alabama's Tennessee River Valley, Lynne had a heritage different from that of Johnson, who descended from north Alabama's hill and mountain people and their antislavery tradition. River-valley bottomland was where cotton and slavery grew.

At the time of the *Washington* v. *Lee* trial, John O. Boone, black, was director of the Southern Regional Council's three-year study of Deep South prisons. Boone understood the values of slavery. Heavyset, soft-spoken, and seemingly easygoing, he is more than six feet tall and has a broad face that inspires belief. A graduate of Morehouse College and Atlanta University, he had worked for fourteen years at the Atlanta Federal Penitentiary. After that he had been chief classification officer for the federal penitentiary in Terre Haute, Indiana.

I turned Boone over to the state for cross-examination. Referring to the Atlanta federal prison's desegregation experience, he was asked, "And how long did it take?"

"Overnight," came the answer.

Asked why he thought the federal experience was applicable to state prisoners, he replied, "I have met some of your ex-inmates. In fact, I have encountered hundreds and hundreds of them in federal prisons."

Q. Are not the type prisoners usually found in federal penal institutions different?
A. No, sir.
Q. Than those in state.
A. No, sir; they are the same men.

Even the state's witnesses were helpful. Jefferson County's (Birmingham's) sheriff, Melvin Bailey, a former policeman under Bull Connor, resembled Li'l Abner. He was too whole-

some to be real, and too outsized to argue with. I had backed
Bailey for sheriff in 1962. He was up for reelection now and the
black vote was growing rapidly. He listened carefully as Judge
Johnson leaned forward. "Is there any instance in your experience where it is necessary to classify solely because of race . . .
in order to maintain and operate your prison properly?"

"I would have to say no," Bailey responded.

"Any other witnesses for the defendants?" Judge Rives asked.
And sure enough, the state thought it had one.

Frank Lee had succeeded his father as sheriff of eighty-one-
percent-black Greene County. When Frank moved up to commissioner, Frank's brother, "Big Bill," succeeded him. The Lees
prided themselves on not needing guns and, according to some
people, when they sent word to The Wanted, the guilty parties
stumbled over each other in the race to turn themselves in. Now
Commissioner Frank Lee, for the defense—despite his lawyer's
references to Alabama's "vicious, violent, rebellious and deadly
men"—testified that there was not one gun in all of Alabama's
state penal institutions.

Lawyers on "my side" can't afford to write off judges on "the
other side." There are too many of them. Besides, it is not the
nature of southern Protestants to write off people. Without "sin-
ners" there would be no one to convert. Now, a decade after the
bus boycott case, Judge Seybourn Lynne joined the two jurists
with whom he had so sharply disagreed. They unanimously ordered the desegregation of hundreds of institutions.

The honors farms, educational programs, youth centers, and
hospitals were to integrate immediately. Six months were provided the Draper Correctional Center, Julia Tutwiler Prison for
Women, and hundreds of county, city, and town facilities.
Maximum-security institutions, including the high-walled Kilby
Prison where Caliph Washington and Johnnie Coleman awaited
execution, were placed under a one-year deadline.

Alabama appealed.

〜〜〜〜〜〜〜

The first black Supreme Court justice, Thurgood Marshall, a civil rights lawyer, had years of Deep South courtroom experience behind him. So did the senior Justice Hugo L. Black, a former Alabama defense lawyer, prosecutor, and lower court judge. They knew Alabama's prison system as well as did the state's lawyer, Nicholas S. Hare, a bespectacled, reasonable gentleman with the amorphously nice manners which typify Black Belt upbringing.

Hare sought "reasonableness and time." I sought speed and a court order. I argued the tragic reality that "no man in Alabama in public office, subject to appointment by the governor, can, in fact, exercise his discretion and his duty without an order of the court."

On March 11, 1968, the Supreme Court ruled with us. Justices Black, Harlan, and Stewart agreed separately and pointed out that nothing forbade prison officials from "acting in good faith and in particularized circumstances, to take into account racial tensions in maintaining security, discipline, and good order."

Justice Black knew as well as I did that it was poverty and ignorance and the segregated system itself which aggravated racial tensions and led to disorder. During the argument before the justices I referred to a coal-mining county located north and west of Birmingham. "In Walker County there is no municipal jail of two rooms . . . it is difficult to segregate."

Black knew Walker County well. He looked down with a twinkle in his eyes and asked: "They are the ones that are called calabooses?"

A. They are the ones that are called calabooses, yessir.
MR. JUSTICE BLACK: What have they been doing in those places when they have a black and a white?
A. Well . . . I reckon in those small towns they just haven't had a Negro and a white man get drunk on the same night. I don't know. [*Laughter*]

We both knew that when we got the instruments of power straightened out and poor blacks and whites got an equal start and a fair shake, they would get along all right, even in Walker County, even in a calaboose, even on Saturday night.

In April 1968, Johnnie Coleman, one of the plaintiffs in *Washington* v. *Lee,* was retried in Greene County, and by then the jury rolls had been desegregated. Black lawyers Orzell Billingsley, Jr., and Peter H. Hall struck all white males. The white prosecutor struck the white females. Twelve blacks remained. On April 4, 1968 (the day Martin King was assassinated), they voted not guilty. When Coleman was freed the blacks in the courtroom burst into applause. In the evening they burst into tears.

Caliph Washington is free and married. He lives in Birmingham, but it took stay after stay to save his life. Once Judge Johnson halted his execution with a scant twenty-four hours to spare. Twice his conviction for murder was reversed. On January 12, 1971, Alabama's Court of Criminal Appeals set it aside for the final time. Judge Aubrey M. Cates held that blacks had been systematically excluded from the 1957 Bessemer grand jury which indicted Washington. To show that exclusion, Judge Cates relied upon the record in *Billingsley* v. *Clayton!* Orzell's father's case saved Caliph Washington's life. And so it went, beyond reason and prediction, in the struggle for equal justice.

During the years in Atlanta the lives of at least nine men condemned to death were saved by Supreme Court rulings in cases I presented. No client was executed. But each of those victories was tarnished by the certain knowledge that through the years countless innocent "poor devils" had been sacrificed to the Southern Justice System.

We filed desegregation cases against those who ran the jury systems of fifty-five Deep South counties. We aimed at areas that had high percentages of blacks. Alabama was my primary target. We filed suits against twenty-seven of its sixty-seven county jury systems. In twenty of them, court orders are still in effect. I lost two of those Alabama cases. Five were dismissed after the jury rolls had been reconstituted. Of eight suits in South Carolina, none were lost, six resulted in agreed settlements. Two counties are presently under court orders. Nine suits were filed in north Florida and five counties are under court order. One was dismissed after the jury rolls had been reconstituted, and three were lost.

In Virginia, where seven suits were filed and seven more were ready for filing, a favorable state supreme court ruling provided immediate change in all of them. Four suits were filed in Mississippi and Tennessee. Some counties changed without suits. But where suits were not filed, it is likely that the unjust system still produces an occasionally noticed outrage and day-by-day constant and grinding injustice.

Virginia lawyer Philip J. Hirschkop went after more than segregation. He sued for reformation of the entire state prison system and won.

Most of these cases were "not very sexy" and it was "hard to get people interested" in them. They involved rote work. Prejudice against southern whites was another part of the problem. In Mississippi, for example, the cynicism of many northern civil rights lawyers made it impossible for them to believe that southern whites could change, so there was no reason for them to move against jury systems. I did retain Memphis, Tennessee, attorney Louis R. Lucas to file a few jury desegregation cases in north Mississippi. In 1970, my friend from Birmingham, George Peach Taylor, took over the Jackson, Mississippi, office of the Lawyers Committee on Civil Rights Under Law. Then they moved against segregated prisons, jury systems, and public employment, including Mississippi's all-white highway patrol.

Already the Justice Department had sued to integrate Alabama's state employment. Judge Johnson asked me to act as a friend of the court, and Reber F. Boult, Jr., a brilliant young lawyer who worked for me in Atlanta, prepared the briefs. Again Johnson broke precedent and ordered that employment in several state agencies be integrated.

Later, my friends Morris S. Dees, Jr., and Joseph J. Levin,

Jr., of the Southern Poverty Law Center, caused the integration of the lily-white Alabama Highway Patrol. Their client in *Paradise* v. *Allen*, twenty-four-year-old Walter Paradise, had been told that he was "too young to be a state trooper and too old to be a trooper cadet."

Dees, the son of a Montgomery County, Alabama, dirt farmer, worked his way through the University of Alabama. He acquired lists of students' birthdays and their parents' addresses. Would parents like a birthday cake hand-delivered to their child? They sent checks. With day-old birthday cakes, purchased from Tuscaloosa bakeries, Dees gave the students happy birthdays and, as he banked profits, happy days for himself.

Using his mailing-list experience, Dees and fellow law student Millard Fuller made millions of dollars in direct-mail sales.

They did not forget that the Deep South's poor, black and white, had common enemies. So Fuller sold Dees his interest in the company and went into full-time religious and equal rights work. After Dees swapped the firm to the Times-Mirror Corporation for several million dollars' worth of stock, he and Levin established Montgomery's Southern Poverty Law Center.

~~~~~~~~

On November 27, 1974, Camille and I were returning to Birmingham for Thanksgiving and another Alabama football victory over Auburn. Just south of Montgomery, Camille saw the flashing blue light of a state trooper's car. She pulled over. The courteous, spiffy black patrolman whose radar had clocked her speed at seventy-three miles per hour, gave us a warning ticket and set us on our way with "Have a nice day—be careful."

Almost a decade had passed since Viola Gregg Liuzzo's automobile veered from the nearby Selma-to-Montgomery highway.

In Hayneville the verdicts of integrated juries no longer are handed to Kelly Coleman. The new clerk, also female, is black. The superintendent of education, who replaced Hulda Coleman, is black too.

That winter we drove past miles of rolling, untilled Black Belt fields, dotted with those unpainted, rotting, tin-roofed, frame shacks. The white folks still own that land. The black folks still work it. Around the world the rich, the well born and the able, and their corporations are buying up land or taking it, and governments too, as had the cotton men in Bloody Lowndes. Someday there will be a march of ragtag people seeking forty acres and a mule, and the Lowndes counties of the world are made for marching.

When we drove past the still-unpainted Cash Store, the sheriff was chatting with four white men in front of the courthouse. I could almost see twenty-five-year-old Jonathan Daniels and twenty-six-year-old Richard Morrisroe crossing the lawn with their just-freed companions. But now the sheriff was John Hulett, black, one of my clients in *White* v. *Crook.*

4

When Justice William O. Douglas achieved the longest tenure in Supreme Court history (October 29, 1973), *New York Times* reporter Linda Charlton asked him, "Which of the thousands of decisions" during those 34 years, 196 days "had the most impact on the country and its citizens."

Douglas thought for several minutes. He replied, "I suppose . . . the reapportionment cases—*Reynolds* v. *Sims,* which [former Chief Justice Earl] Warren based on a dissent [Justice] Black and I had written twenty years earlier."

I had filed *Reynolds* v. *Sims,* the case which made "one person, one vote" the law of the land, in midsummer 1961. It was one of the cases I had brought with me when I went to work for the ACLU. Of course I didn't know how the case—then named *Sims* v. *Frink*—would come out, but I did know that Alabama's legislature was run for the Big Mules of out-of-state-owned industry by a few powerful men from the Black Belt. And of those Black Belt counties, Lowndes was, as always, the worst.

Each Lowndes County resident—there were 15,417 of them—had forty-one times the state senate strength of each of

Jefferson County's (Birmingham's) residents. In the house, the ratio was sixteen to one. Since the Lowndes population was 81 percent black, and not one black could vote, the actual voter disparity was astronomical.

Back in 1961, 25 percent of the people could elect the Alabama legislature, but, even ignoring the disfranchisement of blacks, that figure was deceptive. In forty-one of Alabama's sixty-seven counties, more than 100 percent of the age-eligible white population was registered to vote. In Black Belt Green County, 127.4 percent of the eligible whites were registered.

When candidates for governor gave lip service to reapportionment, Black Belt legislators "understood." They could lip-read. Sometimes it even seemed they could mind-read. During Jim Folsom's first term he really tried to break their hold on the state, but they kept their power and broke his heart instead.

Like most judges, Alabama's were in harness. Its supreme court justices, led by Judge Ed Livingston, insisted that they had no power to order the legislature to do much of anything, let alone to enforce the state consitution, which mandated one-person, one-vote representation and a new apportionment every ten years.

The federal government was no help. The Big Mules were the Republican party. Through their Black Belt alliance they controlled the state Democratic parties of the Deep South and through them the Congress, the military, and much of the "free" world.

As with countless other wrongs, reapportionment was a matter of "state's rights." "We Dare Defend Our Rights" was Alabama's motto, and as far as democracy was concerned "Now Is Not the Time" was Alabama's creed. The state's social clock was set to Later, but I was thirty-one and unwilling to synchronize my life to Alabama's time.

Representing twelve other members of the Young Men's Business Club of Birmingham, George Peach Taylor and I filed *Sims* v. *Frink* and signed up as plaintiffs as well as lawyers. In Birmingham even the hint of economic pressure could change the minds of plaintiffs, but since we were parties to the lawsuit, only we could fire ourselves.

In midsummer 1961, Birmingham was home and I intended to spend my life there. Already I understood one revealing phrase from my childhood. "Eat all your food, clean your plate, think about the poor starving Chinese" provided me with an adult understanding of Albert Schweitzer liberals. How easy it was for individuals and even entire generations and classes and nations and cities of people to concentrate upon faraway fantasies rather than circumstances closer to home. Adults during my childhood sent their old clothes *and* Albert Schweitzer to Africa. They worried about the poor starving Chinese. The Chinese decided to starve no more. They had a revolution. So now we worried about the nonstarving, but Red, Chinese.

And while we contemplated arms, not alms, for Africa, Birmingham closed its parks, de-seated its park benches, drained its swimming pools, poured concrete in the holes of its public golf courses, witnessed the beatings of countless blacks and the castration of one, suffered scores of unsolved bombings, and voted its habit for Police Commissioner Bull Connor and his designees. Birmingham had seen preacher Fred L. Shuttlesworth and singer Nat ("King") Cole slugged, the latter onstage. It had sued *The New York Times* for libel, denied all, denounced the world, and fought in courts and in the streets to maintain "the old-South" way of life it had never known.

With the New American Revolution under way in their streets, Birmingham's white residents desperately pretended to live unchanged lives.

In the federal district court of Judge Frank Johnson, my reapportionment case slumbered, for no federal district court had reapportionment "jurisdiction." Just after World War II, when Illinois voters had sought equal legislative representation, Justice Felix Frankfurter had led the Supreme Court into dismissing their claim. He rationalized that even though urban voters were discriminated against, "courts ought not to enter this political thicket."

Frankfurter could always find rational reasons for refusing to do the right thing. Repeatedly he led his fellow justices, law professors, and most of the legal profession down the path of "reason" to nonaction. Frankfurter turned the words *comity, abstention, nonjusticiability,* and *political questions* into reputable legal doctrines. Through skill, a long life, and a dedicated cadre of law clerks,* he captivated the minds of legal scholars, and his philosophy—as effectively as Judge Ed's—barred from courts the poor and the oppressed who really needed their protection.

Then, in March 1962 (in *Baker* v. *Carr,* a Tennessee case), the Supreme Court opened the jurisdictional gates. Immediately we moved to enter the "political thicket." Judge Johnson set April 14 for our first hearing.

That day I urged immediate action. Otherwise, I noted, "We may be in this court trying this case for a major portion of the next two years of our lives!" †

By midsummer 1962, the three district court judges (Johnson, Rives, and Mobile District Judge Daniel H. Thomas) ordered partial reapportionment and fashioned the nation's first remedy in a reapportionment case. Even though the moderate relief

---

*Most lawyers and law clerks revere their first employers and many very bright law clerks go through their law professor or attorney lives carrying with them the perpetual appellation, "he was a law clerk to . . ." Some even organize into informal associations which comprise pressure groups on history, their members spending their academic lives advocating the judicial views of their mentor. Thus there is some truth in the phrase "once a Frankfurter law clerk, always a Frankfurter law clerk." Many law clerks actually love their mentor, but there is a trace of self-interest in enhancement of their Great Man's reputation, for, in the teaching of law, reflected reputations linger.

† I was sixteen years wrong. The district court retained jurisdiction and the case is still alive and well, being used periodically to reapportion Alabama's legislature.

they ordered was too little to satisfy us, it was too much for the
Black Belt.

Probate Judge B. A. Reynolds of Selma (one of the sued election officials) retained private counsel and appealed to the Supreme Court. That changed the case name to *Reynolds* v. *Sims*.
It would also provide justices Douglas and Black with a chance
to cut into Frankfurterism's thicket to reap and enjoy the harvest
of their early dissent.

Soon after I filed the lawsuit, labor lawyer Jerome A.
Cooper—Justice Black's first law clerk and the law partner of the
justice's son, Hugo, Jr.—came to my office, which was in the
same building as his.

"Chuck, this case may cost a good bit; if it will help for
the steelworkers to share expenses, we'll come in on your
side."

It would, and they did. None of us charged fees. Despite that,
lawyers Robert S. Vance, David J. Vann, and C. H. Erskine
Smith from Birmingham, and John W. McConnell, Jr., from
Mobile, representing other voters, intervened on our side.*
When Black Belter Reynolds appealed, they cross-appealed,
saying the district court had not gone far enough, fast enough.
So I had the luxury of defending the judgment of the nation's
most distinguished district court while I simultaneously urged

---

*After I left Alabama, Vance developed a Robin Hood law practice which cut
millions of dollars from insurance companies and banks. In 1966 he became
chairman of Alabama's State Democratic Executive Committee, staying in
office despite the continuing and sometimes open opposition of George Wallace. He is now a judge on the United States Court of Appeals for the Fifth
Circuit.

Erskine Smith always helped. An organizer of the Civil Liberties Union of
Alabama, he handled numerous civil rights cases until his premature death.

McConnell had been student body president at the University of Alabama.
Later, Vance had defeated David Vann for the same post. As generous with
time as with money, Vann, who is now Birmingham's mayor, handled the
numerous mathematical facts and theories then applicable to computing representation.

the Supreme Court to make "one person, one vote" the law of the land.

~~~~~~~~

Perhaps their distrust of juries causes some corporate lawyers to believe and many law professors to teach the myth that appellate skills are akin to theirs. Any lawyer who can convincingly argue facts to a jury or law to a trial judge can argue effectively in the Supreme Court. Those afraid to try, including many law professors and some Supreme Court justices, tell a different story. The Supreme Court rules do not. Admission to the Supreme Court Bar requires three years of law practice and three recommendations, and that is more than the Constitution requires of justices. They need not be lawyers.

Frederick Bernays Wiener, said to be the nation's top appellate advocate, had moved my admission to practice before the Supreme Court on October 9, 1961.*

It was now two years later, the morning of November 13, 1963. The chief justice transmitted comfortable warmth. His manner, more like that of a kindly uncle up for reelection to the county commission than of a hard taskmaster, seemed to emphasize his lack of prior judicial experience. But his skills under-

---

*Wiener and I had become friends through happenstance at an American Bar Association meeting. Fritz Wiener had worked in the office of the solicitor general; he had argued often before the Supreme Court; and his book on appellate advocacy was widely accepted. He may have come to regret our friendship. In 1967, when I represented anti-Vietnam War Army Captain Howard B. Levy in his war against the army, I telephoned Colonel Wiener, U.S. Army retired, an expert in military law, for advice. He replied: "If I knew where the library was and you didn't, I wouldn't tell you how to get there."

In 1969, I saw him in the Supreme Court clerk's office. "Hello, Fritz," said I. Silence.

"How are you, Fritz?"

Silence.

I tried once more. Then I went about my business.

cut the argument that bar leaders should judge the "qualifications" of judicial nominees or otherwise control judicial selection.

Charles, ten, and Camille were there to watch and listen. The courtroom is high-ceilinged and plush. Through flowing maroon draperies the justices suddenly materialized. That may have impressed Charles. It did me. We had explained to Charles that this case—*Reynolds* v. *Sims*—might determine the kind of government under which he and his friends would live. He humored us and listened attentively.

I was nervous. Too soon after I began, the white light on the lectern would appear to tell me I had five more minutes. When the red light flashed the rules required that I stop (even if in midsentence) and sit down.

I knew where I wanted the law to go and what I thought should be said to get there. I had read every book, law-review article, and judicial opinion which alluded to reapportionment. Every fact was familiar to me, yet I was nervous. There is an edgy wariness which asks: "Am I *really* prepared? Have I *really* done all I can do? Do I have *every* document which I might need?" And then: "Must I listen to another rationalization about representation based upon acreage and economic interests?" And finally: "I know more about this damned case than anyone else in the whole world!"

Armed with an outline, I quickly moved to the lectern. The chief justice was flanked by justices Black and Douglas. The faces of the other six justices disclosed interest or hostility, I wasn't sure which. When the chief justice looked down, smiled, and said, "Mr. Morgan," I no longer cared, for if this was a "people's court," those judges were the jury, and my first Supreme Court argument was under way.

We had entered the "political thicket" of legislative apportionment knowing that representation had been allocated to "the shipping interests, . . . labor and business . . ." That was wrong. I told the justices, "One fact comes through, the easiest judicially maintainable standard of apportionment should . . . be population. . . ."

First one justice, then another, interrupted with questions.

Land could be no proper basis for representative districts, I responded. An acreage apportionment "naturally" provided "a rural basis." That seemed simple enough, for "there is more farm land than city land." There also "are fewer farmers than city people," I explained, adding that a rurally dominated government could not be "responsive to the people. The essence of our government is responsiveness to the people," and it all "boils down to a question of trust in people. . . .

"If we assume the power of self-government is the power of people to think and to reason and vote and properly elect their own representatives, the majority should surely have the right to elect representatives in both houses of the legislature." If only one legislative house were to be apportioned on a population basis, the people would "have the equal protection of one-half the law."

Again and again I insisted: "Population is the standard that must be met."

The chief justice interrupted. "[C]an we issue an order on reapportionment that will have a lasting effect and will avoid gross inequalities?"

"Yes, there's no doubt . . ."

He interrupted again. "I think the Court must conclude, then, that both houses have to be on a state population basis, as you said a moment ago. One house one way and another, another way is unacceptable."

There was another question, then another.

The white light was burning. Time was almost up.

"The district court is competent to handle the continuing order," I said; "it is exhibiting the requisite speed in doing so." I concluded: "We feel the rights of all Alabamians and all Americans rest on the decision of this Court with respect to whether or not *people* have, on the basis for which this country was founded—for each man—one vote."

On Monday, June 15, 1964, I flew to Oxford, Ohio, to speak to the Mississippi Freedom Summer Volunteers. That morning word came from the Supreme Court. While the taxicab to the airport waited, I ran into the Court to get my copy of the opinion. In the taxicab I read Chief Justice Warren's words, echoing my argument.

> Legislators represent people, not trees or acres. Legislators are elected by voters, not farms or cities or economic interests.

He reemphasized democracy.

> As long as ours is a representative form of government and our legislatures are those instruments of government elected directly by and directly representative of the people, the right to elect legislators in a free and unimpaired fashion is a bedrock of our political system. . . .
> Citizens, not history or economic interests, cast votes. Considerations of area alone provide an insufficient justification for deviations from the equal-population principle. Again, people, not land or trees or pastures, vote.

He dismissed Frankfurterism.

> We are told that the matter . . . is a complex and many-faceted one. We are cautioned about the dangers of entering into political thickets. . . . Our answer is this: a denial of constitutionally protected rights demands judicial protection; our oath and our office require no less of us.

A month later Camille, Charles, and I stood near the clubhouse exit at Yankee Stadium. Hundreds of children clamored for autographs. When the Yankees' manager emerged, they shouted, "Yogi! Yogi!"

The chief justice, out of uniform and unrecognized, walked to a waiting automobile. I pointed him out to Charles, who waved. Earl Warren waved back.

~~~~~~~~

As we headed back south, the "final" decision in *Reynolds* v. *Sims* became a starting place for the in-court struggle for the rights of black voters. By gerrymandering black majority counties with majority white counties, majority white districts were created in a manner which mandated that newly registered black voters would be outvoted.

Then, on October 2, 1965, the three judges of the district court struck down the legislature's plan. "If this court ignores the long history of racial discrimination in Alabama," they wrote, "it will prove that justice is both blind and deaf. With . . . [that] as a backdrop, the cavalier treatment accorded predominantly Negro counties . . . takes on added meaning. The intent [to join] . . . predominantly Negro counties with predominantly white counties for the sole purpose of preventing the election of Negroes" was thwarted as that part of the plan was struck down.

Most of those who marched from Selma had gone home, as had the soldiers and the marshals. But Montgomery's federal judges, the most perceptive federal agents in the Deep South, manned their outpost and refused to allow "Alabama's Negroes . . . to find, just as they were about to achieve the right to vote, that that right had been abridged by racial gerrymandering."

~~~~~~~~

Almost a decade later, Linda Charlton, the reporter to whom Justice Douglas singled out *Reynolds* v. *Sims,* laughed and recalled for me the instructions she had received from her editor at *Newsday* on the uneasy eve of her departure south from New York to report upon the struggle of blacks for their equal right to vote. Her editor thought he was reassuring her when he said: "Put ten dollars in your bra and ten cents in your shoe. The bill is for bail. The dime is to call Chuck Morgan in Atlanta." An editor I didn't know was sending me a case I didn't need and which didn't exist.

It was about then that the Black Belt's governor, George Wallace, sent me a message of a different sort via statewide television. He told a joint session of the legislature: "The people of Alabama expect you and me to protect this state from an apportionment plan submitted by the attorney of the American Civil Liberties Union—said to be in exile—Chuck Morgan."

During the following spring (1966), Tuskegee attorney Fred D. Gray was elected to Alabama's house of representatives from one of the newly created districts. He was Alabama's first black legislator since Reconstruction. That had quite an impact upon the state and those who lived in Gray's Black Belt district—including George C. Wallace, who had begun his political career in the office to which Fred Gray was elected.

5

In the late afternoon of June 6, 1966, James H. Meredith, Jr., was shotgunned down by a bushwhacker near Hernando, Mississippi, fourteen miles south of Memphis, on U.S. Highway 51. His solitary march into Mississippi had been designed to diminish the fear of other blacks and to encourage them to register to vote.

Four years earlier, the loner Meredith had forced the Movement to champion his entry into the University of Mississippi when most civil rights lawyers believed it would be better left until last. Meredith, unconcerned with their well-reasoned timetables, confronted local and national civil rights organizations (and Robert Kennedy's Justice Department) with his intention to enroll. So confronted, they had to help. By putting his life on the line, Meredith spun forward mankind's social clock. Now he was inert, in pain and bleeding at the roadside. The shot which felled him summoned the Movement to its last march.

At 7:30 A.M., on Delta flight 454, June 7, 1966, Hosea Williams, Martin King, Ralph Abernathy, Bernard Lee, and I flew to Memphis.

"There's a slight turbulence in the air," the pilot advised.

"It'll be a lot more turbulent on the ground," Hosea laughed.

White Memphis policemen barred newsmen from Meredith's hospital room.* They started to search us, stopping when it dawned on them that Martin King wouldn't be armed. After Meredith, King, and CORE's Floyd McKissick agreed to continue the march, they were joined by SNCC's Stokely Carmichael and others, who included John J. Hooker, the liberal candidate for governor of Tennessee. If blacks had not been registered to vote, his liberal political friends would have urged him to be elsewhere. But many were registered and Hooker accepted the risks of decency. Meredith was glad to see him. But the moment they shook hands, the banter ended. Meredith cried out in pain: "Only the hand! I've got a hole in the arm there!"

Immediately Hosea Williams drove down the highway clocking mileage and looking for campsites. From logistical answers policy questions might rise. Should northern whites be housed in the homes of Mississippi's black rural poor? Who should make arrangements for legal representation? Should anyone notify the FBI? Who should check in with local leaders? Which local leaders? Who should raise funds, sign checks, and coordinate between SCLC, SNCC, and CORE?

Many of the telephone calls which had to be made could be made only by Martin King. For no matter how tired or sick or

---

*Roy Reed of *The New York Times* and Bill Kovach of the *Nashville Tennessean* managed to sneak in.

Reed had been with Meredith on his march. A moment before the shooting Reed had walked into a roadside store to purchase a Coca-Cola. When the wire service photographs of Meredith lying on the highway reached Claude Sitton, *The New York Times*'s national news director, he studied them, then shouted: "Where in the hell was Roy Reed?"

When Reed moved from Atlanta years later, we gave him the memento which *Los Angeles Times* reporter Jack Nelson procured: Sitton's classic editorial reaction inscribed upon a mounted gold-plated Coke bottle.

overwhelmed with work King was, many white liberals would not respond to his aides, who shared with him a common dream.

That afternoon, we ate fried chicken under the smiling, bearded countenance of Colonel Sanders, and drove south from Memphis down U.S. Highway 51. As the station wagon of Memphis movement leader James Lawson neared the point of Meredith's ambush, the long silence was interrupted by Martin. "You always wonder who'll be next, don't you?"

After another long silence, we bantered about who would preach at whose funeral. The preachers won. We parked on the shoulder of the highway, piled out of the station wagon, prayed, and sang "We Shall Overcome."

Earlier in the day, Dick Gregory had arrived in Memphis and had begun his own march down Interstate Highway 55, which runs parallel to U.S. 51. When bystanders told him they had heard on the radio that Dr. King was on his way from Memphis, Gregory walked back to meet him. He walked and walked and walked some more. When we drove back to the Lorraine Motel we found Gregory sitting on the steps examining his blistered, swollen feet. He had been on the wrong highway.

That night in Martin King's crowded room, Stokely Carmichael, SNCC's newly elected chairman, presided.

Martin, in sock feet, wearing pants and an old-style undershirt, ate from a tray on the bed and listened to Hosea Williams plead for nonviolence.

"Shut up, chubby," came the deep, even-toned voice of Ernest Thomas, an organizer of Deacons for Defense and Democracy, a black Louisiana-based self-defense group.

Stokely Carmichael defended their right to participate. Again, Hosea disagreed. Earlier that day Martin and I had talked about black "militants" who never struck or otherwise injured white men. The Deacons and Stokely spoke of "self-defense." They had plausible arguments. Elsewhere, others seemed to want violence for its own sake. Their rhetoric left Martin more puzzled than put out.

When the Black Panthers shouted, "Off the pigs! Kill the

cops!" and the cops killed them, I understood the cops. When
Ku Klux Klansmen killed with stealth and denied that they had
done so, I understood the Ku Klux Klansmen; they were guerrillas. I didn't understand those who merely chanted the rhetoric
of violence—and thereby invited reprisals. Unless they worked
for the cops or others who sought to frighten white folks into
putting black folks further down. Or, unless their threats, like
the threats of many who speak of suicide, were pleas for life.

Propped up on his elbows, Martin King answered even those
who believed in the use of violence for self-defense.

"I believe in nonviolence not only as a religious and moral
matter, but also as a matter of tactics."

The room was as quiet as a wiretap.

"If you want a violent march, go have one. You have a violent
march, but don't expect me to join in your march. Don't try to
bring me into your violence. We'll watch. We'll pray for you as
you head off into Mississippi."

He stopped talking. No one coughed or moved.

Finally a Deacon broke the silence. "We'll take your way,
Doctor, til we know it doesn't work."

What worked was the Christian religion.

Later the black leaders went to two Memphis churches and
drew the strength, sense of purpose, and unity they knew they
would find there. Since black preachers were paid by blacks,
they were free to lead, and those with courage did so. In much of
the Deep South, churches were the only places blacks could
freely assemble. With spirituals and hymns as freedom songs
and nonviolent demonstrations as a way to shuck off the past,
southern blacks found a tangible way to be "born again."

I remained at the motel as Martin King's designee to mediate
the group which was to unite the Movement behind a written
statement of goals. "Negro Americans" was changed to "black
people" and back to "Negro Americans." The document was
termed a "statement of purpose," then a "manifesto." But it was

the conflict between such cliché phrases as "the mainstream of American life" and "the making of their own destinies" which cut across the Movement.

Near midnight we met in the large conference room above the motel office. The NAACP's Roy Wilkins contended that the marchers should seek still another set of civil rights laws.

Carmichael slammed his hand on the table. "That cat the President's a bigot!"

"Don't give me that 'that cat the President' stuff, Stokely!" Wilkins shouted back.

Floyd McKissick sought order. The Urban League's Whitney Young proposed reason. Wilkins walked out.

Martin sighed, shook his head, smiled wearily and adjourned the meeting.

≈≈≈≈≈≈≈

The phrase "black power" had been used by Stokely and SNCC members the night before the march, but it would not be unfurled until they were down the highway at Greenwood. To many whites it would sound like the other side of "white supremacy." Soon politicians and columnists would analyze the "new mood." They desperately wanted to believe Booker T. Washington's description of Negroes as "the most patient, faithful, law-abiding and unresentful people . . ." But there were rumblings from northern ghettoes, where blacks lost hope and found bricks.

"That cat the President's" quest for "victory" in Vietnam, the riots, and the resulting shame which was shared by cold-war liberals split the Movement.

6

Lester Garfield Maddox, politician, was no more improbable than Lester Garfield Maddox, restaurateur. Born into the honest, God-fearing white working class, in early childhood, he was taught the central lesson learned by poor whites: "It takes hard work to make a payday." Nobody gave Lester Maddox a thing. For him there would be no college education, no inheritance, no trip abroad, not even *Mister* Maddox.

After a short stint in Bessemer, Alabama's, steel mills, Lester married and went into the food business with his wife. Finally, with their handshake and friendly manner, the Maddoxes developed their pride and joy—the Pickrick Restaurant— where they served good-quality food at reasonable prices to white working-class families. They made better-than-middling money in fried chicken and that made Lester Maddox middle class.

Faith in himself and in white folks caused him to advertise in Atlanta's daily newspapers. Which he hated. His advertisements contained attacks on the newspapers which ran the ads and messages of "segregationist populism" *—all of which merged with announcements of his daily menu as though he was offering a feast of inexpensive, delicious, high-quality, all-white, anti-Communist drumsticks.

After his 1961 tape-recorded interview for the *Atlanta Journal*, Reese Cleghorn quoted Maddox: "God set up the boundaries of the habitations of people, by continent." The problem, as Lester saw it, was that "our" blacks wound up on the wrong continent.

"History speaks for itself," he said, speaking for history. "We've never had an integrated society anywhere that was as successful as a segregated society, in any country, any time. . . ."

Brazil and Italy were his examples of integrated but unsuccessful societies. He opposed Brazil and Italy. He also opposed "the big financial people": the Carnegies, the Fords, and the Mellons, who were behind it all.

After passage of the Civil Rights Act of 1964, Maddox drove blacks from his Pickrick Restaurant with pick-handles.

I first met him that summer at his trial in Atlanta's federal courthouse. His eyes seemed to goggle and his manner was that of a person who was inquiring whether I, too, intended to do him wrong. I accompanied the "Inc. Fund" (NAACP Legal Defense Fund) lawyers who did intend to do him in. That day he was cordial and subdued, but courtroom manners are as easy to don as a pious appearance and a Sunday suit.

The federal court ordered him to serve every well-behaved member of the public who could afford to purchase his reasonably priced food. Lester told the black public, the "Communists," and the federal government to go to hell, to Brazil, or to wherever. He would sell out the Pickrick Restaurant before he'd sell

---

*Prior to 1894 populism was nonracist. After disfranchisement, the movement turned to racism, but there were a few latter-day nonracist Populists, such as Alabama's Folsom and the dynasty which began with Louisiana's Huey P. Long.

out his principles, so he barred two young blacks who sought service under the injunction and said: "The Communists have put me out of business. . . ." Then Lester sold the Pickrick (at a profit). Like Wallace, who won by surrendering his alma mater, the University of Alabama, to superior forces after a brief stand in the doorway, Lester Maddox was to win by giving up his restaurant and his career.

~~~~~~~

Near Pine Mountain, Georgia, where Callaway Mills produces the family's textile fortune, the Ida Cason Callaway Gardens blossom every spring. The resort, gardens, golf courses, and fishing lakes which sprawl across the countryside are cared for by lawyers, whose complicated statutes and trust agreements turn tax hedges into hedgerows.

Local blacks and whites cried when Franklin D. Roosevelt died in nearby Warm Springs, and many of those who remember FDR still vote Democratic.

The Callaways turned Republican.

Howard H. ("Bo") Callaway, a natural heir to Georgia's good life, entered politics with vistas as broad as those of a Phi Delta Theta pledgemaster. He graduated from West Point, and his military bearing, whiny-twanged Bourbonism, and inherited wealth combined to command attention. As a member of the state university system's board of regents, Bo had a chance to indicate an avid interest in maintaining segregation.

Many rich unaffected white southerners worked for segregation, and segregation worked for them. They joined private clubs and sent their children to private schools, while The Issue kept working-class whites and blacks apart and down.

Until 1964, ardent segregationists remained nominal Democrats. More than ten years had passed since Jim Folsom told me, "Boy, them goddamned Dixiecrats'll sleep with 'em at night and eat the breakfast they give 'em the next morning. But they'll never let 'em sit down to eat with 'em. That's the difference. Letting 'em sit down."

The Dixiecrats despised Eisenhower's Republican judiciary, but it was only when Presidents Kennedy and Johnson seemed really committed to integration that rebel yells became the war cry of "conservative" Republicanism. Goldwater's candidacy made it easy for them to find their proper political seats, and Bo Callaway's was in Congress.

Maddox, by then a three-time loser at the polls, also supported Goldwater, but he remained a Democrat. By 1966 he had become a symbol of resistance, and history conspired with fiction to turn the Georgia governor's race into a classic Faulknerian confrontation.

Bo believed that blacks and liberal whites, when presented with a choice between himself and Lester, would choose him. Bo was no Snopes. A Bourbon wouldn't use a pick-handle to dig a ditch, let alone to chase a "nigger." With Bo in office there would be segregation and order and *image* in Georgia, but to get Bo into office as the "lesser-of-evils candidate," the Bourbons needed someone for Bo to be "less evil than." History's central casting had sent them Lester.

~~~~~~~

Georgia had begun its turn to "one-person, one-vote" democracy in 1963 when the Supreme Court struck down county-unit voting, which had given the voters of small counties a disproportionately large voice in the selection of statewide officials, including the governor.* That system had protected poverty, promoted segregation, and produced as its star galluses-snapping Governor Eugene Talmadge. It was Ol' Gene who had said, "The Georgia farmer has three friends: God, the Sears, Roebuck catalogue, and Gene Talmadge." He had been close to

---

*Under the county-unit system, each of Georgia's 159 counties had at least two votes for governor. Since the most votes any county could cast was six, Fulton County (Atlanta) and the state's other urban areas had virtually no voice in state government. A lawsuit filed by Atlanta's brilliant liberal lawyer Morris B. Abram resulted in abolition of the county-unit system.

the truth but not close enough. Sears had moved up in the world, and Southern poor whites always had a hard time keeping friends, especially after they elected them into social proximity with high-class white folks. So now poor white Georgia farmers had only God, and there were those who believed even He had left them, in order to attend National Council of Churches meetings with—and they spat out the words—"Martin Luther Coon!"

Since the federal courts allowed the general assembly a "reasonable" time to reapportion totally, incumbent legislators took all the time the law allowed—and then some. So in the 1966 Democratic primary elections, even though the majority of the people were to elect the governor statewide rather than on a county-unit basis, the rural counties of Georgia had one last chance to elect a seriously malapportioned legislature.

During World War II, young lawyer Ellis Gibbs Arnall interrupted the Talmadge reign. Governor Arnall's liberal, honest political leadership—the one brand of politics the state had not tried—resulted in his being termed "radical" by some and a "nigger-lover" by others.

In 1966 Arnall decided to be governor again. During twenty years out of office he had built a diverse, relatively small, but lucrative corporate law practice. Included as clients were a life insurance company (a major share of which Arnall owned), an arm of Coca-Cola, and even Walt Disney Studios. Power flows to those who represent major business interests, and in the Democratic primary Arnall was the man to beat. He was well known. He had sufficient financing to run a front-runner's race.

During Jim Folsom's first term (1947–51) in adjoining Alabama, he had looked to Arnall's record as governor for guidance, as had other southern progressives. I can remember Folsom talking wistfully about the antitrust suits he should have brought, "like Arnall." Now, I suppose, Arnall wistfully thinks about the 1966 campaign he should have run in order to generate the electricity which crackles around a surefire winner. But it didn't really matter.

Bo Callaway knew that he was a surefire loser if Arnall got the

Democratic nomination. Arnall asleep was more exciting than a wideawake Callaway. Besides, Arnall would split the business community and he would sweep the votes of newly registered blacks. So the Republicans adopted the campaign plan which Richard Nixon was to use in 1972: they sought to name the Democratic nominee.

Callaway had been nominated by petition and there was no Republican primary. His campaigners quietly urged Georgia's new-breed Republicans to vote in the Democratic primary for the weakest Democrat—Lester Maddox.

And that is what they did. An unknown but exciting young farmer from Plains, James Earl (they called him "Jimmy") Carter, ran a surprisingly strong third. Simultaneously Republican crossovers canceled the ballots of the 135,000 newly registered blacks, and in the runoff Maddox beat Arnall 443,055 to 393,004.*

Bo Callaway's trick had worked and he was riding high. Blacks and many white liberals, especially those termed "loyal Democrats," would not (simply *could not*) vote for a pick-handle-wielding segregationist. Neither could Georgia's image-conscious business community.

To Bourbons, particularly to Black Belters, politics always had been the southern white man's polo—exclusively his Great Game. The entry of illiterate blacks from the sidelines required basic changes in the rules which even well-meaning moderate white politicians did not understand.

Reaction to the Maddox primary victory was immediate. Atlanta's wealthy, soft-spoken mayor, Ivan W. Allen, Jr., set the tone for the unexpected. He termed the results "deplorable." He blamed them on the "combined forces of ignorance, prej-

---

*The *Atlanta Constitution*'s Bruce Galphin analyzed the runoff returns. In Atlanta's Eighth Ward alone there were 1,693 naked crossovers. In prosperously new-rich, new-Republican Sandy Springs there were 1,438. In fifty-five counties the Maddox primary runoff vote exceeded his general election vote, even though the turnout was higher in the general election than in the runoff.

udice, reactionism, and the duplicity of many Republican voters." He refused to surrender "to the rabble of prejudice,
extremism, buffoonery, and incompetency!"

A speaker at an Atlanta banquet served notice "that you cannot pressure us, buy us, or blackmail us into voting for Bo Callaway by giving us Lester Maddox as an only alternative."

The *Atlanta Constitution*'s publisher and syndicated columnist, Ralph McGill, saw a write-in campaign and the lawsuits
which would accompany it as "a healthy, educational experience
for all concerned." Arnall, whose name was to be written in,
refused to disavow or support the movement. He said the "conscience" of the voters and their view of the "long-range best
interest of the state would govern." If the people wanted a
write-in movement, "that's their business."

"I can't support Lester Maddox," Martin King said to reporters. "And I can't vote for Callaway. He is against the poverty
program and the minimum wage, and I don't think he'd be any
better than Maddox. We're in a bad way. But I would think you
could write in somebody."

❦❦❦❦❦❦❦

"I don't want no racist governor, I don't want no company
man. . . ." The guitars and folk singers twanged and sang the
message of Write-In Georgia. It was one month before election
day. The crowd of more than one thousand, many of whom
tapped time, packed the ballroom of Atlanta's Biltmore Hotel
and overflowed into the hallways. ". . . no company man; all I
want is Ellis Arnall and I'll elect him if I can."

The hopeless campaign was under way.

If neither Maddox nor Callaway acquired a clear majority, the
election would be thrown into the Democratic-controlled general assembly. There Callaway was the likely loser, but, as the
Atlanta Constitution's Ralph McGill wrote, after that process no
winner would carry even the "hint of a mandate or general
approval."

Despite concern about the safety of rural Georgia blacks if

Maddox won, Martin King and those who had risked their lives to acquire the vote decided to educate Republican literates by penalizing them for their crossovers.

In the Deep South at least twenty-five percent of the adult population couldn't read or write. Despite that (and because of it), a Georgia statute forbade any person from providing assistance at the polls to more than one illiterate person. Atlanta lawyer Morris Brown and I brought suit to strike that statute down. On Friday, October 28, the three-judge district court ruled it unconstitutional and in violation of the Voting Rights Act of 1965. They raised the number whom one person could assist to ten. They ruled that "poor spellers" could take a sheet of paper with their candidate's name on it into polling places. But they refused to authorize the use of printed paste-ons or stickers, and I couldn't visualize impatient election officials willing to wait while angry, literate voters stood in line behind illiterates who had to laboriously copy from crumpled sheets of paper, E-L-L-I-S G. A-R-N-A-L-L F-O-R G-O-V-E-R-N-O-R.

Only that precise phrase and spelling or, "For Governor, Ellis G. Arnall," could result in a properly tallied vote. Georgia law required that the names of write-in candidates be reported "exactly as they were written, deposited, or affixed." In the 1964 presidential election there had been write-in votes for "Robert F. Kennedy" and "Robert Kennedy." They were counted separately, as were "George Romney" and "Governor Romney"; "William Scranton" and "Wm. Scranton"; "Adlai Stevenson" and "Adlaide Stevenson"; "Geo. Wallace," "George Wallace," "George A. Wallace," "George C. Wallace," and "Gov. Wallace." (The two votes cast for CBS television newsman Walter Cronkite were spelled correctly.)

The morning after the court's ruling, ten days before the election, I drove eighty-seven miles south to Macon to feed unpalatable law to 774 vitally alive campaign workers and to tell them what I had told the judges. Despite state-imposed illiteracy, Georgia had scheduled the world's largest spelling bee.

Upstairs at Five Forsyth Street in Atlanta, campaign workers were in and out of Write-In Georgia's headquarters at all hours. They spent time and money they couldn't afford on a campaign they could not win, in a cause which at first only they seemed to understand.

Maddox attacked Callaway's class interests. "I know what it is to struggle and do without. . . . It's no fault of a millionaire he doesn't understand people. . . . I know how to say 'no' to a wife who wants a new dress . . . the Wall Street crowd is trying to prove they can buy the office of Governor."

As Maddox's crowds increased, Callaway sensed danger. Like Maddox, he attacked instinctively. A week before the election, Callaway's men revealed the results of an "Oliver Quayle survey" which showed Callaway ahead of Maddox 44 percent to 27 percent.

For four weeks Write-In Georgia had been told their cause was futile. *Atlanta Constitution* editor Eugene Patterson, relying upon the Quayle figures, wrote that almost all of the 22 percent of the undecided voters would have to swing to Maddox for the election to be thrown into the general assembly.

Convinced these figures were wrong, I telephoned Quayle. His last survey had been completed on October 22. It showed Callaway ahead of Maddox—but by 42 percent to 34 percent. I asked him to telephone Patterson, who, two days later, noted the "mistake" and commented that Callaway was "running like a dry creek . . . where Maddox's poor-boy campaign had taken hold."

~~~~~~~

On election day (November 8, 1966) hundreds of complaints poured into Five Forsyth Street. At one polling place scores of illiterates demanded assistance. From all over Georgia there were reports of people trying, too often unsuccessfully, to vote for Arnall.

That evening, Write-In Georgia's leaders and others from the office, the press, and the Movement dropped by at our house.

Television networks hire competing political analysts, and in

New York, my friend John F. Kraft was to predict for ABC. I watched as Kraft agreed with the earlier projections from the other networks—Callaway's election was assured.

Moments later the telephone rang. It was Roy Reed of *The New York Times*. He was in the state's heaviest-voting suburban county, which used IBM's new punch cards and computerized Votomatics.

"The computer's broken down!"

Many voters scrawled obscenities rather than "Arnall" on their Votomatic cards. For them, the write-in had prompted write-them-all-off.

I telephoned Kraft. I told him the computer was disgusted. It was eating the ballots. I didn't care what ABC's sample showed, Callaway wasn't going to acquire a majority.

Kraft hedged when he resumed broadcasting, then withdrew his earlier prediction. But it still appeared that Callaway was in.

Our dejected guests departed early. At 1:00 A.M. the telephone rang.

"Chuck, this is John. You were right!" *

I fumbled for a pencil and notepad. He gave me the figures. I rolled out of bed and went to the den to finish work on the complaint, which I had already drafted.

To remove the selection from the Democratic legislature, Callaway would rely upon a recently enacted statute which pro-

---

*John Kraft died in 1973. He loved the people who made up his random samples. A quiet, shy hulk of a man, he picked personal and political favorites carefully and stuck with them.

I used Kraft's "probability" techniques in the argument of *Whitus* v. *Georgia,* a case which helped restructure that state's jury system. In a footnote, the Supreme Court wrote, "While unnecessary to our disposition of the instant case, it is interesting to note the 'probability' involved in the situation before this Court. . . ."

Thus Kraft's theory entered legal history and provided me "authority" to cite to lower federal courts. In a challenge to the jury system of Mobile County, Alabama, the Court of Appeals for the Fifth Circuit approved the use of random sampling techniques for proving racial discrimination in the selection of juror names.

vided for runoffs from general elections as though they were primaries. To win he would have to bar write-in votes.

To us, legislative selection by a properly apportioned general assembly was satisfactory. I sought immediate and total reapportionment and a choice from the top *three* candidates—Callaway, Maddox, and Arnall. Without total reapportionment, we wanted a brand-new, wide-open, special election. Until his successor was elected, incumbent Governor Carl E. Sanders could serve.

Lois Coplan, my bright, committed assistant, who later became a lawyer, already knew what many lawyers never learn—a full night's sleep is not mentioned in licenses to practice. At 4:30 A.M. I finished the suit papers. Lois picked them up and headed to Five Forsyth Street.

By the time the federal court clerk's office opened, Lois was ready and waiting. They accepted the complaint, motions, and memoranda which said there had been a failure of election even though downstairs in the newspaper rack the *Atlanta Constitution's* headline read: CALLAWAY CLOSING IN ON MADDOX: GOP SWEEPING TO HOUSE VICTORY.

The votes finally tallied out to 449,894 (47.07 percent) for Callaway, 448,044 (46.88 percent) for Maddox, and 57,832 (6.05 percent for "Ellis Arnall," who on November 8, 1966, at age fifty-nine, had been renamed "Armdill," "Arnade," and "Arnald." The last picked up seven votes in Atlanta's East, Point suburb, twenty-six votes in Precinct 1-E and five in 4-D. In 1-E, "Harner" got ten votes and "Arour" got thirteen.

Statewide, the spelling variations were incalculable, but Georgia's good spellers thwarted Callaway. The "experts" were astounded. The newspapers reported that the message had finally gotten through. "Informed sources" said if there were a runoff election, Callaway was considering asking Negroes to vote for him.

"This is God speaking!" The voice boomed from the speaker phone. It was five in the afternoon and the whiskey had begun to flow. The voice—not that of Martin King, to whom we some-times irreverently referred as "De Lawd"—proceeded with om-niscient accuracy to name the people present and the brands of whiskey in the bottles lined up on my desk. When the voice, also not that of J. Edgar Hoover, suggested that the reporters and lawyers present get back to work, I looked out across the street and up. It was Ralph McGill. He stood laughing and looking down at allies from the window in the *Atlanta Constitution* office across the street.

Roy Reed of *The New York Times* charitably referred to my "cluttered *coffee*-stained office" when he reported the postelec-tion scene, and I suppose some of those stains had come from coffee. As Reed put it, "Meanwhile, friends of the write-in movement, lawyers, amateur and professional politicians, and civil rights leaders continued this week to buzz through the cluttered, coffee-stained office of the American Civil Liberties Union here to consult with Charles Morgan, Jr., the energetic southern director of the organization.

"Mr. Morgan is the brains behind much of the legal maneuv-ering that has kept the election in court since Nov. 8.

"And a new campaign bumper sticker has appeared on liber-als' cars. Spoofing Mr. Callaway's 'Go Bo' slogan, it says, 'Go Bo—And Take Lester With You.' "

Three days after the election, a district court hearing had been held on our suit and Callaway's (the two had been consolidated by the court). Five days later the three-judge panel invoked the "one-person, one-vote" rule to strike down legislative selection. When Callaway's attorneys proposed a December 6 runoff with write-in votes barred, the judges turned them down. The Geor-gia election case was moving rapidly to the Supreme Court. It was set for argument on December 5, 1966.

Our attack on the state's racially discriminatory jury selection laws (*Whitus* v. *Georgia*) was set for argument on December 7, so, facing two Supreme Court cases within three days, I moved to Washington's Congressional Hotel. The city was abandoned on that dreary Thanksgiving weekend.

At 10:00 A.M. on December 5, the members of the Supreme Court stepped through the ceiling-high draperies and quickly moved to their seats. Usually they set aside one hour for oral argument. This case dealt with basic voting rights and state-federal relationships, so three hours were scheduled.

Georgia's assistant attorney general, Harold N. Hill, Jr., was first up. He relied upon the 142-year history of the state law, as though law, like fine wine, improved with age. The federal Constitution provides for presidential selection by the House of Representatives if no candidate achieves an electoral college majority. Hill argued that Georgia's election process was analogous—the election process ended on election day—and to break "ties" states could flip coins.

As usual the justices began by choosing up sides. Justice Fortas asked Hill: "Is it all right for a state to have the man who comes in second be elected governor?"

Douglas asked him: "Is it constitutional to provide that the legislature may select the governor if no candidate receives two-thirds of the vote?"

Then I was up.

During the campaign, Georgia's attorney general had announced his legal judgment that a stand-off would be decided by the (malapportioned) general assembly. His opinion had the force of law. Because I was trying to defeat the remedy proposed by Callaway's lawyers, who wanted a runoff election with write-ins barred, I argued that the attorney general's opinion had misled the voters. The election should be declared "null and void."

Mr. Justice Black, a skilled advocate, bore down: Did I know of an election where some voters hadn't been misled?

No, I replied, but the Georgia misleading undercut the electoral structure and the very rules by which the election was held. Besides, I said, returning to the basic theme of the case, Georgia's constitution "deprive[d] voters of a direct voice in the election" and "filtered" their votes through unrepresentative legislators.

I noted that "a man with a Ph.D. from the University of Chicago and nineteen honorary degrees was misled and [I asked] what of the 135,000 voters who were registered under the Voting Rights Act? . . ."

Black smiled. He gently suggested, "Maybe they had more common sense knowledge about elections than the Ph.D.s." There was laughter, but I knew that Black was probably right.

At another point I was heading into a corner.

Justice White: "And I suppose you would argue that a state could not adopt a parliamentary form of government?"

I answered, "I really find myself being almost forced into that position, and now that I'm almost into it I want to get out of it and I don't want to argue it."

Now laughter filled the courtroom. "Very wise," remarked the justice.

Six days after the argument, the Supreme Court split five to four in favor of general assembly selection. Justice Black reasoned that since the November 8 election had failed, the state's procedure for legislative selection could be employed.

That morning, more than 100 of the state's 259 lawmakers were gathered at a legislative forum in Athens. When word of the decision came, dozens of them rushed to congratulate Maddox, their new leader in their ages-old cause.

Bo Callaway, whom Ralph McGill described as a "stainless-steel young man, without emotions or feelings for people," stood alone.

In Atlanta there were reports of other lawsuits. I scotched them. We were "disappointed" that there was to be no new election, but this battle was over. When the general assembly reconvened on January 9, 1967, it abided by the Supreme Court's orders, and selected Lester G. Maddox as governor.

~~~~~~~~~~

Blacks, along with liberal whites, had sent more than a message to Georgia's Big Mules. They had made them hear.

Before he died, Ralph McGill wrote of that "futile" campaign when we fed that "dead horse." To McGill that had been "public education at its best." He quoted a young person's guitar-strummed campaign song:

> Oh, I went to the poll, pencil in my hand.
> Didn't want to vote for either man.
> What they had said was ugly and bad.
> They made Democracy feel real sad.
> So I took my ballot, wrote in a name.
> And Georgia hasn't been the same.

Chorus:

> Oh, no, Georgia hasn't yet been the same,
> Since I walked right in, wrote in a name
> And walked right out again.

7

To poor whites in the "Solid South," power, like the moon, seemed inaccessible. They knew that the vote was the key. But they rarely found the doors, let alone the right locks. In almost every case their candidates turned out to be not poor men's guides, but rich men's guards whose desire to redistribute power (meaning "wealth") ran as deep as their own hip pockets.* The Big Mules had "access," or, as they said when contributing their dues to those political Pinkertons, "a chance to present our views."

Blacks, like poor whites, knew that political power was in the hands of insiders who controlled the nominating process. Like white leaders, some black leaders saw politics as a way to get "a piece of the action." But their piece was as tiny as their price,

---

*As Ralph McGill wrote in *The South and the Southerner*: "The people of the South have suffered much, but most of it has been piled on their backs by their own leaders. Nearly all of this misdirection and deceit has come from the region's politicians, many of them so grotesque it seems impossible they could have been influential."

and all blacks faced the maze of century-old barriers which had been erected against all outsiders—especially dedicated blacks.*

White Alabama had always made its position clear, but pragmatic liberals tried not to understand. Their doctrine of sweet reason was part of the Harvard-Yale syndrome—a rational process which allowed intelligent, educated people to refuse to believe that Wallace really intended to stand in that schoolhouse doorway. That enabled them to deal with him less harshly than the law required. And by refusing to believe he really intended to be President they were able to use his candidacy to complement theirs.

But it must have been hard to swallow the slogan "White Supremacy, For the Right" which was arched around the Alabama Democratic party's white rooster emblem. It was too hard for me. In 1962, while living in Birmingham, I had worked with Orzell Billingsley on a lawsuit designed to strike "White Supremacy" from the ballot. We were unsuccessful. So, prominently featured atop every ballot remained the message the swastika had conveyed to Jews, and even when we voted against the South's most basic compromise, by the act of voting, we endorsed and became part of it. Some of us also remained apart from it, but not because we refused to understand The System and to face up to the wrongness of our participation in it. We also knew that the phrase, "free, white, and twenty-one," like "white supremacy," meant white folks were free to vote for President if The Man was favored by the Big Mules and their Black Belt allies.

During 1965, the year of the Voting Rights Act (and the year before the Meredith march and the Maddox-Callaway race), I proposed to the Alabama Democratic Conference—the state's

---

*From 1872 to 1900 blacks often were allowed to cast general-election ballots. But their ballots, even when counted, meant little since they had been excluded from the nominating process. The general election provided them real choices only during the Populist rebellion of the 1890s. After 1900 they were disfranchised.

top black political leadership—meeting in Mobile, not merely the abolition of that slogan but also the creation of a third force—a black-voter-based, integrated political movement. Then, during the spring of 1966, in Birmingham's Sixth Avenue Baptist Church, I urged them never again to cast their ballots for a candidate who paid lip service to segregation. That way they could win even if they lost. Campaigns educate voters, and as far as The Issue was concerned, generations of Deep South whites and blacks had heard nothing but "Hell, no!" "Not now!" and "Never!"

The state consitution forbade Wallace a second term. He ran his cancer-consumed wife. The white-bloc vote overwhelmed the newly registered black-vote bloc, made Wallace Alabama's "first man," and gave him access to the state's treasury for his next presidential campaign.

⁂⁂⁂⁂⁂⁂

In January 1966, the Democratic executive committee removed the words "White Supremacy" from the ballot. At their next meeting they elected Loyalist Robert Vance (my friend from college days who had intervened in *Reynolds* v. *Sims,* the one-person, one-vote case) to be their chairman.

Vance, no Wallace supporter, went to the White House to see what Lyndon Johnson wanted him to do. He hardly expected the instructions he received: "It is the President's desire that you place no obstacles against Wallace's entry into the race."

For precisely the reason that the Loyalist Vance saw Wallace as a problem, the pragmatist President saw him as an opportunity. If properly used, Wallace's independent candidacy could remove the Deep South states from the Republican column and wreck their Southern Strategy.*

---

*Even though Johnson's ploy seemed logical to many Democrats and was "understood," the explicit nature of LBJ's complicity in the 1968 Wallace campaign was **not** revealed.

Historically, a bolt from the state party had been the one sure road to political obscurity. As a child, Wallace had seen that fate attach to Senator ("Cotton Tom") Heflin, an anti-Catholic who opposed Al Smith in 1928.* Twenty years later, when Alabama's "State Rights Democrats" marched out of the Philadelphia convention hall singing "Dixie" and shouting "Good-bye, Harry," two young alternate delegates, George Wallace and George Hawkins, had stepped forward to take their seats.

Twenty years after that the issues hadn't changed. Neither had the players. But the Loyalist Wallace had become the world's number-one Dixiecrat, and Loyalist Democrats now controlled the state executive committee. LBJ needed Wallace to run on the third-party ticket, but if Wallace broke the state party's loyalty rule and supported himself over LBJ in Alabama, he would not be able to run for governor in the 1970 Democratic primary.

To help LBJ, Vance solved Wallace's problem. The Loyalists did away with their loyalty rule, the existence of which was the sole reason for the Loyalists' existence. That made it possible for Wallace to run as the nominee of the American Independent Party in forty-nine states while he also ran as the Alabama Democratic party's presidential nominee.

To be able to vote for LBJ, Vance asked David Vann to organize a third party. Vann's Alabama Independent Democratic Party (AIDP) would run Loyalist presidential elector candidates pledged to the nominee of the 1968 National Democratic Convention. In this way, Alabama's loyal Democrats would finally have a chance to cast a whole ballot for their candidate for President.

The national party emblem was a donkey. Vann adopted it as

---

*Alabama lore has it that Heflin summed up his religious beliefs when he shouted: "The Pope's off the coast at Mobile in a submarine, waiting to steam in and take over!" Previously he had clarified his racial views by shooting a black man who refused to surrender his seat on a District of Columbia streetcar.

the AIDP's emblem. Because Alabamians could vote for the national nominee under that donkey emblem, Vance's party, even though the rooster was its emblem and Wallace was its candidate, was in technical compliance with the Call (the formal document of invitation) to the 1968 National Democratic Convention.

So in Alabama in 1968 (according to Vance's consensus plan), by voting a straight ticket under the rooster emblem, you would vote for Wallace for President and, simultaneously, for the Democratic state and local nominees. To vote for the national party's presidential nominee, you would vote in the AIDP's column under the donkey emblem. Then you could move back across the ballot to mark the names of each state and local candidate. That would be hard for highly literate whites, let alone illiterate blacks, who could vote the straight ticket for local candidates only by marking an X at the top of the rooster (Wallace) ballot. If they marked their X at the top of the AIDP's donkey slate, and walked out, they would have voted for the national party's presidential nominee but for not one state or local candidate. This ingenious scheme satisfied every Alabama and national party political interest except one—that of the poor, illiterate black citizens of Alabama.

~~~~~~~~~

Light-skinned, fast-talking, and tough, Dr. John Cashin drove fine cars and "took nothing off nobody." He lacked the "humility" some require of "good politicians," let alone "good niggers." But he had drive—and lawyers.

On December 29, 1967, Cashin, lawyer Orzell Billingsley, and other black political leaders met with David Vann and Robert Vance in Montgomery's Jefferson Davis Hotel. Vann and Vance explained their wondrous political creations. Cashin said no. Two weeks later, he and Billingsley incorporated the National Democratic Party of Alabama (NDPA).

Orzell Billingsley and I understood the state's election laws as well as anybody—which isn't saying much. If the state could have written its statutory scheme in Japanese, it would have. One thing was certain: Political parties didn't have to hold primary elections to select candidates. The convention system was allowed. In the primary, the maze of state election laws was enforced by the Alabama Democratic party's white polling officials. There was no runoff after the general election. If black candidates could get their names onto the November general election ballots and, where there were many registered blacks, split the whites between the Republicans and Democrats, they could be elected.

On May 7, 1968, primary-election day, many blacks and liberal whites didn't vote. They convened in large and small meetings in or near courthouses and in churches to nominate candidates for local office and delegates to their state convention. They were subjected less to criticism than to curiosity. Even George Wallace peeked into one of their meetings.

Blacks who worked from "first sun" to "sundown" meandered in on what we had come to call "CPT," or "colored people's time." After near-formal Sunday-like greetings, they convened and selected delegates to the upcoming state convention in Birmingham and nominees for local office. Platforms were unknown to Alabama's other parties. But at their state conventions these mostly black, mostly poor, mostly Black Belt delegates would endorse a program which, like that of the Populists, spoke of such "radical" matters as land ownership, taxation, jobs, and equal justice.

With candidates pledged to the national Democratic party's nominee, their emblem and the slogan "Vote Under the Eagle"*

---

*Two years later, Secretary of State Mabel S. Amos authorized two other parties to use the eagle emblem. The Montgomery federal court put a stop to that. Mrs. Amos testified that the illiteracy of blacks "didn't enter [her] head." She said she had "been reared with Negroes. I had a Negro mammy and I loved her better than I do my own momma."

My associate, Reber F. Boult, Jr., asked her if she understood the difficulty illiterates had voting without emblems. She responded no, but she did remember that for many years voters had been urged to "Scratch the Donkey" and "Vote the Rooster."

could provide black illiterates with a way to a straight ticket vote against George Wallace, for the national Democrats, and for blacks and liberal whites who were running for local office.

The refined, but simple, idea offered the poor a pathway to power. Using it, blacks could elect constables, county commissioners, justices of the peace, and sheriffs, especially in the Black Belt, from where the Big Mules exercised much of their control over the nation. Besides, the NDPA could provide Loyalists like Vance and Vann rational political reasons to move in the decent anti-Wallace direction in which they desired to go.

The idea grew like kudzu, for local folks knew that local officers exercised more direct control over their lives than did Congress, the Supreme Court, and even the President of the faraway United States.

~~~~~~~~

Inside Chicago's Conrad Hilton Hotel, the television lights glared at us. So did most of the 110-member Credentials Committee. They sat in two semicircular tiers looking like a scrapbook snapshot of a scrubbed-up politburo. The course of the Alabama credentials challenge was as predictable as was the outcome of the Democratic convention and the coming confrontation in Chicago's streets.

I did not want to be there. Cashin had insisted, but all of us had lost a part of ourselves with that year's assassinations. Young Americans had accepted the leadership of John Kennedy and he had been killed. Then Martin King had been assassinated. Then Robert Kennedy. Later, when I wondered at the cynicism and malaise of the young, Camille suggested that they were political

---

Asked about the Alabama Conservative party's "eagle," she reported that the party chairman "said everybody called him dovish and he wanted to make that look a little bit more like an eagle. And since Mr. Chuck [me] . . . proved that it was an eagle I decided we would change it just a little bit. . . . He's not so peaceful-looking now."

Q. Well, so now he's changed from a dove to an eagle, is that not correct?
A. Well, yes, he's a little bit sterner.

foster children, moved like orphans from foster home to foster home until finally they were unable to give love.

On the night that Martin King was shot down, in the rage and despair which led others to burn their own houses down, I had sent out for a fifth of whiskey and drunk it, crying. After Robert Kennedy, we almost ran out of tears.

Now, I stared up from the long counsel table no less hopeful than an accused black man with a story to tell Judge Ed. My task was to build a record for use in federal court.

The evidence Vance presented (later characterized by three federal judges in Montgomery as "of the most slender nature, largely circumstantial and in part 'hearsay' ") "proved" that the NDPA in Cashin's home county had held no meeting on primary day, May 7, to choose convention delegates.

Vance sprang affidavits on us. A newspaper reporter swore he had seen no meeting; the chairman of the county's board of commissioners had no record of reserved meeting space; and, Vance argued, the proprietor of the courthouse coffee shop said, "I know John Cashin. He wasn't in here at all!" His affidavit actually read, "At no time on May 7, 1968, did I hear anything resembling a mass meeting to select delegates to a political convention being held."

To campaign at the Stockyards, we had to pass through "Checkpoint Charlie," past the electronic machines and armed guards and barbed wire until, finally, we were inside. Earlier, pro-Wallace forces had declined to take the loyalty oath, and Vance's and Vann's delegations combined. Now they appeared en masse. On Monday evening (August 26), Cashin and I entered the New York caucus to seek support for the NDPA. I visualized white Bob Vance dancing on from stage left, buck and wing, twirling a straw hat with his delegation rising behind him in a chorus to sing, "We're the *real* blacks."

Later that night, Humphrey flexed his delegate strength and made a test of the Alabama challenge. The NDPA piled up 880 ¾ votes "with 134¼ delegates abstaining." The Vann-Vance delegation won with 1,607

The next evening, when Mayor Daley's clubs crashed down, I

left the madness of Chicago to return to absurdity in Alabama. When I took the deposition of the Madison County courthouse coffee shop operator, who I believed was the state's eyewitness, I learned that he had sworn to and Vance had argued the absolute, literal truth. He hadn't *heard* the Cashin group, and he certainly hadn't seen them because the eyewitness was blind.

~~~~~~~

I filed *Hadnott* v. *Amos* on September 13, 1968. Our appropriately named lead plaintiff was large, jovial, black Sallie Mae Hadnott—candidate for Autauga (which adjoins Montgomery and Lowndes) County Commissioner.

Three days earlier, the secretary of state, Mabel S. Amos, had hiked up her state party loyalty, cited a state attorney general's opinion, and sashayed into her office to announce that the NDPA's candidates could not run. Mrs. Amos and several county probate judges said the NDPA hadn't complied with a recently enacted statute which required that all candidates "declare their intention" to run prior to March 1. Besides, she said, echoing the affadivits Vance had flashed at Chicago, NDPA mass meetings and caucuses had not been held on primary-election day. Cashin's county was one of those which, she alleged, had held no meeting.

Cashin's group really had met under the rotunda of the courthouse in Huntsville. When they "started to proceed with more business . . . someone suggested . . . 'heck, why should we stand here, when we can sit down.' " So they finished that meeting in the courthouse coffee shop.

Now, Secretary Amos, as an afterthought, threw in noncompliance with the state's "corrupt practices" statutes—the failure of the NDPA candidates to provide her with the names of people to handle their nonexistent campaign finances.

If the absentee ballots were printed with the NDPA column left off them, and the three federal judges were to rule with us, they would have to throw those ballots out. I preferred that they not face that psychological hurdle. Already the campaign resembled a psychological steeplechase. "I don't see how you can run a campaign when you are not on the ballot," I argued to the judges at the hearing held three days after I filed suit. "Alabama's newspapers have constantly said that these plaintiffs did not comply with the law."

I aimed at George Wallace. When Ohio officials had said he filed too late under that state's law, Supreme Court Justice Potter Stewart had ordered him relisted until the full court decided his case. What the Supreme Court had done for Wallace, the district court now did for the NDPA. They ordered that no absentee ballots be printed without the NDPA column on them until after they heard the case.

During the hectic days which followed, we took depositions in Montgomery, Birmingham, and Huntsville.* The state acquired affidavits from county probate judges, one of which came from Greene County's James Dennis Herndon. He swore that neither "publicity" nor "notice" of a primary-election day mass meeting had been "posted in any public building" there.

"No such meeting" had been held "in a hall, room, or open place at or in the immediate vicinity of the voting place of my precinct or voting district within this county."

I was in Atlanta on Friday, October 11, when the word came.

---

*We also found a "sums-things-up" letter from the chairman of Alabama's Conservative party in the files of Secretary of State Amos:

Hi Mabel

Enclosed are the 150 party emblems—per your request. Please send the $150 back to me (the ones which had the motto marked out).

Congratulations on your diligent efforts, which resulted in the disqualification of some liberals.

Regards,
Bill Mori

Two years later when Mori altered his party's emblem to resemble the NDPA's, he sent copies of his eagle to Mrs. Amos, and wrote: "P.S. I bet you won't file this letter for any crazy lawyer to subpoena."

Wrong again.

The district court ruled against us two to one.* The state could proceed with its election process.

My colleague Normal Siegel hurried to the airport on the first lap of our race with the printers. If the ballots rolled off the presses with the NDPA's candidates names off of them, it probably would be too late to get them back on. In Montgomery, Deputy Court Clerk Jane Gordon kicked off her shoes, slipped on her pink slippers, and worked into the night putting the voluminous record in order for our appeal to the Supreme Court.

In Atlanta Reber Boult and I prepared papers to be directed to Justice Black. Shortly after 1:00 A.M., Norman returned with the record. Five hours later he was off to Washington.

It was Saturday, but when the Supreme Court's doors opened, Norman was there. By Sunday night we had turned out the jurisdictional statement and brief, the motions, and other necessary documents. Weather had closed the Washington airport, so Nan Guerrero from my office, toting the last chance for eighty-nine NDPA candidates, flew to Philadelphia. From there she took the bus. Monday morning she arrived, exhausted, at the ACLU's Washington office. She was greeted with "You haven't got a chance."

That morning after Justice Black recused himself (his sister-in-law, Virginia Durr, was one of the NDPA's nominees for presidential elector), his eight fellow justices ordered:

> The application for temporary relief is granted pending oral argument on the application which is set for Friday, October 18, 1968, at 9:00 A.M. The case is placed on the summary calendar.

---

*Judge Johnson dissented, saying that "[t]he best of laws . . . can be invoked in an unworthy manner. . . ." This time it had been invoked strictly as an "afterthought." To him, the NDPA's late filing of Corrupt Practices Act forms didn't matter, for it simply was "not tolerable" to allow Alabama's officials "to make their first foray in the enforcement direction against a small, new and almost surely impecunious group of candidates seeking to form a new party in Alabama."

At 9:13 A.M., October 18, Chief Justice Warren said, "Mr. Morgan, you may proceed."

I turned to the eight-by-four-foot reproduction of the Alabama ballot on the stand behind me.

I was carrying a cane as the result of a recent knee operation. Now I used the cane as a pointer when I began explaining the ballot's eight complicated columns to the extraordinarily literate men on the bench.

"How many electors are there in Alabama?" asked one of them.

"Ten electors," I replied.

"There are only eight in column one," a justice responded.

"No, sir, there are ten in this column, column three, and column seven, and also column five, which is the Republican party. If an illiterate person walks in, he can flip this lever here and then he would have to wander all across this ballot to find whoever he wants."

Justice Stewart asked how voters could learn who the presidential elector candidates would support for President. "Often it is a mystery," I responded. "I voted for John Kennedy in 1960. We had eleven electoral votes. Six of the eleven of my votes went for Harry F. Byrd."

I concluded with the understatement, "It is not very easy to run for office sometimes in Alabama."

~~~~~~~~~

Early the next afternoon Camille and I watched the televised Alabama-Tennessee football game at the Hay Adams Hotel. The call came. A ruling was expected as soon as the chief justice finished his meeting with some Swedish diplomats. I raced outside and flagged a cab, but the Swedes were in no hurry.

The second half was well under way when the deputy clerk handed me a copy of the order. It required the relisting of the NDPA's candidates. They had sixteen days for their campaign.

As I sat there, the deputy clerk dialed the telephone. "Do you understand?" he asked Alabama's deputy attorney general after reading him the order.

In Knoxville, Tennessee, L. Drew Redden, the lawyer for Mrs. Amos, read of the decision in Sunday morning's newspaper. The following Wednesday, he received a copy in the mail.

To be sure that every Alabama election official understood, Reber Boult sought permission from their lawyers to communicate with them directly. Permission denied. No need. The attorney general's office had notified the probate judges.

As the ballots rolled off the presses, appeals to "Vote the Eagle, the NDPA Symbol" from Julian Bond, Coretta King, and Ralph Abernathy were carried into the Black Belt on black-music radio stations. Sample ballots marked with an X under the eagle were prepared. They would be passed out in churches and, after that, from hand to hand.

On election day (November 5) I went to Birmingham. My father was feeble with Parkinson's disease and, when my mother and I took him to vote, his quivering hand lacked the strength to pull down the lever on the voting machine.

In his arms he had taken me to vote for Franklin D. Roosevelt. Now it was my turn. He laughed and whispered, "Straight Republican!" I put his hand on the lever and we pulled together to cast his vote for Richard M. Nixon.

8

Life always had been tough for the 11,050 Negroes in Black Belt Greene County, near the Mississippi line. Greene was one of the five poorest counties in the United States, and almost all of its blacks (they made up 81 percent of the county's 13,600 people) were poor. The 2,550 whites ruled with an iron hand. Legend has it that while a black man was being lynched in adjoining Pickens County, lightning struck and transferred his image to the courthouse window. When the sun strikes at a certain angle you can see him hanging there, or at least you think you can.

Greene County needs no legends. When its white folks wanted to destroy the indictments returned against them by a carpet-bagger grand jury, they simply burned the courthouse down. Now a century had passed, and blacks again were working to take the courthouse away from them. But the Reverend William McKinley Branch, the NDPA's candidate for Congress, noticed something strange. The white candidates for the four County Commission seats were not campaigning.

Harry C. Means, forty-four, who lived in Boligee with his wife and four children, noticed that too. An excellent farmer, Means had attended Tuskegee Institute. He served on the "loaning committee" of the Farmers Home Administration. The secretary of agriculture had appointed him to the Wheat, Grain, and Soybean Advisory Committee, and for a black Greene County farmer, that was a high honor. Now Means campaigned hard, as did his NDPA companion Frenchie Burton, sixty-four, who still "farmed some." Burton's wife had been the first black woman to register in the county, but he had never been in politics. He, Means, Levi Morrow, Sr., and Vassie Knott were running for "places" on the County Commission. Burton was mighty proud when, two days before the election, he saw his name on a sample ballot.

Cattle- and hog-farmer Levi Morrow had lived in Greene County all of his sixty-five years. Although he had finished only the sixth grade, his twelve children, ages twenty-one to forty-one, were all educated. Once or twice a week when Morrow campaigned in Eutaw, the county seat, he saw his white opponent in the sheriff's office. "It . . . appears to me," he said, "that these people play dominoes in the sheriff's office every day."

At 8:45 on election morning, Branch walked into his Forkland polling place and marked his X under the eagle. As his eyes ran down the ballot, he saw his name and the names of all NDPA candidates for statewide office. Suddenly Branch understood why the white, state-party nominees—"rooster party candidates," Branch called them—had not campaigned. The names of their black opponents for local office were not on the ballot!

Means got the bad news from neighbors. It was "a surprise and a great letdown to me," he said. "So many people promised they'd vote for me—I thought I was going to win."

For Morrow, going to vote was "like going to the table and comin' back hungry."

So Greene County's six NDPA candidates for local office— four for the County Commission and two for the school board— had purchased campaign literature and gasoline which they couldn't afford. They had shaken hands and wasted time and, no doubt, provided local white folks who saw them campaigning good thigh-slapping laughs at how they'd "tricked 'em again."

That afternoon, Greene County's Probate Judge Herndon told the *Birmingham News*, "Don't ask me why this group didn't appeal. Maybe they didn't pay their lawyer. I don't know."

≈≈≈≈≈≈≈

Vann's (AIDP) slate of Humphrey-pledged presidential elector nominees got 196,579 votes. On the Alabama Democratic party ticket, Wallace swept the state with 691,425. Nixon ran a poor third.

Statewide the NDPA received 54,144 votes. It carried Greene (only the local candidates were barred from the ballot) and adjoining Sumter county, and ran well across the Black Belt. In Marengo County, which also borders Greene, the NDPA elected five justices of the peace, three constables, and the chairman of the board of education. Later, in Greene County, when the ballots were rechecked to see how many straight ticket "X-under-the-eagle" votes had been cast, the NDPA's total ran to 2,036

The highest vote received by a white candidate was 1,709. If the names of the NDPA's local candidates had been included on the ballot each of them would have won. Then blacks would have outnumbered whites four to one on the County Commission—and that one would have been the probate judge, James Dennis Herndon.

Although average citizens rightly doubt it, the standard of conduct the law sets for public officials and lawyers is higher than what it sets for average citizens. But three years of legal education, work as a lawyer, and ten years as a probate judge may have taught Herndon the lesson Rhett Butler provided Margaret Mitchell's heroine in *Gone with the Wind*. "Influence is everything, Scarlett. Remember that when you get arrested. Influence is everything, and guilt or innocence merely an academic question."

Academic or not, a week after the election I charged Herndon with contempt of the Supreme Court order in *Hadnott* v. *Amos*.

I asked that Court to try him; to declare elected the seventeen NDPA candidates who won but were disqualified in Sumter and Marengo counties; and to order an unprecedented special election in Greene County.

In Washington the solicitor general, former Harvard Law dean Erwin N. Griswold, so lost in the forest of Frankfurterisms that he never could decide what to do about Herndon, did tell the Court I was right about the rest of the case. In Montgomery, the Justice Department obtained an injunction to prevent Greene County's white incumbents from entering new terms of office, and to a chorus of "I didn't know," my associates Reber Boult, George Dean, and Justice Department lawyers deposed them.

After dark on Christmas Eve, I finished taking the statements of the Reverend Mr. Branch and the Greene County black candidates. They left Five Forsyth Street for the long drive across Georgia and Alabama, saying they were not worried about being late for Christmas.

～～～～～～

On Monday, January 20, 1969, we were greeted by a cold, crisp wind and the inauguration. After taking the oath to "faithfully execute the Office of President of the United States" and to "preserve, protect, and defend the Constitution," Richard Nixon advised us to "lower our voices." We "suffered from a fever of words; from inflated rhetoric that promises more than it can deliver; from angry rhetoric that fans discontents into hatreds; from bombastic rhetoric that postures instead of persuading."

He rhetorically urged us to "stop shouting at one another." We should "speak quietly enough so that our words can be heard as well as our voices."

"[T]he Government," he promised, "will listen."

～～～～～～

My case against Herndon and *Hadnott v. Amos* was to be the first Supreme Court arguments heard during the Nixon administration. The city was packed and it was a long way from our rooms at a northern Virginia Holiday Inn to the Supreme Court. The highway and streets were icy, and even though we tried to start early, I was unable to find my co-counsel, Orzell Billingsley. As I was leaving the motel lobby, he came in from the cold, stomping, huffing, and laughing. Democrat Orzell had attended Nixon's inaugural ball and another party or so. Since they had lasted into the night, Orzell had lasted into the night. Now he looked sharp, said, "I feel sharp," climbed into the waiting taxicab, and fell asleep. That was fine with me. Since I was to argue the case, all Orzell had to do was look sharp.

During my presentation, I turned to the depositions which had been added to the Record. I told the Court: "They all subscribe to newspapers, but nobody seems to even read them, except the defendant Herndon, he did admit that.

"They have all got television sets and they have got two television stations that they receive clearly, one from Birmingham and one from Meridian," I continued.

And "they never campaigned for office."

Their decisions had to be conscious and deliberate. Herndon and his fellow whites had to have known exactly what was going on. As I told the Court, I could hear them saying, *"Leave those names off that ballot!"*

It was Alabama's turn. While Drew Redden, to my left at the podium, spoke, I saw justices White and Marshall chatting and laughing. Even if I hadn't had to answer Redden I would have paid attention, for he is a good lawyer. Then I thought I heard a familiar sound. A moment later I clearly heard a deep, long, loud, natural snore. Out of the corner of my eye I saw that Orzell's head had fallen to his chest. Again he snored, this time with a slight whistle.

Under the table I tapped him with my cane. He came awake with a start. Then he returned to slumber with what may have been the loudest snore in American legal history. Again I rapped him, this time sharply. It was no use.

Orzell had stayed awake for me in opening argument. He

would stay awake for me in closing argument. That was as far as he would go. Orzell Billingsley, Jr., had followed Richard Nixon's advice: he refused to suffer "from a fever of words."

Justice Marshall interrupted during my rebuttal. "So your only precedent is the dissenting opinion in this case?"

I began to respond, "Our only precedent—" but Marshall smiled and cut me off with, "Judge Johnson *is* a good judge."

"[A]s the President said yesterday," I concluded, "the laws have caught up with our conscience and what remains is to give life to the law. I think that is what this case is really all about."

At the Holiday Inn we toasted Orzell. He laughed. "There's no need to stay awake when you know how its going to come out."

~~~~~~~~

On March 25, 1969, the Supreme Court, in an opinion by Justice Douglas, overturned the district court majority point by point and instructed that the seventeen NDPA candidates elected in Sumter and Marengo counties "be treated as duly elected." A new election was ordered for Greene County, "promptly."

Regarding Judge Herndon's contempt, the Supreme Court postponed its decision in order to "await timely initiation and completion of appropriate proceedings of the District Court." As to Herndon, justices Douglas and Harlan dissented. They believed that there was "probable cause to conclude that Judge Herndon knowingly and purposefully evaded our order. . . ." That being the case, they believed he should be tried by the Supreme Court itself.

Greene County came alive.

Martin King was dead, but Ralph Abernathy, Hosea Williams, Coretta King, and Andrew Young campaigned for the local NDPA candidates. Julian Bond helped out, as did Winifred Green and Constance Curry of the American Friends Service Committee.

From the pulpits of black churches came calls for courage and unity. The parishioners canvassed voters and organized car pools.

In later years, July 29 would be celebrated as Freedom Day. That Tuesday in 1969 was a day of hard work. At dawn, black people prepared for their trek to the polls. Many men dressed in their black wool "Sunday suits" despite the heat. The women dressed up too. Some rode. Those with bent bodies were carried. Ancient people, joined by their children and their children's children, went into voting places and marked their X's under the eagle. And one person, one vote came home to roost.

That night in Greene County they celebrated Christmas, the Fourth of July, and Emancipation Day. For the first time in the Deep South's history, the black majority assumed control of both the County Commission and the school board, the two instruments of countywide government.

~~~~~~~~

My work in Greene County was almost over, but in the fall of 1970, I was back in the district court to challenge Alabama's voter residency requirements and other measures designed to diminish the NDPA's vote.

I had come with another purpose, too. Herndon had remained untried. Not one public official—let alone a judge—had ever been convicted of criminal or civil contempt of a federal court's desegregation order. Herndon knew, as did all white public officials, that whatever "equal justice under law" meant, defiant white folks were more equal than others. Herndon had seen George Wallace stand in his alma mater's doorway, go unpunished, and become one of the nation's most popular politicians. Herndon's patriotic obligation ran to Our Southern Way of Life. To discharge his duty all he had to do was to leave the names off that ballot and claim, "I didn't know."

In the courtroom I looked up at the three judges. "[Y]ou have families, and I have a son. We tell young people about The System. And we go out and tell them to take their struggles into the courts and out of the streets."

Judge Johnson stared at me over the top of his half-glasses. The other two judges leaned forward.

"Now, you get paid, and I get paid, to be here to protect rights to vote." I reminded them that they had risen through politics to the bench. "Nobody in this courtroom would be here if we didn't have a right to vote." The protection of that right is "what federal courts are for and what they say lawyers are for." The Herndon question was a matter of "the integrity of the judicial process!

"We have got James Dennis Herndon sitting over in his county . . . since March of 1969. . . ." As I spoke, the anger I'd felt on election night in 1968 returned. My voice rose in sarcasm: " 'Decision *postponed*,' said the Supreme Court!"

The three judges ordered Judge Herndon to appear on December 14, 1970, to show why he should not be held in contempt.

Jerris Leonard, the assistant attorney general for the civil rights division of the Justice Department, was present in the courtroom, for despite Nixon's Southern Strategy, Leonard did believe in the equal right to vote and serve on juries (but not in school busing). He was there to designate me a special assistant if the court required that.

My beliefs and instincts run to the defense. I had never prosecuted a criminal case. Now, in briefs, I carefully spelled out each of Herndon's rights. When the court convicted Herndon, I wanted him to stay convicted, without a chance of appeal. So, with the FBI at my disposal and more "walking-around-sense, circumstantial evidence" than I could use, I proceeded to trial.

The trial took two days. The white county commissioners whose careers were at stake had heard "rumors" about the Supreme Court's order in *Hadnott* v. *Amos*, but nothing more. To "What did Judge Herndon know, and when did he know it?" Herndon's answer was nothing and too late. His omission of the names from the ballot was "the result of ignorance." His lawyers had not specifically informed him of the Supreme Court's order. He had read of some "Supreme Court action" in the newspaper.

He had "heard some stories." But he had made no effort "however slight" to find out whether the Supreme Court order affected him or not.

A.   I didn't make any effort.
Q.   None?
A.   No.

So, answer by answer, Herndon wrapped himself into a cocoon of ignorance which bound him as tightly as if he had confessed.

Three weeks later we were back in the Montgomery courtroom. The white candidates whom Herndon had tried to help in 1968 were not present. He had stood up for them. Now, except for his lawyer, he stood alone, and in eleven days (on January 18, 1971), regardless of what this court decided, Herndon's career as probate judge would end. The Reverend William McKinley Branch had defeated him to become the South's first black probate judge.

There had been a one-person, one-vote overthrow of the government. Tom Gilmore, black, had interrupted the line of natural succession to defeat Sheriff Big Bill Lee (whose brother, Frank, had been the defendant in the prison desegregation case). Blacks had been elected sheriff in three counties, and in Greene the offices of clerk of court and coroner were to change hands, as were two more seats on the school board.*

Now, flanked by his two black-robed associates, Circuit Judge Godbold looked down. "The evidence in this case reflects that James Dennis Herndon had actual knowledge. . . ."

My associate Norman Siegel nudged me. Co-counsel George Dean and Reber Boult settled back in their chairs.

For civil contempt, Herndon's fine was the $5,452 back salary the black candidates had lost. That money went to them.

---

*No whites would enter office then, but in the next election the incumbent white tax assessor ran on the NDPA ticket and was reelected.

"This conduct on the part of Herndon, which was knowing and willful, constituted criminal contempt of this Court." For that he was fined $300 and sentenced to one year on probation.

Outside, James T. Wooten of *The New York Times* asked me if I felt sorry for Herndon. I thought about the common phrase "they all do it"; about those people, some of whom I had known, who had been beaten and killed in the struggle to vote; and about Wallace and those who, like him, showed contempt for the Constitution itself.

"No, Jim. I feel sorry about him, not sorry for him."

More than four years later (in the fall of 1975) Steve Suitts, who directed the ACLU's Alabama affiliate, telephoned me in Florida. He told me that at the founding meeting of the Greene County chapter of the ACLU, unlike the sophisticated gatherings elsewhere, they opened and closed with prayer. Halfway through their business, Steve said, an aged black man rose and interrupted with, "Now let us say a prayer for Chuck Morgan." And they did.

When Steve told me that story I remembered Herndon's comment which I had read on election night, 1968. Asked why the black candidates' names weren't on the ballot, he had said: "Maybe they didn't pay their lawyer." Like too many lawyers, poor Herndon hadn't learned what real pay is.

9

Since the celebrated Dreyfus case, gentile governments—even in civilian court political prosecutions—have sought to allay suspicions of anti-Semitism by appointing Jewish prosecutors to prosecute Jews. There were no Jewish prosecutors at Fort Jackson, South Carolina, when Dr. Howard B. Levy was court-martialed for speaking against the Vietnam War and refusing to teach medicine to Special Forces troops. So a Jewish lawyer was imported from Fort Gordon, Georgia, to prosecute Howard Levy.

At the court-martial, the prosecutor would argue that, "While freedom to think is absolute, of its own nature, the right to express thoughts orally or in writing . . . at any time or place, is not." That summed up part of Levy's problem. Of the needs of the poor, opposition to the war in Southeast Asia, and his son's right to speak, Levy's father would say: ". . . I knew he wouldn't stand apart from it. . . . [I]f he feels it is right, he must stand by it, and he's got the guts to do it." The World War II veteran would sigh, "I wish I had the guts to do it."

Howard Levy had read and remembered. That was also his

114

problem. On February 22, 1964, *The New York Times* quoted
President Johnson: "The contest in which South Vietnam is now
engaged . . . is . . . to be won by the government and the
people of that country for themselves." Eight days later Levy
read that the President intended to "rely on the South Vietnamese to defend themselves against Communist guerrillas."
He was "not prepared to commit the 15,500 Americans now
advising and training South Vietnam's army." Six months
passed. On August 5, 1964, Levy read: PRESIDENT ORDERS
"LIMITED" RETALIATION AFTER COMMUNIST PT BOATS RENEW
RAIDS.

During the week of the Fourth of July, 1965, Howard Levy
was to leave for Fort Jackson. On Sunday, the fourth, he read in
The New York Times of "an increase . . . to . . . 75,000 men
[American advisers and trainers]—21,000 of whom are combat
troops." In London, the *Sunday Mirror* reported the remarks of
South Vietnam's leader, Marshal Ky: "People ask me who my
heroes are. I have only one—Hitler. I admire Hitler because he
pulled his country together when it was in a terrible state in the
early thirties. But, the situation here is so desperate now that
one man would not be enough. We need four or five Hitlers in
Vietnam."

When Dr. Levy, civilian, began his first trip south, his parents worried. Their view of that faraway province was like that of
the ACLU's Roger Baldwin. But Sadie and Seymour Levy soon
learned that they had as much to fear from their United States
government as they did from any Deep South state.

Army hospitals were so short of dermatologists that Howard
Levy was very welcome. Because of that shortage, "Captain"
Levy was allowed to bypass the military training which physicians usually received at Fort Sam Houston, Texas. On July 13,
1965, he was in uniform and in charge of Fort Jackson's dermatology clinic. Soon the officers club billed him for dues.
Membership wasn't required so he refused to pay. Told that
"the hospital's image is at stake" and, "after all, the club is only
for golf and officers!," Levy replied that he already was busy, in

civil rights work. "Besides, I don't play golf. And I don't like officers."

On Levy's first Saturday (July 17, 1965) in South Carolina, he ate breakfast at a Columbia lunch counter and read in the local paper: "At Newberry, ten out of thirty-three Negroes denied registration." He paid his check, climbed into his untrustworthy Chevrolet, and headed out on I—26.

William Treanor of the Newberry Summer Community Organization and Political Education (SCOPE) project "was down at the courthouse with some people when Levy came up just to see what was going on, and I spoke to him then, and I invited him to come up and assist us in any way he felt he could, during his off-duty hours."

And that is what Howard Levy did. Fellow officers and gentlemen whiled away the hours playing cards and golf and tennis at the officers club. Every night and around the clock on weekends, Dr. Levy worked in Newberry County, always wearing civilian clothes. Treanor said he watched as Levy went from house to house to "explain . . . to people who never had the opportunity to vote before, the importance of their voting in the upcoming city election and, you know, the power of the ballot . . . that we try to get across to people who have not had any instruction before, you know, just a better democracy."

On Monday, July 26, a white volunteer was beaten. Levy and Treanor went to the jail in nearby Whitmire to bring the victim home. As Treanor later testified: "A mob of thirty-five or forty white men . . . threatened us with physical violence and swore at us and insulted our racial backgrounds." They shouted that Levy was "a white Ethiopian." But Levy "refused to be intimidated." He was "pretty courageous . . . because he certainly didn't have to be there or anything."

Levy became good friends with Treanor, a veteran who had served in military intelligence and who still corresponded with his friend, Intelligence Sergeant Geoffrey Hancock.

Stationed in South Vietnam, Sergeant Hancock believed that antiwar "people back in the states" didn't "understand." On the night of September 10, 1965—twenty-one days after the killing of Jonathan Daniels in Lowndes County, Alabama—Treanor suggested that Levy respond to Hancock's most recent letter. Levy had a drink and wrote:

Dear Geoffrey,

. . . I am one of those "people back in the states" who actually opposes our efforts [in Vietnam] and would refuse to serve there if I were so assigned.

. . . I do not believe that you can realistically judge the Viet Nam war as an isolated incident. It must be viewed in the context of the recent history of our foreign policy—at least from the start of the cold war.

Basically there are two arms to our foreign policy . . . 1) The stated part—to contain "Communism" & 2) the unstated part—to support "stable" governments so that our foreign investors may profit. . . . You see, . . . left liberal governments often have the interests of their countrymen at heart and this runs counter to our interests. . . . [E]very time a Latin American government tried to implement a true land reform program . . . we . . . found some reason to balk & not approve the project. This isn't surprising since . . . U.S. companies own or control much of the land in these countries. Yet without land reform nothing will work in Latin America.

Of course our propaganda mills, the newspapers & the mass media, cover up our sins. Invariably communists are found to take the blame. Do you really believe that the Dominican Republic was in danger of a Communist overthrow? . . . The same is true in the Congo. Is Tshombe a great patriot? Few in the Congo think so. Yet we support him. Could it be because he can be "counted on?" I think so.

Let's attack it from another, more radical, approach. What if the majority of a people decide that Communism is good for them. . . . We might . . . try to prove that our way is better but by any stretch of any moral principal can we deny them the choice? Is Communism worse than a U.S. oriented government? The fastest growing economy in Latin America is Cuba. Everybody reads & writes in Cuba. Everybody has medical care. Was this true with the . . . American backed governments? Not on your life. Is it true in other American backed governments in Latin America? Far East? Near East? Where? . . . Are the North Vietnamese worse off than the South Vietnamese? I doubt it. If they are why do many back the Viet Cong? Guerrilla terrorism? Unlikely. . . .

Geoffrey who are you fighting for? Do you know? . . . Your real battle is back here in the U.S. but why must I fight it for you? The same people who suppress Negroes & poor whites here are doing it all over again all over the world & you[']re helping them. Why? You . . . know about the terror . . . inflicted upon Negroes in our country. Aren't you guilty of the same thing with regard to Vietnamese? A dead woman is a dead woman in Alabama & in Viet Nam. To destroy a child's life in Viet Nam equals a destroyed life in Harlem. For what cause? Democracy? Diem, Trujillo, Batista, Chiang Kai-shek, Franco, Tshombe—Bullshit?

As I mentioned earlier I don't contest your position that we can win. The question is win what. If we must destroy a whole people to win them then I don't understand. . . . Who are we winning for? The government in Saigon? Which one? It may change before you receive this letter. I could hasten to remind you that despite your obvious courage & enthusiasm Viet Nam is not our country & you are not a Vietnamese. At least the Viet Cong have that on their side. . . .

In any event let me wish you good luck & safe conduct in your present situation.

Yours truly,
Howard Levy

The letter was to become one of the army's most prized possessions—its prosecution exhibit number five.

~~~~~~~

Occasionally Howard Levy's shoes went unshined and his insignia were askew. His hair wasn't crewcut, but it wasn't long, and whenever he had time and thought about it, he had it cut. He didn't salute well, but he'd had no military training. He wore the physician's white jacket and nobody in the hospital saluted anybody anyway. At the entrance to Fort Jackson, where his

bumper sticker placed the guards on notice that he was an officer, they smartly came to attention and saluted his bumper.

Fort Jackson physicians, civil rights activists, and local state,
and national police knew of Howard Levy's nigger-loving views.
They also knew he was an excellent physician. He freely taught
dermatology to interested army doctors, nurses, and corpsmen.
He took his regular turn in the emergency room and minded his
medical business. Because he made no public speeches he was
no "embarrassment" to the army.

~~~~~~~~~

Whatever other soldiers did well, Special Forces did best.
These were highly motivated volunteers, selected on the basis of
mental as well as physical ability. Like the CIA, they were modeled on the OSS of World War II. Begun in 1952, Special Forces
had grown from 1,800 men to more than 9,000. Their basic
fighting unit—a twelve-man "A-team"—included an officer in
charge, a second-in-command, an operations and intelligence
sergeant, and at least two weapons sergeants, two demolitions
men, and two aidmen.

Each A-team member was crosstrained in at least one other
guerrilla skill (and preferably all of them), but aidmen were the
most important. They were the very brightest of the army's best.
Their average GTS (IQ) score, 127, was higher than that required for entrance into Officers Candidate School.

Former Special Forces Sergeant Donald Duncan said aidmen
"got the confidence of the people by treating them. . . ." Unlike
nurses and corpsmen, however, Special Forces aidmen, these
nicest of the nice guys, sometimes were supposed to kill those
whose hearts and minds they could not win. But army physicians
were supposed to save lives. Even when all other officers had
been killed in combat, the physician-officer was not to assume
command. The highest-ranking noncommissioned officer was to
do so. By separating killing from lifesaving, armies benefited,
and treaties, including the Geneva Conventions and the Doctors
Draft Law, had been written to keep that separation absolute.

Despite that, the army approved the aidman program which Colonel Richard Coppedge, chief surgeon for the Special Forces Warfare Center, devised. Coppedge described the aidman program as "a political use of medicine; certainly its effects are political." But he believed that the doctors were acting as politicians in order to do good. He also believed that Levy was "the kind of person" Special Forces needed. But the army had drafted Levy's skills; his heart and mind he kept for himself.

The new Fort Jackson Army Hospital commander, Colonel Henry Franklin Fancy, arrived in midsummer 1966. He kept to himself, so Levy saw little of him.

On October 2, Counterintelligence Corps Special Agent James B. West, a white, stout, middle-aged resident of Prosperity, South Carolina, one of the towns where Levy had worked to register blacks, visited the colonel. That was a "rather shocking occurrence," for, according to Fancy, the special agent said that "Levy had attended certain meetings in New York City." A "suspect" organization "behind these meetings" had a possible "association with Communism. This was the suspicion, of course. . . ."

Not only was this the colonel's first command, but for the first time in his life he was associated "with a person . . . who had, in effect, been accused of being or was suspected of being a Communist."

Five days later he went to the G-2 (intelligence) office, where he looked at part of Levy's dossier, the rest being held at Third Army Headquarters. By the time the special agent returned to visit him again, the colonel knew that Levy had been denied a security clearance because of his "communistic leanings."

When the army had asked Levy for a statement for his Armed Forces Security Questionnaire, he had written, "I am in accord with the democratic form of government as outlined in the Constitution of the United States, even though I disagree with much of the method and policy that the U.S. government sometimes pursues."

He described his political beliefs as "liberal left." To the best of his knowledge he'd "never attended any meetings of any subversive organizations or groups . . . that conspire to overthrow the U.S. government by violent or unconstitutional means."

Levy's alert and inquiring mind had led him into eight *public* meetings of the Militant Labor Forum in New York City. He had not joined.

"I am not a pacifist," he wrote; "however, I do have certain pacifistic leanings. I am able to envision situations in which I could conceivably refuse to obey a military order given me by a commander. This would be in such a situation in which I felt that the order was ethically or morally incorrect. I would add that this cannot be a criteria of loyalty inasmuch as in such an unusual situation it might be more loyal not to obey the order. There is ample historical evidence to suggest that this has sometimes been the case. I don't think that one can honestly predict such a response in advance of the specific situation."

Immediately after their first meeting, Special Agent West reported to his superiors that Colonel Fancy "will call SUBJECT in and reprimand HIM for HIS previous dereliction of duty and give HIM a direct order as well as a written order to train Special Forces personnel without injecting HIS political opinions or directing derogatory remarks toward these personnel, and then if HE fails to obey . . . take appropriate action. . . . Source will not tolerate any interference with the training of these personnel, and requires everyone concerned to cooperate to the utmost."

So, on October 11, Dr. Levy was ordered to teach basic dermatology to Special Forces aidmen.

Later the colonel said, "I gave him the original of my prepared order . . . and asked him to read it carefully, which he did and I asked him if he understood the contents and he said that he did. He then stated that he felt that giving such training to the . . . aid men [*sic*] was like giving candy to babies. That he did not approve of the use to which it was put."

Heroics are difficult in bureaucratic settings. But Levy was convinced that the CIA-directed Special Forces were "killers of peasants and murderers of women and children," and "liars and thieves."

As a physician, he believed that the lives of "Communists"

and "foreigners"—even those with dark skins—were as important as the lives of white Americans. "A dead woman is a dead woman in Alabama & in Viet Nam," the physician had written to Intelligence Sergeant Hancock. "To destroy a child's life in Viet Nam equals a destroyed life in Harlem."

Colonel Fancy later testified that Levy "stood and told me that he did not feel that he could ethically conduct this training because it was against his principles. . . ." He said "he could not ethically bring himself to train this class of personnel in the basic elements of his specialty."

At first Colonel Fancy sought to proceed against Levy "administratively" for "dereliction of duty." His executive officer drafted the minor "Article 15" charge.* After the drafting of the charge, the colonel was called to the G-2 office. Told that Levy's full dossier had been returned from Third Army Headquarters, "[t]hey recommended that I read it, which I proceeded to do."

Fancy withdrew the Article 15 charge. He decided a general court-martial was "more appropriate." There was "a brief conference with the commanding general familiarizing" him "with the situation"; but, said the colonel, the "general did not tell me what action to take."

The action he did take raised Levy's potential maximum sentence from a half-month's restriction on the post to five years in the penitentiary at hard labor. Four more charges were added. They drove the maximum allowable sentence up to eleven years.

In mid-December 1966, when Howard Levy heard that he was to be court-martialed, Richard Miles, a friend involved in voter registration work, suggested that he telephone me.

Most medical graduates whom I knew, even more than lawyers, entered their profession to acquire money and prestige.

---

*Under Article 15 of the Uniform Code of Military Justice, dereliction of duty entails minor administrative rather than judicial punishment. The maximum penalty is one-half month of withheld pay, privileges and duty, and restriction to the post.

Those who wanted money the most specialized. And I believed that those who wanted the most money for the least work and the least risk specialized in dermatology. I didn't want to represent Howard Levy. But because he had worked in the SCOPE education drive, I asked my associate lawyer Laughlin McDonald a South Carolinian who was heading home for Christmas, to interview him.

Laughlin recommended that we take the case. And I discovered that Levy was a physician because he loved medicine and people and life. And because the young physician loved life, he wouldn't teach medicine to those who took life; so the men who ran our country wanted to put him in jail.

∽∽∽∽∽∽∽

For seventeen days at Fort Jackson, South Carolina, and Fort Bragg, North Carolina, in rundown clapboard buildings three wars old, I was allowed to question many of the witnesses. The soldiers marched up to the table, clicked their heels, and saluted. The army had numbered tables with "fire priorities" so everyone would know which tables were to be removed first in case of fire.

Our priority was the order Levy had disobeyed. All military commands are presumed lawful. The burden of proof is upon the disobedient, and no presumption of innocence helps. But the military takes pride in its pretrial process, its "system of discovery," so it was there that I set out to prove that the order and the charges based on it were racially and politically motivated.

During pre-trial hearings I asked Colonel Fancy if the elevation of charges resulted from his reading of the G-2 dossier. "In large part," he replied. The dossier had caused him to "revise" his "estimate of the situation."

Colonel Fancy had obtained all of his information on Levy's "previous political beliefs" from his review of the G-2 dossier and the questions asked by Special Agent West.

When I questioned West, the system of discovery became discretionary. He testified that his duties were to "investigate treason, sabotage, disloyalty, disaffection, and [not to] handle anything which would be criminal in nature, such as murderers or robbery." The special agent denied that he had told Colonel Fancy that Levy was a Communist or anything else. "Well," he said, "I would not make a statement, even if I thought it; of course, it is not for me to think or to know. . . . I do not give any information I receive." But, "anyone intelligent such as Colonel Fancy can deduct from the questions I ask what I am getting at. I ask what I am getting at insofar as the questions I am asking. Insofar as telling the colonel that he is this, he is that, or who said he said this, I do not do that."

Then I inquired about "the kinds of questions . . . asked."

West replied, "I cannot give you the techniques of the questions."

I tried a different tack. "Did you make any investigation of Captain Levy relating to his activities or affairs around South Carolina?" *

Special Agent West leaned forward. He was wary and reluctant. Discovery ran into a stone wall as he carefully and slowly answered, "I did not myself."

Q. Do you know whether or not someone else did?

A. I cannot answer that. I had better delay answering that until I can see, because this possibly could be a security matter. I do not have that. I do not know that.

Q. Well, now, I am not asking you whether or not someone else did at this point. I am asking you whether or not you know whether or not someone did.

A. Well, I will have to decline to answer that.

---

*Although he had lived in the town of Prosperity, Newberry County, South Carolina, since 1961, West could not recall the SCOPE voter registration project during the summer of 1965: "Not in Prosperity, no. Not as far as I know. It could have been." He had no recollection of Dr. King's people "coming into the county in 1965, in the summer."

He did know the local "Sheriff of the Police Department," but he testified that he did not then know of Levy's participation in the voter drive, having that knowledge later from "only what I have read."

Q. As to even whether you have knowledge of whether someone else did?

A. Right.

MR. MORGAN: At this point we request that the witness be
instructed to answer the question.

The prosecutor objected. "[T]his relates to certain matters
that provide the basis for the classification that we have in the
dossier, and apparently there are certain operational techniques
and operations by certain other agencies that may be classified. . . ."

The colonel who presided sustained the prosecutor's objection. The special agent sat silent.

I asked him if his immediate superior was an army officer.
"Sir, I cannot answer that," he responded. "I am not at liberty
myself to answer that."

I asked him if he kept notes. He answered, "No, our notes are
destroyed in our office. We have only a field office. My office is
in Atlanta and they are destroyed after thirty days after the
report goes in after they see them here."

And so it went as we moved inexorably to trial. The existence
of open justice within the military system was less certain than
Howard Levy's future. Ruling after ruling went against us. Repeatedly we were denied access to 100 of the 180 pages of the
G-2 dossier—the very documents upon which the charges were
based. They were classified "Confidential," not even "Secret" or
"Top Secret," yet the army's silent sentries guarded them as
though they contained the ultimate secret tactic for the ultimate
world war.

Four of the five counts charged Howard Levy with saying or
writing something, not with doing (or not doing) something.
Two charges alleged "conduct unbecoming an officer and a gentleman." * The "conduct" was verbal. Two charges set forth

---

*In the mid-1800s when the navy's first Jewish commodore, Uriah P. Levy
(no kin), challenged a fellow officer to duel over a woman's honor, a discerning

violations of the Uniform Code of Military Justice's "general article." Again, the conduct was verbal.

Moreover, the general article covered everything not covered elsewhere—more than fifty enumerated offenses ranging from "abusing a public animal" to "wearing unauthorized insignia."

For three hundred years military forces had used these vague statutes. And now semantics further clouded the view. "Wars" were termed "police actions," and "invasions," "incursions." The "Defense" Department, in a burst of Dale-Carnegie–Norman-Vincent-Pealism, had even named Fort Jackson's obstacle course the "confidence course."

During the initial stages of basic training some words were not euphemized. At Fort Jackson I watched row upon row of young men, heads shaved, fresh from home and their mothers' teachings. They stood at attention in the early morning, while grass was still wet with dew. A sergeant roared, "What's the lesson of hand-to-hand?"

The young men responded in staccato unison, "To kill!"

"What does that make you?"

"Killers!"

~~~~~~~~

The training in dermatology which Colonel Fancy had ordered Levy to provide Special Forces aidmen was basic. So was the education which intelligence provided the colonel. At the pretrial hearing I asked him about the special agent's questions.

Q.   Did he use the word Communist?
A.   Whether he did or not—I know what you are getting at.
Q.   You knew what he was getting at, too, didn't you?
A.   I believe this is the chief worry of the country at this time. . . .

---

court-martial found him guilty of "conduct unbecoming an officer," but ˙ not guilty of conduct unbecoming a gentleman."

Q. And, of course you are concerned about that problem
yourself personally, aren't you?

A. Yes.

According to Colonel Fancy, the special agent suspected that
Levy was talking to blacks "on rather unpatriotic terms." I prod-
ded. The colonel defined patriotism "broadly, as supporting the
principles and aims of the United States, and when I use the
term, unpatriotism, I mean not supporting those principles and
aims." He testified that "[W]hat Mr. West told me was to the
effect that Captain Levy had been having some dealings with
Negro personnel, which dealings and discussions were of an
unpatriotic nature. . . . I like to feel that all of my officers are
patriotic," he said, "and when this suggestion was made to me
that there was a possible problem here, I became concerned.
This was an officer of my command."

As he testified, Colonel Fancy's voice had a flatness to it which
indicated unassailable certainty. He was neither quarrelsome
nor excited.

The colonel, who practiced governmental medicine, believed
that the Communist threat was abroad in the world, in the nation, at Fort Jackson and, most importantly, in *his* dermatology
clinic. He was concerned about "the Communist line," which he
described as "the political and other types of beliefs that are put
forth by our enemies the Communists."

I probed.

Q. Recently, you made a speech to Special Forces Aid Men
[*sic*] who were graduating, did you not?

A. It is my custom to . . . I believe I said in general terms that
the fight against communism goes on, not only in Viet Nam but in
this country as well. By all of us in the Armed Forces and—or
words to that effect.

Q. Do you recall saying that the Hospital stood behind these
men?

A. I am sure I did.

Q. Can you give me an example of what you appraise as communist agitation which brings on chronic anxiety in the country?

A. Well, I believe that the forms that this sort of agitation takes are varied and well described in the source material. I can't quote these at this particular time. . . . [O]ne example might be a labor union that is infiltrated with communist sympathizers. Certain labor unions ordering or provoking strikes against industries, hospitals or what have you.

This would produce anxiety in the people that worked in the industries or hospitals.

. . . .

Q. Can you think of one example of that happening?

A. I can't offhand, but I am sure it has happened.

Q. How can you be sure, if you can't think of it?

A. This is my recollection that this has happened and that I have read about it.

. . . .

Q. What about racial demonstrations?

A. I . . . feel that this might be fruitful ground for communist sympathizers to use the techniques of agitation and produce anxiety in the community.

Q. Do you see much evidence of that in the Civil Rights Movement?

A. I have very little to do with the Civil Rights Movement. From what I have read, this seems perfectly possible.

Q. And, you stated something about the reference to belief in God as being one of the elements of a communist line—of disbelief being an element of communist line, is that correct?

A. Well . . . one of the requirements of communism is that religion as we know it in the free world has no place in their philosophy.

Q. It did not have much place in some of the founders of this country, did it?

A. It had a considerable place.

Q. I said, in some of the founders of this country. You understand the First Amendment to the Constitution was written to protect the right of man to be an atheist?

A. I thought your question had to do with the religious beliefs of the founders of the country.

Q. Are you familiar with those?

A. What?

Q. Are you familiar with the religious beliefs of the founders of this country?

A. My impression from reading and what I have gathered over the years is that they were what we could consider religious people, by our own definition of the term.

Q. Thomas Jefferson?

A. He was one of them.

Q. And Benjamin Franklin?

A. Well, when I say founders of the country, he came a little later.

Q. No, . . . Benjamin Franklin was also a founder.

A. I am talking in generalities here because I have difficulty in viewing the details on this. It is not my specialty.

I asked him if he thought the Communist line was opposed to involvement in Vietnam?

A. Certainly.

Q. And, do you think that much of the agitation about American involvement in Viet Nam is . . . communist based?

A. I believe so.

The colonel did not believe that all Americans who opposed the war in Vietnam were Communists, so I probed into the basis of his judgments.

Q. Have you read any books on Viet Nam?

A. Certainly.

Q. Name one.

A. I will retract the statement. I have not read any books on Viet Nam, but I have read the news media and articles in magazines and in . . . courses that I take in the Army, I have heard material delivered in the form of lectures, but I have not read a book particularly on Viet Nam.

The Uniform Code of Military Justice was the book thrown at Levy. Uniform and codified, the Code was military, so it had everything to do with discipline and little to do with justice.

If forced to a choice, any trial lawyer with walking-around sense would choose the right to select a jury over the rest of the Bill of Rights. Eight of the ten khaki-clad, career colonels and majors whom the commanding general selected to serve as the jury were from the South. Five were from South Carolina. There were eight Caucasians, one Oriental, and one Negro; their average age was forty-one, and their average length of service was 19.3 years. The commanding general who appointed them could shorten the sentence they returned, so mercy, if any, was his to grant, and he controlled their careers as well as Levy's. The jurors knew the general was required by law to order trials only if he believed "the charges alleged an offense" and were "warranted by the evidence." So a finding of guilt would justify his decision to court-martial.

The votes of only two-thirds were required to convict. So if I exercised the one discretionary challenge which military law provided me, their number would be lowered to nine and the votes necessary to convict would drop from seven to six.

Even though one juror had lost an eye in a "friendly mine-field," I waived our challenge.

As the trial opened I whispered to Levy, "With all nineteen eyes of the jury upon them, the trial began." The casual cruelty of that remark would come home to me. One day after lunch I walked back to court with Ramona Ripston. She had been dispatched from the New York Civil Liberties Union to help me during the trial. We watched the one-eyed major, who I now knew had trouble with his good eye. He was due to go back into the hospital. Standing a hundred feet to our right he was fingering the leaves on a low-hanging tree branch and studying them as though trying to photograph each leaf and fix it in memory. He nodded and smiled. As we walked by we nodded and smiled. Then we spoke softly of the "free men" on that jury, of the war, and "friendly minefields," and of that soldier's sentence to life with one eye.

The trial opened on a blazing, hot Wednesday, May 10, 1967, at Fort Jackson.* One prosecution witness after another paraded in, saluted the jury, and said Levy had said what the army said he had said. Now at my left and to the right of the officer-fathers who faced us, Levy's father was sitting on the witness stand. In one hand he was holding a small, faded American flag which had belonged to his son during childhood. In his other hand he was holding the family Bible.

I had to cast Levy into and then beyond the context of the jurors' lives. They had to see him as an excellent civilian doctor. Even if a bad soldier he had to be no threat to their war and their army. Those ten men could sentence Levy to eleven years at hard labor in a federal penitentiary, so my aim was to build constitutional defenses for appeal and cut the sentence.

The army contended that Levy was trying to subvert black soldiers. Often prejudice is better confronted than averted, and we had to cut through it to cut the sentence. Each day I presented a black character witness, some of whom favored the war.

In addition, I called Joseph H. Feinstein, a tall, scholarly chaplain and Orthodox rabbi, to testify about Levy's loyalty. The army's top law officer, Colonel Earl V. Brown, had come to Fort Jackson to conduct the trial. A sturdily built, gray-haired man of medium height, he sat three steps above us at my left. He rocked forward, looked down and interrupted during Feinstein's testimony, "I am not particularly interested in any witness's idea of what is or is not disloyal. . . . That would be a mere personal opinion. I am sure both sides could present witnesses from many extremes to testify as to that."

"That is one of the points we are trying to make," I replied.

"I will permit him to testify as to whether or not under the circumstances he thought the accused acted disloyal or whether

---

*On the eve of the court-martial we sought to enjoin the trial. Anthony G. Amsterdam argued to the Court of Appeals for the District of Columbia that the statutes under which Levy was charged were clearly unconstitutional. The three judges split three ways but two of them agreed that we lost.

his character is loyal or disloyal," the colonel shot back. "I'll
permit that as a character issue, but not as his ideas as to what is
loyal or disloyal. That is hardly relevant."

I turned back to the rabbi: "With respect to his character, is
he loyal?"

"I believe he is."

"Now, what do you base that belief on?" I asked.

"Objection," cried the prosecution.

"Sustained," said the law officer. "You are going into the same
area."

"I want to find out the reason for his ultimate conclusion," I
urged.

Loyalty "is a very difficult abstract concept," the law officer
replied, "and if we are going to have testimony as to that we will
be going through many, many hours of discussion and debate on
that particular point. I don't think you have any expert who can
testify as to that," he concluded.

Again, I addressed the rabbi: "May I ask you this question?
Have you ever known of any enlisted man or any other officer or
anyone else to your knowledge, that became disloyal because of
Dr. Levy and his statements?"

"No," he answered.

"How about anyone who became disaffectionate?"

"No."

Physician Captain Robert Petres—a prosecution witness who
didn't exactly love the army—had the disarming manner of
seeming not to understand the world around him. After he
marched up to the ten-member panel, saluted the wrong man,
and climbed onto the stand, *Washington Post* reporter Nicholas
von Hoffman dubbed him the "Wally Cox of the Levy trial."

The military prosecutor introduces *every* witness by asking
him if he knows the defendant. He then has the witness point
him out in a series of "I accuse" rituals which aim guilt with a
pointing finger. Always in a preferred position, the prosecutor is
in charge of the relatively isolated courtroom facilities. He also
issues subpoenas, swears in the law officer, swears in witnesses,

and takes care of the administrative needs of the officer-jury which, in civilian courts, are handled by impartial bailiffs and clerks.

To be rid of the finger-pointing ritual, I had offered to stipulate that Levy really was Levy, but to no avail.

The prosecutor asked, "Do you know the accused in this case?" Captain Petres quickly answered, "Yes, I do."

"If he is present in court, will you please point him out and state his name?"

Petres stared up at the law officer. Then he slowly studied the ten members of the court-martial. From there his eyes gazed directly across the room to the prosecution table. After what seemed like five minutes, he looked our way. Half rising out of his seat, he pointed, then exclaimed in the manner of a somewhat befuddled Mr. Peepers, "Captain Howard Levy, there!"

That brought laughter even from the career officers.

During my cross-examination I asked Captain Petres:

Q. He never made you disloyal, did he?
A. No, sir.
Q. He never made you disaffect, did he?
A. What does disaffect mean?
Q. I don't know.
LAW OFFICER: Mr. Morgan, if you don't know the questions, don't ask them.

. . . .

INDIVIDUAL COUNSEL [me]: Could I have a meaning from the court what disaffection is? [Throughout the trial the law officer had been providing advisory rulings.]

LAW OFFICER: Should have asked it before you asked the question.

INDIVIDUAL COUNSEL: I asked for a ruling on disloyalty the other day and you said you would supply it before the case went to the jury. I am trying to make out a case of proof on disloyalty and disaffection. I have difficulty understanding what the words mean.

LAW OFFICER: Well, if you are going to ask the question you had better get the definitions before you go any further.

Then, after continuing colloquy in which an out-of-court hearing was requested, the following occurred:

> INDIVIDUAL COUNSEL: I understand, Colonel. I am trying to get from you now, a ruling as to the legal definition of disaffection.
> LAW OFFICER: And I am going to tell you now that you don't need it at this time. *All you have to do is ask this witness what he means by the use of that word.* [Emphasis added.]

I turned to Captain Petres.

> Q. What do you mean by the use of that word?
> A. I never used it.
> Q. Did you never—
> A. Never used the word. I'm sorry.
> Q. Fine.
> LAW OFFICER: Then you will have to rephrase your question to approach something what you mean by it.

I responded, "If I don't know the definition I don't know how to proceed."

> LAW OFFICER: Certainly, there is a legal definition of these terms, but we do not expect the witness to know these legal definitions or to speak only in legal terms.

Then the law officer asked Petres:

> Q. Doctor, you were asked some questions which apparently Mr. Morgan found some confusion on. He used the word disaffection. I am going to ask you that in your conversations or contact with Doctor Levy, did he create in you feelings of hostility toward authority or a feeling that you should disobey or turn away from authority in the hospital there?
> A. No sir.

The law officer then held an out-of-court hearing in which he defined both *disloyalty* and *disaffection,* using such words as *unfaithful, disgust,* and *discontent, ill-will,* and with respect to *disaffection,* the word *disloyalty.* Other words he used were *respect, obedience,* and *allegiance.*

Then he sternly warned me, "I cannot tolerate in any court-room a lawyer posing questions where he is confused by the words."

Before we were through, a rabbi, a physician, ten court members, the law officer, the commanding general, the colonel who commanded the hospital, the staff judge advocate, prosecuting attorneys, and compilers of the G-2 dossier all were allowed a word or so in defining Levy's crime. Neither Levy, who did not testify, nor I participated in that.

In the end the question of what "disloyal" meant was left up to the court-martial jury of ten army officers. We proved that not one of the people to whom Howard Levy had spoken was "disloyal" or "disaffected." Deep down the army feared Levy, not because he was subversive, but because he was not. He was open and aboveboard. It was Levy's heart and his mind and the hearts and minds of millions of others which bothered the brilliant, pragmatic, fearful, nondimensional men in the Pentagon. So they had moved against Levy and risked losing their army as well as their war.

Law Officer Brown smiled, peered down at me, and said, "The defense has intimated that the Special Forces aidmen are being used in Vietnam in a way contrary to medical ethics."

Intimated, hell! I'd shouted it.

We were fresh out of defenses.

Levy had refused to do what they'd ordered him to do. He had said what they said he'd said—and more. He had told the truth. Special Forces were killers of women, children, and peasants. That's who the Viet Cong were. But Law Officer Brown believed truth was "irrelevant" and no defense to the four speech charges.

He casually suggested war crimes as a defense. I thought about that for a moment. War crimes as a defense.

War crimes as a defense!

The jury was absent and Brown seemed to be thinking aloud. He said he'd "heard no evidence that even remotely suggests that . . . and until I do, I must reject this defense." Then he suggested that "a doctor would be morally bound" not to train Special Forces if they were war criminals!

In case after case, those who refused to fight in Vietnam had tried to contend that the United States was committing war crimes. In case after case and court after court, including the Supreme Court, the right to present that defense had been rejected. Now on a Deep South basic training post, an army colonel was suggesting that I prove war crimes as a defense to the charge that Levy had disobeyed the order to train Special Forces aidmen.

The prosecutor was on his feet insisting, "There has been not even an intimation of that in this case. . . !"

"No," Brown replied quickly, "the issue has not been raised."

"It is about to be, I think," I responded.

"As I say," said the law officer, "I will permit you to attempt to raise it."

It had taken all-out warfare, trillions of dollars, millions of lives, and non-German judges to produce the post—World War II Nuremberg trials. Jurors who voted to acquit Levy on the ground of those trials would be voting to convict their war, if not themselves. Their votes also would fix Levy's sentences, and they could salt him away for up to eleven years. So, prior to the trial, Levy and I had decided not to raise the issue.

In Birmingham I had learned what every nonlawyer knows— criminal sanctions are reserved for lower-downs. In the words of an Alabama political song, "It's the same the whole world over, it's a low-down crying shame; it's the rich that gets the glory, it's the poor what gets the blame."

Levy was unrich and for the poor, and he faced eleven years of blame. In the distance I could hear the singsong cadence chanted by men marching double-time. "With respect to war crimes and crimes against humanity," I said, straightfaced, "it might take me an extra day to prove that."

Brown quickly responded, "I'll give you an extra day."

In mid-May 1967, the glory still went to Special Forces. They were national heroes, and a green felt beret rested easily atop the grave of their special friend, my President, John Kennedy. Conservative actor John Wayne was at work producing *The Green Berets,* a motion picture based upon Robert L. ("Robin") Moore's bestselling (3.5 million copies) novel of the same name.

Justice Oliver Wendell Holmes said, "We often need education in the obvious more than investigation into the obscure," so an army law officer should hardly be blamed for telling me that he was "about ready to take judicial notice" that Special Forces were not "engaged in war crimes." The first war-related murder charge against a Special Forces man would not arise for six months and that case would be tried in secret. Two more years would elapse before eight other Special Forces men were charged with murder. In Song Mi hamlet—a.k.a. "Pinkville" (it was colored pink on military maps), a.k.a. My Lai— "noncombatants"—a.k.a. "indigenous personnel" and "VC"— lived day to day as best they could. Someday a twenty-five-year-old war would end. but it was just beginning for a young man named William L. Calley, then in training at Fort Benning, Georgia.

A witness at the Levy court-martial told of the final phase of medical study at Fort Bragg. A future Special Forces aidman received a dog from which the vocal cords had been removed. He shot the dog in the leg and treated the wound. If the dog lived, the aidman passed.

I dispatched counsel to Fort Bragg to come up with Special Forces training manuals. That evening in my hotel room Homer Bigart of *The New York Times* leaned forward, his eyes dancing. In his halting, dignified manner, but without the slightest trace of a smile, Bigart said, "Ch-Chuck, I think all that your young man will come up with at Fort Bragg is the largest h-herd of three-legged, nonbarking dogs in captivity."

We drank to three-legged nonbarking dogs.

What my associates returned with were the written instructions for homemade napalm (concocted from gasoline, soap chips, and other handy items), antipersonnel bombs (a length of iron pipe, sugar, and match heads), and silencers for guns (wire screen).

When *The New York Times* reported that I had issued a call for witnesses to war crimes, the press and the peace movement poured into Columbia. So did telephone calls and telegrams. LEARNED WITH GREAT CONCERN COURT MARTIAL CAPTAIN LEVY STOP GREEN BERET CRIMES AGAINST HUMANITY ONLY PART OF CRIME OF AGGRESSION STOP ANSWER TELEGRAM STOP LETTER FOLLOWS. SARTRE, 9 RUE DELAMBRE, PARIS 14E.

Bertrand Russell's assistant, Ralph Schoeneman, telephoned from London to ask if I wanted the evidence which had been presented to the informal war crimes tribunal which Russell had convened in Europe. "Certainly," I replied.

When the law officer said "certainly not" to my request to travel to Vietnam to take depositions, we turned to the obvious—Army Field Manual 27-10, entitled *The Law of Land Warfare.* It defined a war crime as "a violation of the law of war by any person or persons, military or civilian." The "law of war" arises from treaties to which the United States is a party. According to the field manual, that law "is binding not only upon States as such but also upon individuals and, in particular, the members of their armed forces."

The Law of Land Warfare forbids assassinations *even* in wartime. The payment of bounty for killing, the defacement of the dead, and the use of weapons which cause unnecessary injury are war crimes. So is the wanton destruction of property. The imposition of penalties against civilians is a war crime, as is their mistreatment, impressment, or mass transfer. Proper care of prisoners of war is the responsibility of the capturing person. He cannot simply shrug his shoulders, turn his prisoners over to others who might mistreat them, and, after they have been mistreated, say "I didn't know."

A stranger to me, Columbia University professor Seymour Melman had compiled more than 4,000 American newspaper articles which reported law of land warfare violations. In New York he worked with Ramona Ripston to organize them into exhibits which would show that our leaders had notice of a pattern and practice of war crimes.* Whether factual or not, newspaper articles may place readers on notice and, thereupon, place them under a burden to inquire. The phrase "I didn't know" provides those with notice no defense when charged with complicity. So the 4,000 newspaper clippings more than made out a *prima facie* case. But the giant crate of Bertrand Russell's documents arrived from London several days after the war crimes issue had been decided. Like the "Pentagon Papers" study, they came too late. Levy and I speculated on the crate's contents. We poured a round of drinks, stared at it, patted it occasionally, and continued to speculate. Finally Levy decided, "They've sent Russell himself."

British-born Army Captain Peter G. Bourne, M.D., arrived early and stayed late. As a psychiatrist he had been in charge of a Walter Reed Army Institute of Research study of the effects of stress on Special Forces A-team members. He had worked in eight of the seventy-two known A-team encampments in South Vietnam. He knew what went on there, and by the time he read of the charges against Levy, he was totally disillusioned with the war.

I summoned Army Doctor Bourne to Fort Jackson to serve as

---

*There was some sniper fire from inside the Manhattan Stockade. Some of the ACLU's cold-war liberals were angry at my proceeding with the war crimes defense. Legal ethics require that the ACLU surrender "control" (which includes "influence") over cases it enters to the lawyers who handle them. Sometimes that drives bureaucrats up their walls. This time the criticism ended when ACLU executive director, Jack Pemberton, backed me up (as he always did) and he and Aryeh Neier sent four New Yorkers—Ramona Ripston, Ira Glasser, Alan Levine, and Eleanor Holmes Norton—to help me out.

an expert witness on my unsuccessful contention that the ethics of medicine were protected by the First Amendment.* Overnight he was converted into a planner of our war crimes defense.

The two best-known experts on Special Forces were Donald Duncan and Robin Moore. They were in substantial agreement about the facts. They deeply disagreed about their effect and the propriety of the war. Neither of them wanted to testify. Their reluctance was a major problem, since there are no clerks or marshals in the military justice system. The prosecutor issues all subpoenas, and I didn't want to confide in him. Instead, I helped the two rival author-witnesses volunteer. Peace movement allies at *Ramparts* magazine and elsewhere were enlisted to speak with the former Special Forces sergeant. Duncan's book, *The New Legion,* was soon to be published, as was Moore's book, *The Country Team.* I talked with Moore's publisher. He shrewdly inferred that the trial was a talk show where competing books might be reviewed or discussed.

As the author of *The Green Berets,* Robin Moore was an unlikely defense witness. The former television producer had quit his job as public relations director of the Sheraton hotel chain to write full-time. In 1962 Moore approached a military attaché to Vice President Lyndon B. Johnson with a proposition. Moore had written *The Devil to Pay,* a portrayal of guerrilla warfare in Cuba. He wanted to write a novel about Special Forces in Vietnam. The army agreed to help. They put him through Special Forces training which included counterinsurgency, and guerrilla and psychological warfare courses. With students from seventeen foreign nations, Moore learned almost everything taught. They did exclude him from the course on expedient devices, which, Moore testified, "took in the assassination end of guerrilla warfare. . . ."

So it was out of class that he learned "how to make a silencer

---

*He was joined by Drs. Jean Mayer and Victor Sidel of the Harvard Medical School, and by Dr. Benjamin Spock. Each of them testified for Levy on issues of ethics.

for a machine gun in a hurry if you had to." He learned of tiny finger-sized explosive devices and other unique American tools.

His training finished, Moore, with press accreditation from *Look* magazine, borrowed airfare to Saigon.

In Vietnam he spent from two days to a week in each of ten of the seventy-two A-team encampments. He visited ten others.

He was as much an advocate of Special Forces on the witness stand as he had been at the motel while we drank and laughed our way into the wee hours of the morning. Moore was proud uncle and best friend of our "armed and mature Peace Corps."

"[A]bout the first thing" Moore had discovered in Vietnam was that "Special Forces were working very closely under the operating arm of the Central Intelligence Agency . . . [which] was actually running most Special Forces operations up until early '65. . . ."

Soon assassinations would become the dominant fact of domestic political life. Martin King was still alive. So was Robert Kennedy. George Wallace was scampering about preparing to campaign for the presidency. With Moore on the stand, I referred the law officer to Paragraph 31 of *The Law of Land Warfare*. The section, entitled "Assassination and Outlawry," read: "It is forbidden to kill or wound treacherously individuals belonging to either hostile nation or Army. . . ."

"Is there any way to fight guerrilla warfare by the rules?" I asked Moore.

"Not that I know of," the slightly overweight, likable man replied affably. "I have never seen it work yet."

Q.   What is an assassination team?
A.   Well, it's a team trained to hit targets, a target being the term generally used for an individual to be assassinated for political reasons or whatever. . . . It is an integral part of guerrilla warfare just as is medical people trying to help the people of an area to win the hearts and minds of the people. An assassination is also an important aspect. If you have a political chief . . . and you know . . . that he is damaging our effort it only makes sense to assassinate him if possible.

"Thank God Special Forces are in charge of training those teams," said Moore, "because the Vietnamese do a pretty botched up job of it left to their own advice."

I turned to the subject of terrorism. "Have you ever seen a black card with a white eye on it?"

"Yes," Moore responded enthusiastically. "That was a card which was used by assassination teams to leave on the body of a target or a house of a target after they were assassinated; and they were also used . . . for terror purposes to put them, say, on a Viet Cong political leader's home. They'd tack it up there so he would know he might be assassinated at any time. I have a whole chapter on that subject in *The Country Team*, if you want to get into assassinations, black cards, and all that sort of thing."

Regarding Special Forces aidmen, "every one" Robin Moore had met was a combat soldier. He said, "They have to be able to fight." On an A-team "everyone can do everyone else's job."

I asked him whether aidmen administered sodium pentothal (truth serum) to captured Vietnamese.

A. Yes, that is done.
Q. Is that used by Special Forces Aidmen?
A. The time I had personal knowledge of it . . . it was used by a Special Forces Captain who told his medic to do it.

Robin Moore's testimony was a preview of the news to come during the next six years. He told of crossing the border into neutral Cambodia; of the worldwide use of Special Forces and of their assignment within Latin America; of "country team" operations in foreign nations; of assassinations, terrorism, and the surrender of our prisoners to those whom we knew would torture and mistreat them. These clear-cut, simple war crimes were our policy and our practice. And, as Justice Brandeis wrote, "Our government is the potent, the omnipresent teacher."

Moore also told of the defacement of the dead. Bounty payments made from CIA funds were based upon the number of right ears of the "enemy" which Montagnard tribesmen turned in.*

Then the prosecution took over.

"Mr. Moore, this is a difficult war in Vietnam, is it not?" the prosecutor began.

"Yes, it is," Moore responded. "I have seen torturing, but if an American was present . . . the only way he was allowed to express dissent . . . was that he could walk out on it. . . . And that was the only way he could express it. He could refuse to be there.

"So if he did any more than that, if he tried to stop the Vietnamese . . . chances were he would be relieved and his career would suffer and also it would cause an incident between the Vietnamese senior corps and Americans."

When Moore had finished, the law officer turned to me and snapped, "This witness certainly doesn't bring up the issues we were looking for here."

"Certainly he does," I snapped back.

"I certainly fail to see it."

"Well in the first place—"

He interrupted me, turned to Moore, and said, "You're in a terrible hurry to get off, I take it."

As Robin Moore left Fort Jackson for Fort Lauderdale, Captain Peter Bourne began telling of our army's certain knowledge that the South Vietnamese tortured prisoners.

He told the law officer of our "attitude of studied indifference" and that the failure to report war crimes had resulted from a "general understanding, policy, and practice."

When the law officer inquired into the "rather careless attitude toward life" which "seems to cover all of Southeast Asia,"

---

*Donald Duncan's testimony corroborated Moore's. Duncan testified that the "clipping of ears is a tally count." It is "considered proof that you have killed a man. Usually it is very difficult to cut a man's ear off unless you have him at your disposal completely."

Bourne stared at him in silence. Then, icily, he replied, "I gather that this sort of feeling was regarded in some ways as a defense to what the Japanese did in World War II, but I think we judged them by our standards then and I suppose this is how we judge incidents now." *

"Assassination and terror" are integral parts of guerrilla warfare, testified former Special Forces Sergeant Donald Duncan, as though it were incredible to him that anyone believed "our side" was different from The Enemy. He had spent time in twenty-one A-team camps. The total number of A-team camps about which our witnesses knew was forty-nine of seventy-two. That seemed sufficient to establish a policy or pattern or practice.

"[F]rom the NKVD manual," Duncan had taught Special Forces men "countermeasures to hostile interrogations." Included among the interrogation methods were "such things as lowering a man's testicles into a vise, spinning a man around, putting a pail over his head and beating it.

"We taught that there was no way to keep serious interrogators from getting from you the information they desired." So, he said, "We really taught the course to teach our men their techniques."

Even though Duncan's testimony merely bolstered that of Dr. Bourne and writer Moore, his reluctance to testify had been well founded. Outside the courtroom, while he was on the witness stand, army public information men issued press releases designed to undercut his credibility. Inside, alluding to Duncan's employment at *Ramparts*, the prosecutor asked, "Do you consider yourself more or less an opportunist?"

---

*During cross-examination, Bourne told of our destruction of a leper village. In his direct testimony he referred to another village we burned to the ground. Bourne "found a man inside the house which was already in flames, lying down on the floor."

"Are you planning to burn this guy alive?" he shouted to a nearby Vietnamese lieutenant.

The lieutenant laughed, "He is dead."

"No," Duncan responded.

"What is your salary?"

Duncan responded, "Six hundred sixty dollars a month."

In redirect examination I asked, "What was your salary at Special Forces?"

He answered, "About nine hundred dollars a month, tax-free."

The law officer, after a day-long trial recess, ruled that Special Forces were not engaged in the commission of war crimes. He said, correctly, there was "no court, civilian or military, which would sit in judgment on the President's exercise of his power in disposing the troops. . . ."

There were "perhaps instances of needless brutality in this struggle in Vietnam." But Law Officer Brown found "no evidence that would render this order to train aidman illegal on the grounds that eventually these men would become engaged in war crimes or in some way prostitute their medical training by employing it in crimes against humanity."

※※※※※※※

At 2:00 A.M., June 2, 1967, I flipped on the light in my dreary motel room, rolled out of bed, turned on the coffee, and began to outline my closing argument.

The prosecutor's task was easy. He reread for the career-officer jury Levy's letter to Geoffrey Hancock, the intelligence sergeant in Vietnam.

When I spoke, the officers listened intently despite sweltering courtroom heat. The air-conditioning system broke down (for

---

Bourne reentered the house and found the man alive and well, but tied up. Bourne cut the ropes. Together they escaped as the hut "burned up."

The Vietnamese lieutenant was furious. Bourne, fearing that the man whose life he had just saved would be killed, escorted him to a helicopter to get him out of the village alive.

"Don't rock the boat," the captain told him when he reported the incident. "As soon as it gets to the Special Forces Corps advisor, he will just have to ignore it."

the first and only time during the weeks of trial) as I began my summation. When I finished, it came back on. As usual I talked too fast for the court reporter to pick up many of my words, but the officers understood that I was asking for Levy's freedom, not his martyrdom.

They filed out. I was totally spent. My clothes were drenched with sweat. The accumulated tension of months spent trapped within the military justice system, the knowledge of national wrong and Levy's heroism had sapped every bit of my energy. At home the *Birmingham News*'s editorial cartoon had me and Levy undermining the nation. To the *New York Daily News* and other prowar newspapers we were the war criminals. Reporters were speculating on a speedy verdict and a maximum sentence. As the crowd left the courtroom, Levy's father put his arms around my shoulders and hugged me.

It was then that Homer Bigart's wife, Alice, walked over. She reminded me that Homer had covered many trials for *The New York Times*. "He could never tell you this himself, but I can." She paused and then spoke softly: "To us you are the Beethoven of the legal profession."

After seven hours the officers returned a guilty verdict on three charges. They ordered the two charges based upon the letter reduced.

The next morning, when they met to fix the sentence, the letter charges were dismissed. That automatically cut the maximum sentence from eleven to eight years in the penitentiary. They finally sentenced Levy to three years at hard labor, dismissal from the service, and a forfeiture of pay and allowances.

We returned to our seats. Then it happened.

I had paid no attention to the hospital's executive officer, Colonel Chester Davis, who was sitting in the packed courtroom audience. The law officer briskly passed the necessary papers to the jury. From there they were passed to the prosecutor. Now the papers were coming toward us. I noticed Colonel Davis standing behind us. He was a head taller than Levy and outweighed him by almost a hundred pounds. Court adjourned.

The officer jury was filing out. Davis said, "Sit down, Howard!" I watched the incredulous expression on the face of our quiet and easy-going military defense counsel, Captain Charles Sanders. His jaw set as he saw Davis snap handcuffs on Levy's wrists and jerk him to his feet. Sanders clenched his fists. He started at the colonel. I grabbed Sanders.

A woman screamed. There was a roar from the crowd in the courtroom. Cameras flashed as Davis shoved Howard Levy through the door and into a waiting automobile. The door slammed. Levy disappeared. The automobile sped away. We raced into the street and jumped into automobiles to follow him. Suddenly, scores of soldiers appeared. At parade rest they blocked the roads in front of the courthouse. Behind me *New York Daily News* reporter Anthony Burton shouted, "Fascist bastards!"

I shoved my way through the soldiers and strode purposefully down the road—to nowhere. To absolutely nowhere. Three network camera crews were following me.

Under a burning midday sun, I was absurdly alone, on foot, on camera, five miles from the jail, ten miles from the hospital, and light-years from every conceivable place into which I might logically disappear. I couldn't simply turn around and walk back to that damned court building. I slowed down. As the camera crews caught up with me, I stopped. I quickly reverted to basic Alabama politics where we learned (perhaps from Jim Folsom's example) that, when whiskey isn't available, and all else fails, it is time to have a press conference.

I was concerned about Levy's whereabouts. But I was less concerned than others. When the handcuffs had been snapped on his wrists, Levy had slowly winked at me. On his way into the penitentiary, he so desperately wanted to end that war that he actually smiled. He knew that in those fleeting, photographed, malicious moments, the army had made a martyr and helped a movement.

Howard Levy in handcuffs appeared on the front page of Sunday morning's newspapers, June 4, 1967. By then the Pentagon had ordered him removed from the stockade and transferred to a wing of the Fort Jackson hospital. For the next seven months he had unlimited visitation rights, access to a sun porch, and a telephone.

The army's largess came too late. That photograph slammed the war home to millions of Americans. It became a poster which carried the message: "Join the New Action Army." In New York and San Francisco, demonstrators called for Levy's freedom. In medical schools the debate began and young physicians organized to resist the service.

During the trial I had argued that speaking the truth could never be "conduct unbecoming an officer and a gentleman." An officer could freely speak "objective truth," even if it "totally disrupted the armed forces!"

"Not as long as that army won," the law officer said.

At the Levy court-martial, truth lost, as the army "won."

But the facts had begun their long march. People's perception of the Vietnam War had begun to change. Within nine months the law officer, Earl Brown, having retired to Columbia University, would cosponsor an antiwar advertisement in *The New York Times*. In Columbia, South Carolina, the first of the antiwar coffee houses, the UFO, opened. Intraservice resistance grew as two young Fort Jackson soldiers began an antiwar prayer movement. Ordered to "Stop praying and move on," they refused. Threatened with court-martial, they telephoned me. When I flew to Columbia, the army dropped the charges. According to *The New York Times*, a hastily scrawled note had been placed on the general's bulletin board. It read, "Morgan's Back."

~~~~~~~~

In *habeas corpus* proceedings in nine separate military and civilian district and appellate courts, we fought for Levy's release pending appeal. Civilian court deference to the military justice system, a general's affidavit, and the G-2 dossier kept him behind bars.

The general swore that he'd received information "on about May 31, 1967, from a confidential source who has furnished reliable information in the past, that Captain Levy had expressed the following to a close associate: his intention upon conviction to seek bail, . . . to flee . . . to a Communist country, seek political asylum . . ., remain absent . . . denounce the United States, and . . . after several years . . . contact an American embassy . . . and request permission to return . . . and . . . this request would be granted in view of the lenient treatment of defectors by the United States."

In mid-December 1967, they flew him from comparative comfort to a barred cell behind the thick, turreted, high walls of the disciplinary barracks at Fort Leavenworth, Kansas. At midnight, January 19, 1969 (which was the final moment of the outgoing Johnson administration), the order to remove Levy to the Lewisburg, Pennsylvania, federal penitentiary became effective. Soon after his transfer, I filed a petition for writ of *habeas corpus* challenging his conviction. Reber Boult and Norman Siegel toted it to Pennsylvania. At the Atlanta airport, the boxes, which included the trial record and other papers, were weighed for excess luggage charges. They came to 272 pounds—more than Reber and Norman combined. In antiwar cases even the weight of constitutional arguments was less important that the luck of the draw. In the next few months I lost three more times. Levy remained imprisoned until August 4, 1969, when I finally reached Supreme Court Justice William O. Douglas. He ordered that Levy be released.*

Levy's parents promptly posted the $1,000 bail. They drove us to Philadelphia. From there Howard and I flew to Atlanta, where a celebration was planned. As we approached the building at Five Forsyth Street, our eyes caught the headline on the afternoon *Atlanta Journal*: BERET-COLONEL, 7 OTHERS CHARGED IN VIET MURDER.

Howard smiled. "As I was saying before I was so rudely interrupted."

We went upstairs and had a drink.

---

*In 1974, after we finally won in the Court of Appeals for the Third Circuit, Nixon's Supreme Court appointees joined with a holdover justice to provide a five-to-three majority against us. They upheld the constitutionality of the conviction and of the statutes. However, Levy did not have to return to jail.

10

As the war escalated, so did opposition to it. Four months after Howard Levy's letter was mailed to the intelligence sergeant in Vietnam, SNCC's chairman, John Lewis, black Christian, charged that our government was "deceptive" in the "Dominican Republic, the Congo, South Africa, Rhodesia, and in the United States." By then we had 197,300 troops in South Vietnam and an additional 70,000 men in the nearby Seventh Fleet.

Lewis spoke for himself and for SNCC. In Atlanta, on Thursday, January 6, 1966, he equated the war with the civil rights struggle. He questioned "the ability and even the desire of the United States government to guarantee free elections abroad." The statement continued: "We are in sympathy with, and support, the men in this country who are unwilling to respond to a military draft which would compel them to contribute their lives to United States aggression in Vietnam in the name of the freedom we find so false in this country. . . ."

That statement had not been previously communicated to John Lewis's best friend, Julian Bond, SNCC's communications director, who at eighty-five dollars a week was its highest-paid employee. But as the events precipitating his ouster from membership in Georgia's house of representatives were to demonstrate, Representative-elect Bond totally agreed with SNCC's words. Like Levy and Lewis and others in their generation, Julian Bond, at twenty-five, wanted to make the United States safe for democracy.

There was a time when Julian, with his friend Jim Forman, had gone into the gallery of Georgia's house of representatives and white legislators had danced a jig, pointed upward, and shouted from the floor, "Nigger! Nigger! Mr. Doorkeeper, get those niggers out of there!" Upstairs a white man shoved Bond and struck at Forman, saying, "I'm the meanest man in Meriwether County. Me and my daddy used to snatch niggers off the train and kill 'em."

Whether or not his eviction from the house gallery moved Julian Bond to seek a seat on the house floor, District 126, which resulted from the Supreme Court's one-person, one-vote decision, seemed tailor-made for him. Some of its residents taught at Atlanta University. Many others were unemployed and lived in Atlanta's "Vine City" slums. But 6,000 of that district's 6,500 voters had one thing in common. They were black.

SNCC members, fearing that he would have to compromise his principles, hadn't wanted Julian Bond to run. He would prove himself "different" and them wrong, for he started well ahead of those who see "compromise" as a worthy social end in itself, and (although they rarely say it) a way to remain popular by appearing to be all things to everyone.

Many political careers are modeled on appearances and too few physically attractive people (like the very rich and the very bright, to whom good things come too easily) should be taken seriously. That was not true of Julian Bond. He modeled for RC Cola signs that adorned the Deep South's black cafés and grocery stores, but by the age of twenty, a semester before graduation, his beliefs had led him to leave Morehouse College to become executive secretary of the Atlanta Committee for Ap-

peals on Human Rights. As he followed his beliefs, 1,500 marching young people followed him into the city streets. They sought
the right to drink their Coca-Colas sitting down in Atlanta's
stores, and to enter all-white restaurants and theaters.

In 1965, Julian Bond campaigned door to door. An appearance
by Harry Belafonte and the Freedom Singers helped him over-
whelm his two black opponents 2,320 to 487 and lead the civil
rights movement into politics.

As well as leadership, Julian Bond had artistic talent. By the
time he was twenty-five his poetry had been published in six
anthologies in four countries. It was clear to everyone—
especially white segregationists—that he wasn't just another
"nigger politician." He walked, talked, wrote, and thought with
ease. Where most white politicians stumbled for words, Julian
Bond was self-assured. They labored for humor. He had a
smooth, self-deprecating wit. So, with SNCC's antiwar statement as their stated reason, getting Julian Bond became a way
for white legislators to say "We're still better." And that was the
perfect way to pay the radicals back.

∿∿∿∿∿∿

"Julian," Ed Spivia, an Atlanta newscaster with WGST, began, "the only thing that is keeping the group that has made this
statement from being in treason is the technicality that we aren't
at war. If we should become engaged in war and a declaration of
war be declared, would you still stand by this statement?"

"Well, I don't know," Julian answered into the telephone and
Spivia's tape recorder. "Right now I can stand by it. If it were
treasonable by law I would have to think about it again."

The barrage continued:

Why specifically do you endorse it and what points?
Will you be able to take this oath [of office] with a clear con-
science and endorse this statement?
You don't feel that there are certain, perhaps, moral obligations

that are implied in taking over such an office as you expect to do, which might be in variance with this view which you have just stated?

You are willing to stand by this as long as it doesn't cost you anything, but if it is going to cost you, you are going to be held in treason, then you can't stand by it?

Do you feel that all the folks that voted for you have those same views, or the majority of them?

You don't think that this is what would be necessary in order to fight this war in order to stop the communism from going any further?*

Julian answered with crisp precision. He was not convinced that we were stopping international communism. He had been educated in Quaker schools, so he did oppose killing—by the Viet Cong as well as by United States troops.

Dr. Horace Mann Bond, dean of education at Atlanta University, listened to his son's replies on the radio. Dr. Bond had resigned his membership on the executive committee of the Fulton County (Atlanta) Republican party. He had put up Julian's $500 qualifying fee. He had gone to work for his son, the Democrat. He listened carefully.

"That's it!" he exclaimed. "Julian just lost his seat."

To former governor Ernest Vandiver, Bond's support of the SNCC statement was "appalling." To *Time* the statement was "typically intemperate"; to Governor Carl E. Sanders it was "inaccurate and intemperate"; to Lieutenant Governor Peter Zack Geer, it was a "subversive policy statement." To seventy-five state representatives, it was treason.

They charged that Julian had given "aid and comfort" to the enemies of the United States; that he had violated the Selective Service laws; that he had brought "disrespect" and "discredit"

---

*Spivia's questions later prompted Chief Judge Elbert P. Tuttle to say from the bench that this was "what you might call making the news as well as reporting it."

upon the house; and that the SNCC statement was inconsistent with a legislator's oath of office.*

The weekend of January 7, some black legislators urged Julian to "modify" his views. That knew what Charles Pou, the *Atlanta Journal's* political editor, knew. Pou had written that the white folks wanted Bond to "say he's just a little bit sorry, about endorsing that SNCC statement and all." House Speaker George T. Smith, a portly, soft-spoken man who abstained from all heady spirits except politics, later said that Bond might have been seated if he'd apologized and come begging.

SNCC's Box Zellner, a former client of mine, phoned me in Waveland, Mississippi, where I was speaking at a CORE training session. I said, sure I would join Howard Moore, Julian's brother-in-law, in Julian's defense.

I dodged holes and washouts in the hurricane-damaged highway to New Orleans, hijacked a seat on a flight to Atlanta, and arrived in time to discover that we had a sure-fire winner. All we had to do was keep our heads, tell the truth, build a record for the Supreme Court, and obey the procedural rules of the house. But there were no applicable rules. So, on the morning of Monday, January 10, 1966, I entered Georgia's capitol with the Constitution in my pocket, the facts clear, not an inkling of the procedures to be followed, and the immediate problem of finding a place to sit.

At 10:20 A.M. Julian accepted the petition from the house clerk. He remained seated. The other 204 house members rose, held their heads and hands high, and swore to uphold and defend the constitutions of the United States and Georgia.

The speaker appointed a special twenty-eight-man committee (which included the three blacks, two from Atlanta, whom we

---

*Which reads in its entirety, "I will support the Constitution of this State and of the United States, and on all questions and measures which may come before me, I will so conduct myself, as will, in my judgment, be most conducive to the interests and prosperity of this State."

had requested) to meet at 2:30 P.M. to hear the evidence and to report to the full house. He pledged to complete the proceedings "before we go to bed tonight." There was an attitude of expectation, an understanding that this would be a wondrous day. Even though they were legislators, not lynchers, many seemed to feel excitement and fear—like teen-agers on their way to "egg niggers."

Black Senator LeRoy Johnson sought mercy as well as justice, arguing that Bond's "youth" and his "political experience" should be considered. The two black men who had run against Julian testified that he was loyal. Black State Senator Horace Ward agreed. All who spoke for him were black. All who spoke against him were white.

Now Julian Bond stood and those who had taken the oath sat. Wearing a conservative blue-gray vested suit and striped tie, he didn't look "radical." He gazed up at the recently integrated gallery, where his family and their friends sat waiting anxiously. Then he looked out over the packed house. In a calm, clear, firm voice, he told them that he agreed with the SNCC statement "without reservation."

During cross-examination he was asked about those who burn draft cards. He responded:

I admire people who . . . feel strongly enough about their convictions to take an action like that knowing the consequences that they will face. . . .

I have never suggested or counseled or advocated that any one other person burn their draft card. In fact, I have mine in my pocket and will produce it if you wish. . . .

The legislators were attentive as he tried to explain to them his duty and theirs. "The fact of my election to public office," he said to veteran office-holders, "does not lessen my duty or desire to express my opinions even when they differ from those held by others."

I spoke. *New York Times* reporter Roy Reed wrote:

Mr. Morgan, his great hulk arched over the rostrum and his voice quivering with emotion, said, "If Mr. Bond has committed treason, then the proper place for Mr. Bond to be tried is in a court of law. But that is not what this is all about. The issue here is the right of every Georgian to speak."

As the legislators debated, they centered on SNCC. "[N]ow we find not only our state, our counties, but the legislature itself has been invaded by one whose 'SNCCing' [pronounced "Snicking"] pursues not freedom for us but victory for our enemies!" cried Representative Bobby Pafford.

Outraged, Representative George Bagby referred to seven white men, former legislators, who had been unseated by the federal court's reapportionment order. "[S]hoved in their stead, that this state might see darkness instead of light [was] the infamous Mr. Bond!"

Later Julian and I laughed. They almost acted out the story of the Georgia black woman in the subway to Harlem: "How do you like your new job?" she asked her seatmate.

"Jes' fine."

"How come you like it so well?"

"They're so high class." Her employer had hosted a dinner party for Mamie Eisenhower, Adlai E. Stevenson, Bernard Baruch, and Helen Hayes.

"My, my," the seatmate exclaimed, "what do important white folks like that talk about when they are alone?"

"Us."

The "us" was the "infamous Mr. Bond." He might as well have been absent from the capitol that day. He listened attentively, if impassively, while the white folks talked about him. "I feel that this situation that has arisen here today was a planned thing, and that we are being used!" Bagby cried. "SNCC is in debt! They are in a hole, they are in a rough spot! Well, we are fixing to give them a martyr, and we are fixing to give them a cause!"

The short, fat man pulled himself to full height. His face

trembling with anger, he turned to the television camera. His voice rose. "Well, I want them to know, wherever the SNCCs are today and tonight, that I know I am being used; you ain't fooling me a darn bit!"

When they voted 184 to 12 to exclude Julian Bond from their midst, a "stunned silence" (as one report described it) came over the spectators. The speakers immediately adjourned the house. As we were swept away by surging well-wishers, reporters, and photographers, I heard Aubrey Morris, one of Atlanta's best newsmen, shout a prelude to what would become a chant at the 1968 National Democratic Convention. "Jul-yan! Jul-yan! Mr. Bond!"

Morris pushed toward us, microphone in hand.

Carried on the crest of the crowd, Julian turned his head. I heard him say, "You have not heard the last of this."

And that is how the nation heard the first of Julian Bond. Overnight he became its best-known black political figure, and after an appearance on NBC's "Meet the Press" this college "dropout" became the most sought-after speaker on the college lecture circuit.

Years later we were returning to Atlanta from a fund-raiser for southern black office-seekers. At Sargent Shriver's home in Maryland we had been given lots of liberal hospitality, but no food. As hungry as the poor starving Chinese, John Lewis and I went into the north terminal's stand-up lunch counter at Washington's National Airport. Julian went to the telephone.

A black waitress ignored us when excited stage whispers swept down the counter. "Julian Bond's out there!" All of the waitresses raced into the hallway. Even the cashier abandoned the cash register to see the man for whom we were trying to order a hot dog. Other customers shrugged at one another, astounded.

John and I tried to keep straight faces, but we looked at each other and burst out laughing.

The waitresses returned with Julian. Sheepishly, he ordered for us. The airport hot dogs were prepared with loving care— and they were free.

Georgia's general assembly had made a hero, not a martyr. They did not save SNCC. Even John Lewis and Julian Bond resigned when the organization moved to separatism. But for a few vital years while white World War II veterans in legislative halls turned thumbs down on democracy, SNCC's members were freedom's foot soldiers, going where others dared not go, doing and saying what others dared not do and say, and changing the world, until, in perhaps the most courageous act of all, they disappeared.

Back in January 1966, inside Georgia's capitol, white legislators sought to compensate for what they had done. One described black representative J. C. Dougherty as "calm and dignified and reasoned." Another termed black representative Grace Hamilton a "real smart woman." To reporters an unnamed black representative noted the "extra effort to make the rest of us welcome."

Outside Georgia's capitol, on the Friday (January 14) following the expulsion, 1,000 protesters assembled in front of Populist (and anti-black, anti-World War I) Tom Watson's statue, sang "The Star-Spangled Banner," prayed with Dr. Ralph D. Abernathy, and listened to Martin King and SNCC's James Forman. Then a hundred protesters bolted toward the capitol. As the police turned them back, they shouted: "You ain't got nothing but bullets! We're going to sit up there in the Georgia legislature and make some decent laws!"

Across town, at the ACLU office, we had neither "decent laws" nor "prove it" problems. The facts were clear. Julian's accusers had been his judges. His expulsion resulted from a legislative treason trial which punished him for his words. The federal courts simply had to rule that the First, Fourteenth, and Fifteenth amendments forbade penalizing a legislator for his race or speech.* But on January 12, even before we finished

---

*Martin King and Mrs. Ariel Keys resided in Julian Bond's district. Since their representative had been ousted they had been denied their voice in their state legislature and that amounted to a denial of their right to vote. I joined them with Julian as plaintiffs in his lawsuit.

drafting the complaint, *New York Times* correspondent Sidney E. Zion reported on the dutiful gloominess of the "experts." To me "experts" meant corporate firm lawyers who collected large fees in desegregation cases and lost each of them. They were referred to as "constitutional lawyers." Those who won were called "civil rights lawyers." (Outside the South, "constitutional lawyers" are law professors, their renown more dependent upon defeatism than expertise.) Even Professor Thomas I. Emerson of the Yale Law School "agreed that Mr. Bond had little chance of victory if he took the matter to court." Where he had more (or even any other) "chance of victory" escaped me. Zion reported my response: "The experts are always pessimistic. There may be no case directly in our favor, but there are not any against us either."

Among the representatives against us, James Floyd was a leader. His "good old boy" nickname clung to him as tightly as a kudzu vine to slaked, eroding soil. In the legislative roster, Representative Floyd named himself "James 'Sloppy' " so, today, even humorless professors smile when they teach *Julian Bond* v. *James "Sloppy" Floyd.*

Five days after the legislature adjourned, the state held a special election to fill Julian's vacant seat. The three-judge federal district court had moved slowly. A majority of the judges must have reasoned that if Julian lost, his case would be "mooted," so they dawdled while Julian ran. But no one ran against him. Even Julian's previous opponent, "Dean Dean" (Malcolm J. Dean really was an Atlanta University dean) offered to manage his campaign. "Sure, we're all running," said Dean; "we're running for Julian Bond!"

Julian received 100 percent of the votes. The House Rules Committee met. Again Julian refused to recant. Again he was denied the oath of office.*

And when the district court ruled, we lost. Chief Judge Tuttle

---

*Twice more he ran, and twice more he was elected as his case moved toward the Supreme Court.

dissented. But judges Griffin B. Bell and Lewis R. Morgan applied a Frankfurterian "balancing test" to Julian's speech. They found it was "repugnant to the oath which he was required to take." They said it was "a call to action based upon race; a call alien to the pluralistic society. . . ." It aligned SNCC with blacks "in the Dominican Republic, the Congo, South Africa, Rhodesia. . . ." It accused the United States of murder in Vietnam and of "[p]ursuing an aggressive policy in violation of international law."

New York lawyer Leonard Boudin argued for Julian in the Supreme Court. He and his law partner, Victor Rabinowitz, represented the Emergency Civil Liberties Committee, which had been organized to counter the ACLU's general failure to defend Communists during the McCarthy period. There are plenty of constitutional cases to go around without trying to corner the market. I never even tried to find out who asked Boudin to enter the case. I knew that with Boudin, Julian was well represented. The ACLU's rules forbade joint participation with its "competitors." Despite an invitation from Boudin to continue as co-counsel, I withdrew. Some within the ACLU tried to label Julian an unwitting dupe for Rabinowitz and Boudin, who also defended Fidel Castro's Cuban economic interests in cases in American courts. The harsh infighting in that case provided me with an insight into how tough the liberals' war against real Communists such as Elizabeth Gurley Flynn must have been.

On December 5, 1966, I sat in the Supreme Court waiting to argue another political case, *Fortson* v. *Morris,* the Write-in Georgia, Maddox-Callaway election case, when Chief Justice Warren issued the decision in *Bond* v. *Floyd.* The Supreme Court unanimously struck down the Georgia house's action so as "to give freedom of expression the breathing space it needs to survive." All nine justices said: "Legislators have an obligation to take positions on controversial political questions so that their constitutents can be fully informed by them, and be better able to assess their qualifications for office. . . ."

In January 1967, pursuant to the orders of the Supreme Court, Governor-elect Maddox and Representative-elect Bond, each of whom had stood up for very different beliefs, stood up to take Georgia's oath of office.

True to Tom Paine's words, the tumult did subside. One day in 1975, Julian was confronted by a friendly white legislator who asked: "Listen, Senator, I was here when all that happened. Just what is it you did say about the war?"

11

It took the sit-ins, the freedom rides, the University of Mississippi riots, Birmingham, George Wallace's stand in the University of Alabama's schoolhouse door, the Mississippi Freedom Summer, the Selma-to-Montgomery march, and sundry bombings, burnings, beatings, and killings to jolt the Justice Department into enforcing the Equality Amendments. Then suddenly the Vietnam War became a wall between the Movement and the liberal government. Peaceful social revolutions rarely survive foreign conflicts. Now as the CIA, the FBI, and the rest of that clandestine apparatus took careful aim at public opinion, cold-war liberals pointed editorial lances at Martin King. They wrote that his meddling hurt the Movement; he should ignore the war and stick to civil rights.

But it was not until March 30, 1967, 370 days before a sniper took its leader, that Martin King's Southern Christian Leadership Conference actually voiced opposition to our foreign "war against the poor." SNCC had been the first of the civil rights organizations to articulate the war's relationship to the Movement. Next had come CORE. At an SCLC board meeting in

Louisville, Kentucky, I wrote the statement which we adopted.*
Martin King read it like thunder. "The people of this nation from
the President to every man on every street have turned their
eyes to a small land, thousands of miles from the ghettos of
America. Far from the tenant farmer's shack in south Alabama. . . ."

When reporter John Herbers interviewed King for the April
2, 1967, *New York Times,* only Andy Young and I sat in.

"I love America," Martin told Herbers. "I want to see our
great nation stand up as the moral example of the world."

He planned to move against "hard economic problems which
would cost the nation something to solve." Changes in public
accommodations, school desegregation, and voting had cost
nothing. Desegregation had saved money for school systems,
restaurateurs, hotel owners and shopkeepers. Now, Martin
King was aiming at economic justice, at the distribution of
wealth. He stressed, "You can't really have freedom without
justice; you can't have peace without justice; and you can't have
justice without peace."

~~~~~~~~

SNCC members felt that foreign policy was made in corporate
boardrooms, corporate law firm offices, and other secret corporate places. As I heard them talk, I remembered a song I had
heard in Birmingham. "Do you want to go to war, Billy Boy?"
was followed by, "No inclination do I feel to be maimed for U.S.
Steel, I'm a young thing and cannot leave my mother." †

The FBI knew that SNCC was filled with Billy Boys and that
Cleveland L. Sellers, Jr., was one of the "worst" of them. Born
in 1944, in Denmark, South Carolina, where his enterprising

---

*I was acting as a board member of SCLC. The ACLU did not decide that
the war was a "civil liberties issue" until June 2, 1970.

†The other passage I remember is "from the idea I recoil, to be maimed for
Standard Oil."

mother and father owned a local café and a taxicab company, Cleveland, Jr., distinguished himself as a Boy Scout. A good student and athlete, he spent two years at Howard University in Washington, D.C. Then he left college to become a SNCC field secretary.

Even though draft regulations forbade it, an FBI agent dropped into the office of Sellers's all-white draft board to review his file.* Soon Sellers was ordered to report for a physical examination. He asked for a routine delay. Request denied. When he failed to show up, he was declared "delinquent" and was ordered to report for induction on Friday, March 13, 1967.

That week we filed suit in the Atlanta and South Carolina federal courts. We asked that the induction *of all* blacks be halted until the draft system inducting them had been integrated.

All but one of South Carolina's 161 local board members were white. They were selected by the governor, and we alleged that the mathematical probability that only one of them would be black, if randomly selected, was less likely than "that in a game of contract bridge each of four players would be dealt a perfect hand from a well-shuffled deck of fifty-two playing cards."

In Atlanta, the government of the United States answered that the draft and draftees were beyond the jurisdiction of the court. The Selective Service System's judgments were final and, by law, The Law.

Federal Judge Lewis R. Morgan agreed. The next morning, Sellers was scheduled to appear at the Atlanta induction center. If he refused to appear or to step forward after he did appear, he would be indicted.

I telephoned Chief Judge Elbert Tuttle of the court of appeals and told him we were preparing an application for a stay. The rules required that requests for quick action be submitted to the

---

*FBI agents often review bank, credit card, tax, military, medical, and other confidential records. Usually the citizen doesn't know of the secret review, so he cannot challenge it or any aftermath.

fifth circuit's clerk, who is stationed in New Orleans, but I couldn't get there by morning. Judge Tuttle assured me that he would wait for me to bring the papers to his Atlanta office.

It takes time to draft and type papers. Later that evening I telephoned to apologize for the delay. Could he wait a little longer?

"I get paid to wait, Mr. Morgan. I get paid to decide the cases you get paid to prepare. We both get paid to work late hours. I'll be here when you're ready."

He was.

To be certain that no one lost rights by default, Judge Tuttle was willing to work around the clock and, if necessary, to over-rule the whole world, which he sometimes did. Despite the rules, he granted the stay we sought.

When a panel of the full court of appeals overruled Tuttle, Sellers reported to Atlanta's Armed Forces Examining and Entrance Station. Immediately, three Counterintelligence Corps agents appeared to question him. Sellers telephoned my office. I acted as dispatcher and within minutes my associate counsel, Laughlin McDonald, was at the induction center.

Sellers denounced his interrogation as "intimidation," refused to step forward, and attacked the "conspiracy on the part of the government to induct the whole organization." He was the sixteenth SNCC leader to be called within three months.

During those first seven days in May 1967, there was another, more widely known black also challenging his induction into the army—Muhammad Ali, the heavyweight champion of the world, whom SNCC leader Stokely Carmichael unabashedly described as "my hero."

The Justice Department came down hard on both Ali and Sellers. The House Armed Services Committee's number two man, F. Edward Hebert, a Louisiana Democrat, urged his companions to "forget the First Amendment." The chairman, South Carolina's L. Mendel Rivers, nodded and urged a speed-up in the prosecution of draft cases and in bringing charges against the "Carmichaels and the Kings."

On the night of May 10, Ali spoke to an overflow crowd of

1,600 at the University of Chicago's Field House. "It has been said that I have two alternatives—go to jail or the army. But there is another: justice! If justice prevails I will neither go to jail or to the army."

Justice delayed is "justice" in most antiwar cases. They are usually won after the war ends and the pressure of patriotism is off the courts. It took the Supreme Court two years to say no to our question about racially exclusive draft boards. On June 9, 1969, I lost the Sellers case. Chief Justice Warren did join justices Marshall and Douglas in dissent. Douglas wrote, "The system of using an all-white board may well result in black registrants being sent to Vietnam [to] do service for white registrants." He cited the reference in Sellers's draft board files to his SNCC employment, to a civil rights "trespassing" conviction, the FBI agent's visit to the board, and an item at which Sellers and I had laughed: the psychiatrist who interviewed him at his physical examination had noted, "He is considered to be a semiprofessional race agitator." Innocent of a crime Cleveland Sellers was. A "*semi*professional" he was not.

Before the Supreme Court was through with Sellers, the solicitor general disclosed that in 1965 Sellers's telephone conversations (like those of Muhammad Ali and others) had been illegally intercepted. So the federal conviction for refusing induction was remanded to the district court. Later it was set aside.

But back in 1968 Sellers had been drafted into jail in a state case. There had been a state police massacre at South Carolina State College in Orangeburg, witnessed, but not interfered with, by agents of the FBI. South Carolina needed someone to blame. Stokely was in Africa, Martin was dead, and Ali was out of town, so they locked up Cleveland Sellers for a year.

On the way with me into the federal courthouse in Louisville, Kentucky, Muhammad Ali ate four packages of cheese crackers. Going out of the courthouse, he ate three chocolate cupcakes and thrust the fourth one at me. I'd never eaten a chocolate cupcake on the way to lunch, but, silently marveling over his weight as opposed to mine, I ate up. In the elevator on the way to the *Courier Journal*'s cafeteria, Ali sparred at me, playfully missing by a fraction of an inch, dancing, moving, alarming others—and me.

It was Thursday, March 30, 1967. Ali was soon to be indicted or inducted, so he had few friends in high places. Instead, he had lawyers. Chauncey Eskridge from Chicago was one of them. He served with me on the Southern Christian Leadership Conference's board, but lawyers are by training (and self-interest) nonparochial. Chauncey also represented the Lost Found Nation of Islam and its champion, Muhammad Ali.

Eskridge and I were in Louisville for that antiwar SCLC board meeting. Eskridge had asked me to accompany him to a hearing where Hayden Covington, the lawyer whom Eskridge had retained for Ali, was seeking to enjoin Ali's induction.

A member of Jehovah's Witnesses, Covington had made legal history during World War II by carving a path through the law's wilderness for conscientious objector co-religionists. He charged them minimum fees (some said expenses plus twenty dollars). But before Ali relieved him of his duties, the lawyer's bill would reach a quarter of a million dollars.

Pushing a tray down the cafeteria line behind Ali was a relatively inexpensive religious experience. "Any pork in that chili?" he asked the elderly black woman behind the food counter.

"No, not a bit."

"You sure?"

"It's all beef, I'm sure."

"You really sure? I can't eat it. I'll blow up all over if I eat pork."

She smiled in tolerant exasperation. "No suh, not a bit."

He took the chili, stacked several slices of American cheese upon it, acquired a pile of crackers, two portions of cheesecake, and, in half-pint containers, a quart of milk. At the cash register he turned to me. "Lawyer, you got any money? Any change? I've only got hundred-dollar bills."

As we ate, an attractive blonde woman in her midthirties came to our table.

"Pardon me," she asked Ali timidly. "Would you mind if my little boy took your picture?"

Ali put down his silverware. He stared at her with his "mean" look. "Yes, ma'am. You know I don't like to have my picture taken, especially by white boys."

He glared at her son, perhaps thirteen years old, standing nearby. "Little boys' mothers ought to take pictures. Come on over here, boy." The boy moved shyly to Ali's side. The prizefighter slipped to the knees of his tailor-made suit, took the boy's fist and planted it firmly against his world championship jaw. "Okay," he said as he cocked his head. The mother hurried, the child beamed, the camera clicked, then clicked again while Ali laughed and I wondered about the madmen who sought to put him behind bars.

~~~~~~~~

Poor black boys in the South grew up knowing that athletic excellence was their best chance for freedom. Other obvious opportunities ranged from barbering, bootblacking, bootlegging, and burying to preaching. When young Cassius Clay won the 1960 Olympics, back home in Louisville, his father Cassius Marcellus Clay, Sr., celebrated his son's gold medal and golden opportunity by painting the steps of their home red, white, and blue. Local whites were proud too. Some even believed that young Cassius had an "old family" background. He was said to be the great-great-grandson of the "great" Great Compromiser, Kentucky pre–Civil War senator, Henry Clay. Whether kin to Clay or not—and Ali said not—he spent his boyhood in training so he could fight and win, not lose or draw. Then, as he put it, "I went to the Olympics in Rome, Italy, and won the gold medal for great America and came back to Kentucky and I couldn't go in a downtown restaurant. . . ."

Even losers were welcomed into Elijah Muhammad's mosque

in Miami* where, late in 1960, a Muslim minister explained the facts of faith to young Mr. Clay. He told him why blacks "call ourselves Culpepper, Mr. Tree, Mr. Bird, Mr. Clay, Mr. Washington. These were the names of our slave-masters."

After thirty minutes Cassius Clay wanted to enlist in the Muslim army. He believed the teachings of the Honorable Elijah Muhammad. He agreed with his top spokesman, the soon to be assassinated Malcolm X, who told Clay that a black person was "not to force himself on whites and not to beg whites to come to clean up the rats, but to clean up our own neighborhoods, respect our women, do something for ourselves, quit drinking, and obey the laws of the land and respect those in authority."

I had heard white folks say those kinds of things all my life, but when Ali, a cocky prizefighter, or Malcolm, an ex-convict, or Elijah Muhammad, an uneducated black religious leader, said them, the white folks hated it.

So Cassius Clay became Muhammad Ali. He said his new name contained "two attributes of Allah. Muhammad means 'one who is worthy of all praises and one most praiseworthy,' such as the Supreme Being," and that "Ali means 'man's most praiseworthy.'" After that he often proclaimed, "I am the greatest!" And even though few people knew what his name meant, none doubted his belief in himself.

Muhammad Ali totally rejected the life of the "sporting man." He neither smoked, drank intoxicants, nor broke dietary rules. He fasted; worshiped three times a week and prayed five times a day; refused to endorse products; rejected roles in two motion pictures, *Slave Mutiny* and *The Jack Johnson Story*; and turned down a $500,000 contract to record rock-and-roll love songs.

When Ali refused to apologize to the Illinois Boxing Commission for his views on the Vietnam War, they refused to allow him to box Ernie Terrell. That cost him two million dollars.

---

*The FBI has it differently. According to Agent Robert Nichols, Muhammad Ali first entered a mosque in Atlanta in October 1958. One thing is certain. Hoover's FBI had the Muslims under surveillance even during the 1950s.

Tens of millions had seen the quick deft brutality of Ali's flicking left hand, his slack-armed mockery when he danced away from those who ponderously stalked him, and they had heard him him poetically emasculate his opposition. Besides, conscientious objectors were supposed to be Christian, other-worldly, misty-eyed, humble, and ascetic. Muhammad Ali was Muslim and brash, and he was acclaimed as the number-one warrior in the whole wide cold-war world.

To determine Ali's sincerity as a conscientious objector, the Justice Department appointed a retired Louisville state court judge as hearing officer.* In August 1966, Ali explained to him:

> When I go in a ring, my intentions [sic] is not to be violent in the way of fighting to kill, or going to war, or hurting no one physically; it's not my faith, and we have a referee in the ring, and I'm known as a scientific fighter and as a fast, classy boxer, and we have three judges and we have an ambulance and we have doctors and we are not one nation against another or one race against another or one religion against another. It's just the art of boxing, and more people get killed in at least ten other sports than they do in boxing, but I'm not—I don't consider myself a violent men [sic] . . . [i]f he hit me low, he'll—points will be taken away and in a war you shoot, you kill, you fight and you kill babies and you kill old ladies and men and there's no such thing as laws and rules and regulations.

The Justice Department's own hearing officer, the retired judge, decided that Ali's beliefs were based upon religious teachings and that he was entitled to conscientious objector status. In a rare move, the Justice Department overruled its own hearing officer saying that Ali's

---

*The law provides for appeals by those denied conscientious objector status. After the appeal board forwarded Ali's file to the United States attorney who was destined to prosecute the case, he sent it to the FBI for investigation. After that the file went to the Conscientious Objector Section of the Justice Department, which, before making its recommendation, was required to have a hearing to prove or disprove the applicant's sincerity.

claimed objections to participation in war *insofar* as they are based upon the teachings of the Nation of Islam, rest on grounds which primarily are political and racial. These constitute objections to only certain types of war. . . .

Ali's draft case dragged on through the summer of 1967. From Mecca, California, to Nitro, West Virginia, the letters poured into Selective Service Board No. 47, Louisville, Kentucky. One read: "Dear Skunks: You yellow bellied scum—you are as bad as those picketting [*sic*] against the U.S. and those burning their draft cards."

Not since World War I, when the government under liberal Democrats prosecuted Eugene Victor Debs, had an antiwar defendant presented a bolder target. "How much has Clay paid you to keep him out of the Army?" one letter writer asked the members of Ali's draft board. "You had better resign before some soldier takes a shot at you! You are nothing but a 'yellow belly Negro lover.' And apparently a cheap Jew."

Another smelled "a rat—or maybe a payoff!! That Black Bastard Cassius Clay should be in Viet Nam right now with our fighting men instead of hiding behind some phony heathen religion. He is a disgrace to the sports world—his race—and his country—and so are you for letting him get away with such crap!!"

To those who went to war and to those who didn't, Muhammad Ali became a useful symbol. He was rich and famous, out of the army and out of jail, so to many white folks he was living proof of the lie that the rich and the famous—even athletes—went to war. To blacks, because he was black and different, his fate proved that black radicals opposed to the war were punitively drafted into jail.

With the world's heavyweight champion now the world's number-one Billy Boy, Chauncey Eskridge telephoned me. On June 20, 1967, following his conviction (in Houston, to which he had moved his residence), Ali received the maximum sentence—five years in the federal penitentiary and a $10,000 fine. He was stripped of his title and his passport. Now lawyer

Covington, who had been paid more than $50,000 in legal fees, wanted to strip Ali of an additional $200,000 to handle the appeal. Eskridge asked if I would take the case for $35,000.

I said yes, if Covington was discharged first, in writing. No, I would not accept the $35,000. The ACLU represents rich and poor without regard to their wealth. Even though, as an ACLU staff lawyer, I could take private fee-generating cases, this was clearly "an ACLU case." (Ali did not have to, but he contributed court costs and out-of-pocket expenses. But no fees.) At that Eskridge stammered and backed off, wondering aloud at the intelligence of a lawyer—let alone a friend—who'd turn down such a fee. He said he'd be back in touch with me. Before he accepted my counteroffer, he told me they wanted to retain me privately to avoid a relationship with another lawyer who was prominently identified with the ACLU. I assured Eskridge that that lawyer would have nothing to do with the case. If I entered it, my total obligation would run to Ali, not to the ACLU, or to anyone or anything else.

I wrote Ali's brief in bed. I was at my heaviest weight (280 pounds) and in Birmingham for Thanksgiving 1967, when I fell. I got up and tried to walk, but my right leg gave way. The next day Camille drove us to Atlanta.

Two days of physician-patient negotiations included an anesthesia conference and a near knockdown insistence that the nurse tell me what the pills were that she insisted I take. John Morris of ESCRU, other Episcopalians, and pro-civil rights preachers reassured me. Some even prayed for me. After the orthopedic surgeon revealed that he was on my side and was an ACLU member to boot, I agreed to the operation. When I came to, my leg was encased in a cast. Camille read me a telegram from Aryeh Neier. He said the ACLU executive committee wished me a speedy recovery—four-to-two with five abstentions.

Ali sent a maroon velvet robe and a gloves-cocked photograph inscribed, "Get well soon, Muhammad Ali." After I displayed that picture I was overwhelmed by the hospital service.

At home, surrounded by lawbooks, I wrote the brief and grew a beard. Charles, by now thirteen, had long hair. His heroes wore beards, so he had to be proud of mine.

"Charles," said I in mid-December, "what do you want for Christmas?"

He responded without hesitation, "Shave!"

So went the beard.

And the weight.

I used to gain weight during trials and political campaigns, but on-the-road food and lack of exercise were only part of that problem. I drank too much. What had begun as "fun" had become habit. Chain-smoked cigarettes and whiskey were prime companions during the long, often lonely, hours which went into every case.

But now I remembered Jack Nelson of the *Los Angeles Times* lying in his hospital bed after surviving an embolism. He had stared incredulously as Gene Roberts of *The New York Times* and I drank whiskey while, at his bedside, I wrote Nelson's will. In Los Angeles, Karl Fleming, of *Newsweek*, had his jaws broken and wired together after he was clubbed down in a Watts riot. He could barely shake his head when my friend Eason Monroe and I downed the gift bottle of Wild Turkey which had been left for Karl by actor Robert Vaughn. Jack had quit smoking. Karl had quit drinking. If they could quit, I could quit. And so I went into training for Ali's case.

❧❧❧❧❧❧

Muhammad Ali and I were leaving the federal courthouse in Houston. A television reporter addressed him. "You've been quoted as saying you have no white friends. Is that true?"

"Yes, that's true," Ali responded.

He turned to other questioners. She interrupted, returning to her theme with an air of disbelief. "You really don't have one white friend?"

"Yes, that's true," he responded. "Not one."

On camera beside him, I feigned detachment, knowing what

was coming, trying not to smile, and wondering how he'd handle it.

"Well," she said, nodding toward me. "Your lawyer's white, what about him?"

"Him?" he half turned, paused, then said, "He's not my friend; he's my lawyer."

We climbed into the taxicab to the hotel. Ali turned and with a straight face said, "They'll stop at nothing to drive us apart."

After I lost in the court of appeals in Houston, the case languished in the Supreme Court. Finally our luck changed when the solicitor general revealed that Ali had conversed on wiretapped telephones. On March 24, 1969, the Supreme Court sent the case back to Houston to the district court where Ali had been convicted. The judge who sentenced him was to determine whether that FBI surveillance had contributed to the conviction.

Ali had been denied conscientious objector status because of Muslim "teachings" which the Justice Department said were "primarily . . . political and racial." His 1-A classification had resulted from an FBI summary which contained reference to "an informed source known to be reliable," which was the way the FBI referred to wiretaps.

The Justice Department asked Houston Federal District Judge Joe Ingraham to decide without a hearing whether the records of the wiretaps (termed "logs") should be kept secret. Ingraham agreed. One log should be kept totally secret—even from Ali—the Justice Department argued, for it involved our "national security." Ingraham agreed. In secret, the Justice Department said that the secrecy of the other four logs was in the "national interest." Ingraham agreed. His order allowed me to read four logs if I agreed not to disclose them publicly.

I disagreed. Because Ingraham's conditions were unacceptable, I refused to accept the logs.

Ali and I arrived in Houston with no knowledge of what awaited us, and I set about trying to persuade the judge to overrule himself.

At first the hearing was open and the press was present. Gray-haired, slender, and courteous, Judge Ingraham listened carefully. Then he turned to Justice Department attorney John Martin: "Why should . . . the first conversation not be made public?"

> MR. MARTIN: That is a reason which I find difficult to articulate in public.
> THE COURT: You say you find it difficult to articulate in the [sic] public because it would violate national security?
> MR. MARTIN: We are here asking for this because we feel it might prejudice the national interest, might prejudice the right of third parties involved.
> THE COURT: I said "national security" and you say "national interest." There is a difference. National interests can be very far reaching.

Martin reemphasized the importance of secrecy. The decision to ask for a secret hearing had been made by the head of the Justice Department's Criminal Division and by Attorney General John N. Mitchell himself.

Over my objections the judge ordered the courtroom closed. He excluded the press and the public. Then I was told that one of the logs over which we were arguing was the first conclusive proof that the FBI had wiretapped my late friend, Martin King.

The first line began "Chauncey to MLK, said he is in Miami with Cassius. . . ." I turned to Chauncey Eskridge sitting beside me. "That you?" I asked.

"Yep," he whispered, "but we must have talked for three-quarters of an hour."

As the Justice Department's lawyers argued, I felt that slow-burning anger. I stared at the log. "C said that he is keeping up with MLK [,] that MLK is his brother, and with him 100% but can't take any chances, and that MLK should take care of himself, that MLK is known world wide and should watch out for them whities [sic]. . . ." I heard one of the lawyers say, "There could be damage done to Dr. King's reputation" if the people knew that the FBI was investigating him. During his lifetime, they had done their deadlevel best to destroy that reputation. Now the Justice Department's men clucked "that he was under suspicion of subversive activities, etcetera."

The Xerox copy contained only ten lines. The remainder of the log had been deleted by masking it off before they made the copy. The other three logs disclosed listening devices covering the telephones and residence of Elijah Muhammad. The Justice Department lawyers insisted that they be kept secret because "there are militant members of the Negro community who will attempt to use any excuse to stir up—"

Ingraham interrupted. He did not know that many of the most "militant" were on the payroll of the government. But he noted that, apparently, white men had killed Robert Kennedy and Martin King. Silent, the prizefighter sat beside Eskridge and me. He was the victim of a conspiracy, and the conspirators were men of the law who represented The Order.

In court, anger is a luxury. I smiled.

The judge nodded. Ali "called the right person or the wrong person, depending upon your viewpoint?"

> MR. MORGAN: That's right.
> THE COURT: If this wins him a reversal, then he called the right person.
> MR. MORGAN: That's correct, yes sir.

The only witnesses he allowed me to examine were those called by the Justice Department. I asked for relevant FBI Air-Tels, a type of letter communication. I sought the FBI's secret "June Files," its files on the Nation of Islam, and the documents upon which the Justice Department had based its conscientious objector advice letter and resumé.

To each request, Ingraham said no.

Special Agent Frederick A. Brownell testified that he had sent the details of Ali's conversation with Elijah Muhammad in Phoenix, Arizona, to FBI offices in Chicago, Louisville, Miami,

New York, Washington, and Boston. Brownell said he wanted them to know Ali's "travel destinations." We wanted to know what they had known about Ali's travel plans—and the journey of Martin King to Memphis, his final destination.

Ingraham said no.

But he did let Special Agent Pickett testify. If black had been white, C. Barry Pickett might have been the prizefighter and Muhammad Ali might have been the college student. They were about the same age, but in 1961, while Ali was pursuing the championship, Pickett was working his way through college as an eavesdropper for the all-white FBI. He monitored conversations which took place inside the Phoenix residence of Elijah Muhammad. The religious leader's telephones were tapped. Miniature transmitters were secreted inside the home.

Pickett had been twenty then. Now he was twenty-eight. He and his FBI co-worker, Richard A. Feight, were dressed conservatively like other young men who sold law or life insurance. But they had begun their careers wearing earphones and, during eight-hour shifts, they flicked a switch on the Magnavox recorder. As the tape rolled, they hand-wrote notes. At the end of their shifts they typed entries from their notes onto the bureau's printed log forms, designated FD 297 (1-28-57). Their "instructions" were to note "anything that seemed important to security, things of that nature, to take them down." They were to ignore "trivial" and "everyday conversations." But even the few logs we were provided with contained remarks about Ali's weight, his family's health, the well-being of his automobile, his brother and women, and the Muslims' closing salutation.

Then they destroyed their notes, retained the tapes, took the typed logs to the agents' room, and deposited them in Frederick Brownell's workbox.

Robert W. Nichols, an FBI agent stationed in Atlanta, had been the overseer of Martin King's telephone. On the witness stand he was as relaxed and cordial as an old friend. I led him from the date of the log entry, September 4, 1964, to April 4, 1968, the date of the King assassination. Then, according to my memory and *New York Times* reporter Martin Waldron's notes, I asked if the tap "continued until his death on April 4, 1968," and he answered, "It was my understanding that it went on." The court reporter's transcript had a slightly different answer: "It was my understanding it went on *after that.*"

It didn't really matter whether my recollection or the court reporter's transcript was correct. Either way Hoover probably had a tape recording of the sharp crack of the rifle shot which killed his adversary, Martin King. Hoover probably heard his fall to the stoop in front of that Lorraine Motel room and the cries of terror and anguish which came "after that."

On the King log, under "Employee's Name," there appeared "AT1379−S*(1)." Nichols said this was just a number designation for that particular surveillance. There was no file corresponding to that number. Later he said, "I believe there is a file."

The Justice Department's attorney had said earlier that AT1379−S*(1) "just refers to the device." Agent Nichols said that was wrong, so I asked Agent Brownell, with two decades of FBI experience, to shed light on the number.

> A. "A" I believe stands for Atlanta. This [1379] is the number of the source, and "S" stands for security. The asterisk will stand for—it could stand for anonymous or electronic, but I don't know. I can't remember.
> Q. Do you know what the (1) is?
> A. I don't have any idea.

Repeatedly I insisted that the Justice Department produce "Mister AT1379−S*(1)." The judge said no. He wouldn't even allow an answer to the question, "[W]ho authorized . . . this electronic eavesdropping?"

> MR. MARTIN: Objection. . . .
> MR. MORGAN: I want to know about this particular conversation, who authorized the eavesdropping. . . .
> MR. MARTIN: Object, Your Honor. There is no express authorization.
> THE COURT: Objection sustained.

At the close of the hearing the judge did tell the Justice Department lawyers they should find out what the number really meant and report back. They satisfied him by saying:

> After the conclusion of the hearing on Friday, June 6, 1969, the attorneys for the government were advised by the Atlanta office of the FBI that the number AT1379–S* on Government Exhibit 105 was the number assigned to the telephone surveillance of Dr. King and that this number did not refer to any particular FBI employee. We have so advised defense counsel.

Hoover, out of court, had no objection to publicizing his version of who authorized the King tapes. Newspaper headlines tell the story. The *Atlanta Constitution*: WIRETAP ON KING OKAYED, RFK APPROVED, FBI EXPLAINS; *The New York Times*: FBI SAYS KENNEDY APPROVED WIRETAP ON DR. KING'S PHONE; The *New York Post*: 2 DENY RFK INSTIGATED THE KING TAPS; and the *Washington Evening Star*: CONTROVERSY WIDENS OVER KING WIRETAP.

Hoover had sent word to Robert Kennedy that a Communist was serving on King's SCLC board. Fearing that the information could be used to defeat the Civil Rights Bill, the Kennedys had struck a deal with the man who bedeviled them. Later many liberals could not understand why an idealist like Martin King supported Robert Kennedy for President. But they did not know that in the late summer of 1963 his brother, the President, had taken Martin King into the White House rose garden and into his confidence. He told him he would be wiretapped. Martin King knew that he and the Kennedy brothers, like gamefish in the sea, shared the game fisherman as an enemy.

In Muhammad Ali's case the FBI even lied to its own attorneys. The four "logs" they had presented to the court were extracts from originals, produced by masking off portions of them and then Xeroxing them. I had insisted that the Justice Department's attorneys produce the originals. After that, they discovered they had been lied to by the nation's top lawmen. A copy of the log entry as produced after the hearing follows.

Time	Initial	IC OG	Activity Recorded
6:55PM	✓	IC	Chauncey to MLK, said he is in Miami with Cassius, MMLK spoke to Cassius, they exchanged greetings, MLK wished him well on his recent marriage, C invited MLK to be his guest at his next championship fight, MLK said he would like to attend. C said that he is keeping up with MLK that MLK is his brother, and with him 100% but can't take any chances, and that MLK should take care of himself, that MLK is known world wide and should watch out for them whities, said that people in Nigeria Egypt and Ghani asked about MLK,

Log .... Page	Employee's Name	Date Stamp
Day .... Date		
9-4-64 page 1	AT1379-S* (1)	

On the copy originally provided to the court, the FBI had masked off the handwritten words "sum up in memo"; the agent's handwritten name, Nichols, R. W.; and the comma which followed the initials MLK. That comma indicated that the log entry had been cut off in midsentence. Chauncey Eskridge's recollection had been correct. The FBI had provided us and the federal court with ten lines of a forty-five-minute conversation. But Agent Nichols said that even though he had written "sum up in memo" there was no "memo," and Judge Ingraham was glad to be rid of us. He refused to continue the factual inquiry. I heard Ali harshly whisper his hurt and fury. "This is America!" Judge Ingraham resentenced him to the penitentiary for a maximum of five years and fined him $10,000. Before doing so he asked Ali if he had a comment.

"No, sir," Ali replied. "Except I am sticking to my religious beliefs. I know this is a country that preaches religious freedom."

Resurrected by the Houston hearings, the case took on new life. Muhammad Ali was seen less as a draft dodger, more as an underdog. As sentiment against the war escalated, fate and public opinion inevitably began its work upon the legal system. I lost the case again in the court of appeals, but, finally, in 1971, when Chauncey Eskridge argued it in the Supreme Court, we won a unanimous reversal.

∾∾∾∾∾∾

In Atlanta, the telephone crackled with static. The familiar voice was strained as though broadcasting on shortwave.

"Counsellor, this is Muhammad! I'm on my way to the hotel."

The conversation stopped abruptly as the transmission cut out.

Muhammad Ali owned a briefcase telephone for which he told me, perhaps jestingly, he had paid "fifty dollars down and fifty dollars a month."

There was no need to wiretap that easily overheard wonder of Western civilization. I had mentioned that I wanted Charles to meet him when he was in Atlanta. Ali had remembered.

"Bring your boy down. I should be there in thirty minutes."

Camille corraled Charles and his friends, Alfred Cofield, Stevie Crawford, and "Skip" Cromer, at a city school track meet. There were light on their feet and excellent athletes." Ali met them in the parking garage beneath Paschal's Motor Hotel.

"Are you as fast as they say you are?" asked Stevie, the soon-to-be defensive back for Georgia Tech.

"Touch my chest," taunted Ali. Steve moved forward.

"All of you," said Ali to the four of them.

The immaculately attired world's heavyweight champion took the sweatsuited teen-agers on, collectively. Flat-footed, then weaving, bobbing, dancing, and skipping, Ali was too much for them. They landed not one blow.

~~~~~~~~

Most who write and broadcast about sports cotton to the crowd and its moments of madness. *New York Times* columnist Robert Lipsyte was an exception. On October 28, 1967, he wrote "no matter who a cabal of television executives, Texas showmen, fools and slyfingers offer us, Muhammad Ali is the heavyweight champion of the world." But it is sportscasters, more than sportswriters, who strive for popularity. They are stars who fear ratings and the sponsors who rely upon them. Perhaps that is why they root for overdogs and rarely carry courage from the playing field into the press box. One did so. Only Howard Cosell persisted in calling "Ali" champion, when Cosell's fellows believed him to be an artful draft dodger and seemed spitefully pleased to call him "Cassius Clay," as they counted him down and out. I thought of Cosell's solitary courage later when the crowds of the world chanted "Ali! Ali!" and Gerald R. Ford, President, invited The Champion to the White House.

12

Captain John J. McCarthy of Special Forces had been tried in secret and sentenced to life for the murder of a "peasant." At Fort Leavenworth he and Howard Levy were subjected to unusual punishment: The army made them cellmates. I could understand the kind of army reasoning which put them together, thinking back to the time I had run away from military school and they had brought me back just to kick me out.

I could also understand the logic in Levy's request that I represent McCarthy. I had been denied access to Levy's low-classified G-2 dossier which held no "national security" secrets. Access to the highly secret transcript in McCarthy's case would undercut any "security risk" argument which the army might make to justify its denial to me of Levy's dossier. If the army refused me "Top Secret" clearance, neither Levy nor McCarthy would be worse off than they already were, and McCarthy would be able to assign that refusal as a deprivation of his right to select counsel of his own choosing.

The prison conference room in which McCarthy and I met was so small that it turned whispers into shouts. We sized each other up. He had pale blue eyes. He was wiry, neat even in fatigues, and of medium height. He talked freely, but he knew more about the charge than the transcript disclosed. If he had killed that "peasant"—and he didn't believe that he had—he had done so accidentally, and somewhere that peasant had a service record which would show him to be every bit as skilled and "special" as McCarthy.

~~~~~~~~

In January 1960, on his seventeenth birthday, John McCarthy had enlisted in the army. After he qualified as a paratrooper and finished Special Forces training, he was stationed in Germany. Extraordinarily competent, his expertise included jumping from airplanes at 30,000 feet and opening his parachute 500 feet above ground or water, and, if water, swimming under it.

In October 1964, he completed officer training and was assigned to a Special Forces organization in Okinawa. Next came Vietnam. He returned to Okinawa and from there had a number of short-term assignments. On Taiwan he served on a joint United States—Republic of China team. Later he worked with a group of military men from the Republic of the Philippines. In June 1967, when the army sent Levy to prison, it sent McCarthy to Vietnam as an operations officer.

In the early-morning hours after Thankgiving night— November 24, 1967—McCarthy, who always operated under civilian cover, and a Special Forces sergeant, also dressed as a civilian, went to a "safe house" in Vietnam where "Jimmie," a male Oriental with whom they worked, was quartered.

McCarthy told the sergeant, "Go outside and bring Jimmie."

According to the unclassified portions of the trial transcript, Jimmie was a Cambodian who belonged to the highly secret Khmer Serai (Free Cambodia). In the wee hours of that November morning, McCarthy, Jimmie, and the sergeant left Saigon on the road to Hoa Ndock Tao in a four-door civilian Datsun. The sergeant drove. Jimmie had been caught possessing documents which jeopardized the security of McCarthy's secret unit. Jimmie sat front seat center. At his right McCarthy held a .38-caliber Smith and Wesson revolver loosely in his left hand behind the front seat.

As they amiably chatted there was a loud "explosion." The windshield frosted into honeycombed cracks. Jimmie slumped, a hole through his head, blood pouring from his face, dead.

They hid the corpse under a tarpaulin in a six-foot ditch and returned to the detachment compound. McCarthy went to bed. The sergeant reported the incident. The next morning the detachment commander, a non-Special Forces "intelligence officer," placed McCarthy under arrest.

After sixty days' confinement at Long Binh jail, known affectionately as LBJ, McCarthy was secretly tried.

His counsel, Captain Stewart P. Davis, stipulated that "Jimmie," known by several other names, including Inchin Hai Lam, was dead. He also agreed that McCarthy was one of the three men in the automobile; that his weapon discharged inside that automobile; that previous to that "Jimmie" was alive, and afterward he was dead. The question for the court-martial was How had Jimmie been killed? Murder? Ambush? Shrapnel? A stray shot? A ricochet from the accidental discharge of McCarthy's .38? Davis said, "[The prosecution] cannot connect Captain McCarthy's weapon and the wound."

Davis looks like the movie-star version of a Special Forces man—solidly built, well tanned, his quiet approach to the law and life belying an ability to withstand pressure. After becoming a paratrooper, he graduated from Washington and Lee's law school and served in the Judge Advocate Generals Corps.

Davis and McCarthy made an excellent defense team. The lawyer liked his client, who insisted he had wanted Jimmie questioned, not killed.

Their problem was the pathologist. He had observed no powder burns on the skin on Jimmie's neck near the wound, and in his expert opinion any weapon larger than .25 caliber would have produced both a star-shaped wound and a burn visible to the naked eye. Since he found gunpowder within the wound he concluded that the weapon had been held against Jimmie's body. The .38 would have made a larger hole, and a more pronounced gunpowder "tattoo." The pathologist said a weapon of .25 caliber or less had been held against Jimmie's neck. That ruled out an accidental or stray shot, shrapnel or a ricochet. It also ruled out the possibility that a bullet had been fired from outside the Datsun. But the windows on the left side of the automobile had been down, and a motorcyclist had pulled away from the "safe house" and headed up the highway immediately before them. Inside the Datsun, McCarthy, his .38 cocked in anticipation of hostile fire, had speculated on the mission of that motorcyclist. The sergeant testified that his elbow had been resting on the window frame when the "explosion" occurred. It was then that McCarthy's weapon had fired. Had McCarthy's weapon caused that explosion or had he fired it as a reflex response to another shot?

By saying that the wound could not have been caused by the .38 at close range, the pathologist ruled out answers to these and other questions. Under normal circumstances his testimony would have meant McCarthy could not have committed the crime. But Special Forces men were trained to defy normal circumstances. They were known for their ability to obtain and use small, secret .25-caliber single-shot devices. So the jury believed that McCarthy had killed Jimmie with a secret .25-caliber weapon, and under that theory, the killing could not have been accidental.

They sentenced him to life at hard labor and recommended clemency. That was normal enough. What was unheard of was their refusal to order a forfeiture of his pay and allowances and his dismissal from the service.

I entered the case on June 10, 1968. It took the Army 229 days to prove me "nationally secure." After my clearance on February 25, 1969, I certified in writing that I had read the statutes which provide for "the willful or negligent divulging of classified information to unauthorized persons" and a "penalty of death or imprisonment for any term of years or for life." In a similar situation, in Muhammad Ali's case, I had refused to accept wiretap logs covered by a secrecy order. That also was an intuitive judgment and, in law as in life, "luck."

In Falls Church, Virginia, I was provided a "secure" secretary for dictation, typing, and clerical work. I couldn't work on certain aspects of the case in Atlanta, for the transcript and other documents couldn't leave the Falls Church office building. Later (on February 8, 1970) in an article in the *Washington Post* entitled TERMINATED AGENT MAY HAUNT U.S., Murray Marder would write: "[W]hile comparatively obscure, the McCarthy case carries a larger potential for international complications than the celebrated Green Berets case." McCarthy was locked up in the government's prison, but if Marder was right, the secrets McCarthy knew made the government his prisoner. In court papers I urged that McCarthy be freed, for he had been deprived of his unqualified constitutional rights to an open and public trial.

Soon after the August 6, 1969, headline in the *Atlanta Journal*—BERET COLONEL, 7 OTHERS CHARGED IN VIET MURDER—I telephoned the disciplinary barracks. "John, if you haven't told me the truth, if you lied at the trial, if you've said anything up to now that wasn't true, it is time to recant."

I want to know every fact which a client reasonably thinks may have a bearing upon his case. From the beginning McCarthy maintained his innocence, and even if his story seemed irrational to some, he stuck by it—tenaciously. I would cross-examine and attempt to trip him up, and ask him every question I could think of. He remained unshaken and unshakable.

I explained that Special Forces Colonel Robert B. Rheault and the seven other men charged with murder in Vietnam had as much chance of coming to trial as did the CIA or Richard M. Nixon. The desire to cover up, to keep secrets—not from the Communists but from Americans—would guarantee the release of the Special Forces men. If McCarthy had lied at trial and to me, but now came out with the truth, we could tie his case to Rheault's, and the odds would be a hundred to one in favor of his release.

"I'll be goddamned!" came the response. "If my own lawyer

won't believe me. I told the truth! I don't give a damn if I rot in here, I didn't kill that man!"

When a convict serving a life sentence angers at the sight of a master key to his cell, it's time that he be believed.

On September 29, 1969, the army dismissed the charges against Rheault and company and blamed the cover-up on the CIA's refusal to allow its agents to testify at any trial. Two days later, in *The New York Times*, the lawyer for a Green Beret, Henry B. Rothblatt, said that Nixon made that decision.

In Washington, Stewart Davis conferred with Colonel Pierre A. Fink, chief of the Wound Ballistics Pathology Branch of the Armed Forces Institute of Pathology, and widely known as the physician who performed the John F. Kennedy autopsy. Fink told Davis that he was familiar with the McCarthy file and testimony, but he revealed nothing helpful. Neither did the army attorney who directed Davis to the right file, which, however, he could not let Davis see. But he placed the file on the nearby table and left Davis in the room, saying, "There's a Xerox machine down the hall and a sergeant in the next office."

Alone, Davis opened the folder. On top there was a memorandum from the prosecution's pathologist-witness to "Chief, Forensic Pathology Division, Armed Forces Institute of Pathology." "Because of the small size of the wound and the absence of grossly visible powder tattooing I originally testified . . . that the murder weapon was probably a .22 or .25 caliber weapon."

The pathologist went on to write that he had been "mistaken about the weapon."

Based upon the trial transcript, McCarthy's testimony that he had a .38-caliber pistol, and the driver's description of the sound as deafening, that his ears were ringing, and that he experienced "a temporary loss of hearing," the pathologist had altered his scientific judgment. He wrote, "In conclusion I now think the victim was killed by a single shot from Captain McCarthy's revolver fired several inches away from the back of the neck."

So the accidental firing of the .38 could have killed Jimmie.

Finally, in the secret world of secret cases, we had begun to win.

The report of the pathologist also mentioned correspondence with "the Federal Bureau of Investigation regarding a bullet fragment removed from the nasal pharynx from the deceased." This metal was "enclosed in a plastic envelope attached to the FBI laboratory report."

When we obtained that report it read, "A tiny particle of quartz was stuck to the surface of the fragment." It also said, "No glass was found." Quartz comes from glass and glass can come from shattered windshields, so we wanted to examine the metal fragment. But the FBI and the army had managed to lose it in the *registered* mail.

In a Virginia office building, in a hearing open to the public, I argued for the right of public trial. Then the three officers on the Court of Military Review, accompanied by their security advisor, adjourned to a conference room in the bowels of the Pentagon. Outside, soldiers stood guard while I argued from the secret portion of the record.

On October 29, 1970, we won. Based upon the pathologist's altered testimony, the court unanimously ordered the conviction set aside. One judge went further. To him, McCarthy's "record in intelligence and intelligence-related operations, as well as the military skills associated therewith which he has developed," made it in defiance of "logic" that he would have murdered "the victim in the manner developed by the Government at trial and urged upon us during appellate argument." Terming McCarthy a "proven officer, thoroughly trained in intelligence operations, well-disciplined and sensitive to the ramifications of all his actions, not only with regard to the United States but to other political entities whose interests might be affected," that judge said the court should have forbidden a retrial.

But that decision rested with Major General W. B. Latta of the army's Strategic Communications Command, under whom McCarthy was then serving.

On January 6, 1971, I met the general at Fort Huachuca, Arizona. He concurred in his staff judge advocate's recommendation that a new trial was "not warranted." The charge was dismissed.

Months after John McCarthy honorably left the service, I received an urgent telephone call. He had applied for a job. He told me of the county personnel officer who had received an FBI report on his status.

"I'm sitting in this man's office and the report at which he's looking says I should be in Leavenworth locked in prison. Would you tell him I'm not an escapee or a convicted felon?"

I did so, as I marveled at the efficiency and concern of a government which imprisoned together one man who termed its heroes killers, and a hero whom the government wrongly termed a killer, then ignored its own pathologist's recantation, lost a metal bullet fragment transmitted in its registered mail, and failed to put into its computer the record of the one Green Beret it had certified innocent.

~~~~~~~~~

In the early 1960s other fine Atlanta restaurants refused to serve blacks, but Herrens served them. In the ensuing years, lunch at Herrens became a habit for those who tried to help make up for the white boycott losses it had suffered. There, in midsummer of 1971, reporter Jim Wooten of *The New York Times* took a long sip of his martini and asked me what I thought about Lieutenant Colonel Anthony B. Herbert.

Now stationed at nearby Fort McPherson, Georgia, Herbert had charged that his commanding officers in Vietnam, Colonel J. Ross Franklin and General John W. Barnes, had covered up his reports of war crimes.

Fifteen years earlier, Herbert had been acclaimed the most-decorated enlisted man to emerge from the Korean War. In Vietnam he had built an outstanding record as an on-the-ground combat leader. But in April 1969 (after he reported war crimes, Herbert said), Barnes relieved him as battalion commander. That meant the end of Herbert's military career.

Responsibility for the My Lai massacre had been firmly fixed at the level of Lieutenant Calley. The question of higher-up responsibility fell to the commission headed by General William Peers. Colonel Franklin had served on the Peers Commission. Peers himself had been General Barnes's immediate superior, and, in the chain of command, immediately above Peers there were only generals Abrams and Westmoreland and, the Commander in Chief, Richard M. Nixon.

Right or wrong, Herbert was too high up for comfort and, unlike Calley, he was a hero, not a war criminal. Despite this, as I told Wooten, I'd had enough of war crimes trials. I had nothing personal against those who'd fought in Vietnam, but to me the heroes were those early lonely citizens who had stood against the war. I hoped no other heroes would emerge from that war—and that hope included Herbert.

But that was not the end of it. A few weeks later, sent to me via Washington, New York, and an Army lawyer-major, Tony Herbert showed up in my office. He stood six feet tall, and his muscled frame and crewcut hair labeled him spit-and-polish military. He knew the rules, and abided by them.

Born in Herminie, Pennsylvania, a coal-mining town, he was my age. When I was hitching rides and running away from military school, Tony Herbert was running away from home and trying to join the Marines. He successfully enlisted in the army at seventeen. A poor white boy, he had done well with the options open to him. In his book, *Soldier,* Herbert describes his almost reverential respect for the military which provided him with a college and a postgraduate education and a way out of and up from the lives of coal miners and truckdrivers. But now he too was a victim of that damned war.

He had submitted to lengthy questioning in secret proceedings, but the army refused to give him a copy of his own testimony. He was under constant surveillance. Now they wanted him to submit to a polygraph (lie detector) test. As I listened, I knew that the army was preparing to accuse its accuser. I agreed to take his case.

At Herbert's own insistence, I told Captain Richard L.

Heintz, army counsel, to proceed with Benjamin F. Malinowski, a polygraph examiner at Lincoln M. Zonn, Inc., in Atlanta. Malinowski was now a civilian, but he had taught the army's polygraph experts. He had written their service manuals and had supervised production of their training films. The lie-detector test was the army's idea, not Herbert's. Malinowski had been the army's expert, and if Herbert "passed," the army could hardly reject Malinowski's findings.

Herbert entered Malinkowski's chambers and was wired up. Heintz and I sat waiting, less relaxed than expectant fathers in the reception room of a maternity ward.

"Did you on or about February 14, 1969, advise Colonel Franklin of the killing of Vietnamese detainees?" Malinowski asked.

"Yes," Herbert responded.

"On or about April 4, 1969, did you personally request General Barnes to conduct an investigation?"

"Yes."

Malinowski emerged smiling. He had studied the graphs and decided that "Herbert was truthful when he answered the relevant questions with a 'Yes.' "

∞∞∞∞∞∞

During the cold-war years the nation manufactured a military machine. All by itself, the military machine put together a public relations machine. As secrecy came to mean "national security," truth became, in the words of Jeb Stuart Magruder, "a public relations problem." As the "credibility gap" grew, so did the public relations bridge. Finally, propaganda was so open that on January 30, 1967, even Associated Press reported that Vietnam veterans had been "tactically" stationed throughout the United States to speak to community groups "to convince the American people that the Vietnam War [was] necessary." By then the government was spending $425 million a year on "public information" programs—more than twice the combined newsgathering costs of ABC, CBS, and NBC television, the ten largest American daily newspapers, United Press, and AP itself.

Now Tony Herbert—whom the government once used to sell savings bonds—had become a public relations problem. Logistically the army had him beaten. It could selectively classify or declassify facts and information and, in that way, exercise basic control over public opinion. Under a cover of secrecy its employees could lie without fear. Even without lies, those secrets were "informed sources" for friendly newspeople. I was convinced that Tony Herbert's only chance was to take his case to the people.

Twice I had been a guest on ABC television's "Dick Cavett Show." Cavett is incisive and intelligent. Besides that, I like him. Immediately after an article on Herbert by Jim Wooten appeared in the September 5, 1971, *New York Times Magazine*, Wooten appeared on the "Dick Cavett Show" to answer the questions of guest host Howard Cosell. Within a few days a Cavett staffer called to ask if Herbert would appear. I answered yes. That answer, Jim Wooten, Dick Cavett, and Tony Herbert's candor saved Tony Herbert.

Cavett introduced Herbert to the nation. The crewcut soldier's conservative narrow-labeled suit and narrow tie were out-of-style reminders of a time when the people expected soldiers to tell them the truth. Herbert was articulate, plainspoken, and relaxed.

By midnight, across the nation, telephones were ringing as average citizens woke up their families and friends. Before that program ended, the audience had grown into the largest in Cavett's history.

World War II veterans saw in Herbert the man they wished their draft-age sons would serve under. Inside the army, Herbert was respected, widely known, and feared by bureaucrats. His appeal to opponents of the war was magnetic. He respected conscientious objectors, emphasized the rules, confirmed the antiwar view of the facts, and was waging a personal war against "higher-ups."

By the time that program ended and local stations played the national anthem, millions of Americans had adopted Herbert as their personal hero. Already thousands of them were writing letters to the President and to Congress, demanding fair treatment for him.

When Cavett invited Barnes and Franklin to confront Herbert on the air, the army said no. Instead, it resorted to petty harassments designed to keep Herbert on post. That successfully prevented his second appearance on Cavett's show. Some in ABC's bureaucracy wanted to rerun "An Evening With Fred Astaire."

Cavett was outraged. First he had me on the program to explain Herbert's absence. Then he reran Herbert's first appearance.

The public response prompted President Nixon to order the army to "reevaluate" Herbert's record. That meant Herbert could remain in the service. There would be no court-martial. His record and honor were intact.*

Despite Tony Herbert's war against those who ran the army, he remained committed to the service. During the summer of 1971, while he was under investigation, Herbert served as a rerecruitment officer, signing up soldiers who had decided not to reenlist. For this he won the All-Army Trophy. He was the best they had. But his belief in democracy set him apart from the army which he loved. I understood his kind of patriotism.

It was the genuineness of Herbert's belief in democracy which gave meaning to his military career. I walked down Atlanta's Forsyth Street with him one day in 1971. Herbert didn't even

---

*When Herbert and Wooten's story of Herbert's life, *Soldier*, was published, few reporters were willing to accept the army's version of the facts because they were refused access to all "classified" documents. The book made it to the best-seller list. CBS's Mike Wallace, armed with army-provided documents and witnesses, grilled Herbert on film, edited the interview, and produced an inconclusive but generally unfavorable report on "60 Minutes."

Franklin filed a libel suit against Herbert, Wooten, and the publishers. After cross-examination during his deposition, Franklin dismissed his lawsuit "with prejudice." Herbert's libel suit against Wallace, CBS, and others is being handled by New York lawyers and, interrupted by appeals (including one to the Supreme Court), is proceeding to trial, slowly.

break stride when we saw a newspaper headline which told of our favorite of the opponents in the India-Pakistan War. "Dammit!" I exclaimed. "Why is it we're never on the side of the democracy!"

"Oh, you're for India?" he laughed. "Don't worry about India. We trained the Pakistani Army, and no army we trained can win a war."

~~~~~~~~

We all paid the high price of pragmatism; of hard decisions easily made; of fear of democracy. Antidemocratic militarism had captured our minds. It had spread slowly, undramatically. Adolf Hitler, defeated and dead, had provided us the means to militarize the democracy. From Joseph Stalin had come the excuse.

I had relearned that which, down deep, I always knew. It will be by small failures that democracy will die. If it dies.

As 1971 drew to a close, I knew that our nation would not go with a bang or a whimper. A free people will never fall under a conqueror's heel. But they may march away to a cadence count.

PART
TWO

13

In 1968 Richard Nixon began his campaign with more than 55 percent of the votes. He had lost to John Kennedy in 1960. He had lost the California governor's race in 1962. On his own he had not received majority approval since his 1950 Senate race. Now he ran a restricted campaign and did his best to avoid the people. He eked into power with less than 44 percent of the votes, so he knew that a majority of the people distrusted him and he knew he had better distrust them, too. Nixon was the classic natural-born loser who, while winning, devised a game plan which would give his friends, their values, and even football a bad name.

Elected by a narrow margin from a flimsy base, Nixon faced an unpopular war, assassinations, terrorism, street crime, and changing personal values. His "allies" were a Democratic, moderately liberal, moderately hostile bureaucracy; Congress; the Supreme Court; and the press.

The Domestic Council under John Ehrlichman kept cabinet secretaries from being absorbed into their baronies. The "Mr. Secretaries" could tell the press and the Congress little, for only

John Ehrlichman and H. R. Haldeman knew the real answers, and they answered only to Nixon.

The State Department bureaucracy handled schedules, housing, and ceremonies while Henry Kissinger's National Security Council imposed The Order (i.e., "stability" and "stable governments") upon the world.

Kissinger, Haldeman, and Ehrlichman made an improbable trio, but pipe-smoking John Mitchell was the ultimate contradiction. His political personality was comparable to that of an avocado; his seemingly flighty wife upstaged him even on the telephone. But he was the ultimate enforcer, for while ultimate governmental power is the power to kill people, next best is the power to put people behind bars.

Mitchell's troops included the hardline, domestic, anti-Communists: Richard G. Kleindienst, Robert C. Mardian, and William Rehnquist. Their last (and first) prominence had been achieved during Goldwater's 1964 Marlboro Man campaign. Their job under Mitchell was to protect The Order. To do that they had to change the Constitution and cajole or corral or otherwise quiet those who disagreed.

Later many people viewed Nixon as an aberration, slightly mad and paranoid, an American version of Bavaria's nineteenth-century King Ludwig II (who retired into one of his feverishly constructed castles prior to jointly drowning with his psychiatrist). But paranoia is an irrational fear, and the dangers Nixon faced were clear and ever-present.

By the time he took office, the intelligence-industrial complex was our dominant political and economic force. Usually, liberal (i.e., "internationalist") corporate lawyers were selected as secretaries of state. They knew that "we" could retain "our vital national interests abroad" only in a world of "stability." To make the world safe for "freedom" (their way of saying "investments," not democracy) and to contain The Enemy, they supported foreign governments built upon a homegrown Black Belt model. For their "containment policy" millions of American and American-controlled troops manned a thousand outposts around the world. A constellation of a thousand satellites looked down from the sky, as hundreds of ships and underwater devices scanned the sea.

The Central Intelligence Agency was run by moderately liberal world-view Democrats—talented, temperate men educated at fine Eastern schools. They favored The Establishment by which they had been favored. And like those for whom they really worked, they saw Nixon as a grubby politician.

Nixon understood this. As Vice President he had worked with them. Their Ivy League style aside, he knew that the CIA was a worldwide army of gentlemen company cops, a sophisticated Pinkerton-like police force which dealt contemptuously with grubby politicians in order to break strikes in Italy, backs in Asia, and national economies in Latin America. The "Company" could finance a secret war, conduct a coup, or simply bribe or frame or kill an enemy to protect the "national security" and "our national interests."

Grubby Nixon was. A fool he was not; and only a fool could fail to see the "servant's" opportunity to acquire for himself, his family, and his friends the seemingly permanent power of the very, very rich.

To achieve that Nixon needed order. To achieve order, Richard Nixon became the twentieth century's ultimate assassin. He killed hope. He termed the 1960s a time when rhetoric "outdistanced gains" and when "promises were unkept." He sought to dismantle poverty programs and to effect the Southern Strategy, to put down the domestic "revolution of rising expectations."

Abroad, his policy was the same. Friendly right-wing dictators could contain revolution. But where Intelligence kept the people (and their wages) down, consumer markets could not develop. Détente would open China, Cuba, and Russia.

The liberals were pushovers. They were immobilized by "two-sides-to-everything" rationality. (Too few educated people do understand that to some things there are twenty-two sides; to others none.) Worse than that, the character of liberalism had been surrendered to pragmatism, and many liberals were afraid to confront themselves, let alone the nation.

As with most truly dangerous conspiracies, there was an acceptable naturalness to the one which Nixon led. Thousands of people sensed their duties and performed them. But the clandestine system presented inherent problems. Standing armies and secret police produce their own leaders and skilled assassins. After exciting careers, killing to preserve "stability" in the poor nations of the world, CIA Special Forces and other extra-special men returned to humdrum civilian lives. There they sold life insurance and taught school, reminisced about their past assignments, voted, and daydreamed about tomorrow's call.

A paranoid President?

There is no paranoia. There is no fiction.

Nixon's war against basic law was total and systematic. The courts were his first priority. He replaced four of the nine Supreme Court justices, and Kleindienst-cleared men were named to a majority of the lower federal courts. Simultaneously, Nixon moved against the press. Despite the First Amendment, reporters' sources were sought. Agnew attacked the media. Others applied pressure against television and newspaper owners. Despite the freedom-of-assembly clause, during the first week in May 1971, Nixon had 12,416 protesting citizens locked up in Washington. To justify the arrests the Justice Department's William Rehnquist invented the phrase "qualified martial law."

"Domestic security" wiretaps, warrantless "no-knock" searches, and centrally coordinated surveillance were forms of attack upon the Fourth Amendment's guarantees against the government. To counter the Fifth Amendment's no-self-incrimination clause, Congress provided Nixon with authority to grant limited or "use" immunity to force the testimony of otherwise unwilling witnesses, and to prosecute them, too. Juries guaranteed by the Sixth Amendment stood in the way, so Rehnquist suggested non-unanimous verdicts. Nixon's men undercut the Eighth Amendment's right to bail with "preventative detention." The Equality Amendments stood against the Southern

Strategy, so their enforcement was marked by "benign neglect." Nixon's men even sought legislation to restrict the right to petition for *habeas corpus*.

With the Congress as immobile as its easy-to-forget leaders (Speaker Carl Albert and Senator Mike Mansfield), and with the courts reappointed, only little George Wallace from Clio, Alabama, stood in Nixon's way. He had the Deep South of the Southern Strategy in his hip pocket so Nixon and Mitchell adopted a Wallace strategy. In 1970, they invested 4,000 black-bagged one-hundred-dollar bills in the campaign of Wallace's Democratic primary opponent, Albert P. Brewer. Brewer lost.*

Then Nixon used Wallace. Nixon parlayed the Florida legislature into placing school busing on the primary election ballot. After George McGovern crippled Edmund Muskie in New Hampshire, Wallace eliminated him in Florida.

In Maryland, Wallace was shot down.

As Nixon had hoped, McGovern moved up. Still Nixon could win only if the Democrats' hatred for each other surpassed their distrust of him. To divide and conquer, he employed foreign intelligence techniques of "disinformation" and "black advance," and would later call them "pranks" and "dirty tricks": a forged letter to a New Hampshire newspaper; smear sheets in Florida which labeled one Democratic candidate mad, another a sexual deviate; bogus telephone calls to labor leaders; canceled hotel, meeting hall, and airline reservations; misrouted campaign airplanes; wiretaps, bugs, burglaries; forged, stolen, and planted documents. In the planning stage were riots, kidnappings, muggings, bribes, and other "stunts."

---

*Brewer's principal backer was Nixon's postmaster general, Winton M. ("Red") Blount. Wallace attacked defense contractor Blount as a war-profiteer and wrapped him around Brewer's neck. He summed up Brewer's slogan, "Our Kind of Man," by attacking Blount's palatial house, which was located near Montgomery. It had "twenty-three bathrooms and an air-conditioned stable." Wallace was right. Whomever Blount backed couldn't be the Alabama voters' "kind of man."

And that is how it came to pass that Richard Nixon, above the law, moved toward his second, and final, term.

The contours of his campaign thus shaped, the Commander in Chief soared to meet the totalitarian masters of other empires—men with whom he could deal and feel comfortable. With foreign affairs his forte, peace his goal, the President was above the tawdry campaign which flowed from his fearfully certain knowledge that the people would reject him. The Committee to Re-Elect President Nixon dropped the surname "Nixon." The President and the presidency were one.

〰〰〰〰

Three years had passed since the Houston hearings in the Muhammad Ali case. At that time, I had forced into public the FBI's log of the wiretapped conversation between Martin King and Muhammad Ali, and Attorney General Mitchell had announced that Nixon had *inherent* power to wiretap to protect "domestic security." Mitchell had served notice that those who sought "to attack and subvert the government by unlawful means" were fair game. And, he had remarked, under the separation-of-powers doctrine, no court could question the President.

In Ali's case, the district judge had rejected the phrase "national interest" as a justification for keeping secret the King wiretap log. Immediately, Nixon had turned to Mitchell's two new words—"domestic security." For three years, he relied upon them until, two days *after* the Watergate arrests, the Supreme Court struck them down.

〰〰〰〰

In the dark morning hours of Saturday, June 17, 1972, Frank Wills, a twenty-four-year-old black security guard, walked the deserted corridors of the gaudy Watergate office building on the banks of the Potomac River in Washington, D.C. He discovered a piece of tape across a basement doorlatch. He thought it had been placed there by workmen and forgotten. They did that to keep doors from locking so they could pass through them easily.

Wills removed the tape. When he returned twenty minutes later, there was another piece of tape across the same doorlatch. This time Frank Wills didn't rationalize. He telephoned the police.

Arrested as burglars were Bernard L. Barker, Virgilio R. Gonzalez, Eugenio R. Martinez, Frank A. Sturgis, and James W. McCord, Jr. Each had worked for the CIA. The four, who would become known as "the Cuban-Americans," had previously attempted to overthrow the government of Fidel Castro. McCord now worked for the Committee to Re-Elect the President. On September 15, two other men who had worked in the White House would be named as co-conspirators: E. Howard Hunt, formerly of the CIA, and G. Gordon Liddy, who had received his intelligence background as a special agent of the FBI.

On fast-breaking stories, daily newspapers play follow-the-President. The Watergate story was no exception. White House Press Secretary Ronald Ziegler termed the break-in a "third-rate burglary," a "bizarre" event. The story was buried inside *The New York Times*. To the *Washington Post*, the burglary was a "caper," a kind of Keystone Cops adventure. Promptly, prominent Democrats laughed, "Why would anyone wiretap the Democratic National Committee?" and "Who would want to listen to Larry O'Brien?"

On the day after the arrests (Sunday, June 18) Morris Dees, the bright "amateur" who served as McGovern's chief fundraiser, telephoned me at my vacation home in Destin, Florida. His question was: "Should the Democrats sue the Committee to Re-Elect the President?"

Constitutionally the Justice Department couldn't move against the President, and no southerner in the civil rights movement doubted that the burglars worked for him.

"Sure, sue!" I told Dees.

Before he slept that night, Dees talked with McGovern's campaign managers, Frank Mankiewicz and Gary Hart, and McGovern himself. The next day Dees called me again, this time from Washington. He, Joseph A. Califano, Jr., and other lawyers in Edward Bennett Williams's firm were preparing suit papers. On Tuesday, June 20, with Dees in the background, off-camera, the Democrats' national chairman, Lawrence F. O'Brien, announced that he was seeking $1 million in civil damages.

The Watergate case was under way.

~~~~~~~

All southerners have a lot in common, and in some ways I fitted the stereotype of those in politics. Still tending toward the weight of a chief deputy, I wore seersucker in the summer and often smoked cigars and consumed wondrous amounts of whiskey. It sometimes seemed easier to change myself than society. In the late afternoon of April 4, 1968, hours after the integration of the Greene County (Alabama) jury rolls resulted in the acquittal of Johnnie Coleman, one of the plaintiffs in the prison desegregation case, Camille had telephoned me the news of the assassination of Martin King. My resolve to quit drinking ended. In the rage and despair which led others to burn their own dwellings down, I sent out for a fifth of whiskey and drank it, crying. Finally, rationalizations faced reality, and on June 13, 1971, the day *The New York Times* published the Pentagon Papers, I quit drinking for good.

Simultaneously Camille and I prepared to leave Atlanta. Aryeh Neier, now the ACLU's executive director, had asked me to head up our national office in Washington.

The nation's capital offers ACLU liberals a pleasant, relaxed in-crowd life. I knew many good southerners, black and white, who had been digested into its blandness, choosing to remember the sweet softness of rustling magnolias rather than the red-clay poverty of Deep South life. Despite that, I agreed that we would move after June 1972, when Charles graduated from high school. We loved Atlanta, but the defense against Nixon's Southern Strategy required that the struggle be removed from the courts, carried to the people, and by them transformed into political action. To be in that fight, I needed to be in Washington.

14

By tradition, Labor Day is kickoff day for presidential campaigns. But for Nixon there were no Labor Day parades. His campaign began two weeks late. It was kicked off when the carefully drawn indictment firmly fixing Watergate blame at the Liddy-Hunt level was issued by a District of Columbia grand jury.

Henry E. Petersen, the head of the Criminal Division of the Justice Department, had tried to get grand jury action by Labor Day. His prosecutor, Earl J. Silbert, couldn't meet that deadline. Petersen was told that September 15 would be Indictment Day, so he sent that date up to Attorney General Kleindienst.

FBI clerks spent Monday, September 11, gathering data. In scores of field offices teletype machines rat-a-tatted back to the Justice Department the number of "leads" FBI agents "covered" and the number of persons "interviewed and reinterviewed."

The next morning, bluff, hearty, and blunt-spoken Kleindienst ate breakfast at the White House. Nixon's cabinet members, senior staff aides, and Republican congressional leadership paid rapt attention as the law-and-order devotee told them that

207

in three days the Watergate Seven, and no others, would be indicted.

A few hours later, the Democratic National Committee's lawyer, Edward Bennett Williams, met with Federal Judge Charles R. Richey. Through the civil lawsuit and depositions, Williams and his law partners had tried to bring out the facts. They had even argued for application of the Nixon administration's immunity rules to the Watergate burglars, despite the fact that those arrested could then go free if they provided evidence against higher-ups. But now Williams was trapped by a ruling by Judge Richey which the lawyer believed was unprecedented. (He termed it a "hypertechnical position.") Williams had sought to amend his lawsuit. Too late, said the judge. He was adamant. The amendment attacked Nixon's finance chairman, Maurice Stans, and it was publicly announced. Stans immediately claimed that the charges in the amendment were unprotected by the privilege which attaches to filed court papers. During the next three days he launched a legal and public relations counteroffensive by filing libel suits against Williams's clients seeking $7.5 million in damages.

~~~~~~~~

On Wednesday, September 13, Silbert finished writing his "prosecutive memorandum." When Petersen had picked Silbert to prosecute the Watergate Seven (on the day of the arrests), he had instructed him to make "oral reports, on a daily basis." But now Silbert put in writing his "grave reservations about Magruder's testimony" and his "reluctance to call Magruder as a witness at trial."

At Camp David, Mitchell and Clark MacGregor, Mitchell's successor as Nixon's campaign chairman, and John B. Connally met with Haldeman and the President. They discussed the upcoming indictment. Nixon decided not to appoint a special prosecutor.

At the Watergate office of the Association of State Democratic Chairmen, R. Spencer Oliver, Jr., the association's executive director, met with telephone company employees and FBI agents to discuss the listening device Oliver's *secretary* had just uncovered inside the telephone! Almost three months had passed since the confessed Watergate wiretap listener, former FBI Agent Alfred C. Baldwin III (who had escaped immediate arrest because he was stationed in the Howard Johnson Motel across the street), had told the prosecutors that the tap on Chairman O'Brien's telephone hadn't worked. But he also had told them that there had been a second bug and it was on Oliver's telephone. That one had worked. No one had told Oliver. For almost three months, the device had continued to transmit from Oliver's Watergate office telephone. Its discovery slowed down nothing.

The next day, September 14, Mitchell appeared before the grand jury investigating Watergate. By then the indictment had been drawn, the prosecutive memorandum written, the FBI statistics compiled, the private announcements made, and the publicity planned. According to Mitchell, his grand jury appearance was "very brief" and the prosecutors were "very polite." He said that he had been asked to appear "almost on the basis of an apology."

∿∿∿∿∿∿

On September 15, Indictment Day, the Nixon aide who was in charge of the case, a young former Justice Department lawyer named John W. Dean III, received a "pat on the back" from his President. Neither he nor we knew his conversation was being tape-recorded.

Dean reported to the President that Judge Richey had had an out-of-court "casual encounter" with Silbert. According to Dean, the judge "stopped the civil case so Silbert [could] get the indictment down." Silbert was "going to have a hell of a time drawing these indictments up because . . . these civil depositions will keep coming out and the grand jury has got one eye on this civil case. . . ."

Dean said Richey "had already slowed it down to nothing."

Later Silbert and Richey denied Dean's remarks. The judge also denied Dean's report that he had told a lawyer (with whom, according to Dean, he had met "in the judge's rose garden . . .") that Stans "ought to file a libel action."

Richey said publicly that he feared the depositions, whether or not Dean told Nixon the truth, would "receive continuing attention by the press." He ordered them sealed and closed down the civil suit until after the election. That ruling was in no way contrary to the way other judges often rule. Prejudicial pretrial publicity is a constant judicial concern.

On September 16, like a Nixon campaign handbill, page one of the *Washington Post* proclaimed, U.S. JURY INDICTS 7 IN WATERGATE BREAK-IN. Acting FBI Director L. Patrick Gray III said his agents were still "running leads" up to a week ago. Kleindienst said that the FBI and grand jury had completed their active investigation. Another Justice Department official said the investigation disclosed "absolutely no evidence to indicate that the indicted seven men were acting under the orders of others." The investigation was over.

Kleindienst said the investigation had been "one of the most intensive, objective, and thorough" in years. Justice Department career man Henry Petersen was used to deny McGovern's "whitewash" charge. He cited the FBI's use of "333 agents operating from 51 field offices and in 4 foreign capitals. They developed 1,897 leads, conducted 1,551 interviews, and expended 14,098 man hours." To these figures he added the examination by the grand jury of 50 witnesses and its 125 hours of meetings.

As these statistics were being released, the *Washington Post* headlined, WATERGATE WAS SET UP TO EMBARRASS GOP, AGNEW SAYS. The Vice President's remarks dovetailed with those of Attorney General Kleindienst. He blamed the recently discovered bug on Spencer Oliver's telephone on Oliver himself.

With the Watergate criminal case "under way," with civil suit depositions halted, with the results of the General Accounting

Office's investigation "on the shelf" at the Justice Department, and the Common Cause civil suit (seeking the names of Nixon's campaign contributors) tied up by pretrial maneuvers, only one threat to Nixon remained—the House Banking and Currency Committee investigation of the funding of the burglary. A "reluctant" Assistant Attorney General Petersen, motivated by "law enforcement" and "civil liberties" concerns, wrote the committee to set forth the Justice Department's "views." He feared that a well-publicized investigation would "jeopardize the rights of criminal prosecution [of the Watergate Seven]. . . ." On October 3, the committee voted twenty to fifteen to subpoena no witnesses and to delay the investigation until after the trial.

Due to the pendency of criminal charges, the President declined to comment further.

And so, under the rules of the justice system, the indictment transformed preelection exposure into "pretrial publicity." The case would not be tried until after the election. The cover-up had worked.

~~~~~~~~

Back from South Africa (where I had lectured on the Bill of Rights at the invitation of the anti-apartheid East London *Daily Despatch*), we bought a small town house on Capitol Hill. For the ACLU I leased the first floor of the building which had housed McGovern's campaign staff.

In mid-December 1972, as we prepared to move from Atlanta, the prosecutors told Spencer Oliver, the principal victim of the working wiretap, that they intended to put him on the witness stand. He was to testify "in general" about his conversations on the telephone. The prosecutors tried to set Oliver at ease. They told him they only wanted to ask: Were the conversations personal? Did they involve business? Politics?

Because the prosecutors had no notes, logs, or tape recordings of the conversations, Alfred C. Baldwin III, the wiretap listener, would recall the Democrats' spoken words from memory. The prosecutors had orally agreed not to prosecute Baldwin only if he told "the whole truth." And, by the nature of their jobs, they would have to decide what "the whole truth" was. The Democrats felt trapped. Even if their strongest words had been Biblical "thees" and "thous," they couldn't prove it. They had no recordings. Neither did Baldwin, who didn't know them or their voices. Many other people had used their telephones and no Democrat desired to rely upon the Republican wiretap listener's "memory." And because the prosecutors held office at the pleasure of the President and had not told Oliver about the tap on the Association of State Democratic Chairmen's telephone, he and other Democrats who had been overheard feared their decisions about Baldwin's "whole truth."

Despite the common assumption, Democratic Chairman O'Brien had not been overheard. The primary users of the tapped telephone included: Oliver; his secretary, Ida M. Wells; Alabama's and Maine's state chairmen, Robert S. Vance and Severin Belleveau; and Robert E. B. Allen, the Young Democrats' national president.

Oliver asked me to represent them. He, Vance, and their associates had the law and the Constitution on their side. My task was to keep the Democratic victims of the crime from becoming victims of the trial. To do that I had to cover up—to suppress Baldwin's testified "recollection" of the conversations—and keep his version of the "whole truth" from public view.

To me, the law seemed clear. The disclosure of the contents of the conversations was a felony. A statute explicitly barred their introduction into evidence. Besides the law, the record of what the listener overhears couldn't show the motive (the reason) for the wiretap. Wiretappers, expecting to hear talk of Howard Hughes, may overhear anything from "I'm sorry, that is not a working number" to a confidential report from a medical laboratory disclosing the result of a diabetic family-member's blood tests.

I remember in Muhammad Ali's case how Mitchell, Nixon, and FBI Director Hoover had tried to pin the rap for the Martin King wiretap on the assassinated, and therefore silent, Attorney

General Kennedy. Simultaneously, the FBI had quietly but publicly dumped 2,200 pages of wiretap transcripts into the Newark federal court criminal trial of Simone Rizzo ("Sam the Plumber") deCavelcante. When *The New York Times* published the organized crimester's personal conversations, interspersed with FBI references to "hanky-panky," they successfully diverted public attention from the FBI's own guilt in the King tap.

On December 22, 1972, my associate lawyer Hope Eastman and I lunched with Earl Silbert, a bright, bookish, highly respected Justice Department career lawyer, at the moderately priced Kansas City Beef House on Pennsylvania Avenue near Washington's United States Court House. Throughout lunch Silbert's associate, Seymour Glanzer, was open and friendly. Silbert himself seemed harried, withdrawn, faraway, and, by the time we left, sullen.

Looking back, I don't wonder that Silbert was angry at me, nor do I blame him. Here he was, two weeks before the biggest trial of his life, confronted by a total stranger—a suspicious southern lawyer who flat-out told him he couldn't introduce the Democrats' conversations into evidence. He was on the firing line and he had doubts about his star witness, Jeb Stuart Magruder. That day Silbert was searching for Hunt's notebooks, which were missing from the items taken from Hunt's office in the Executive Office Building. (Silbert's ostensible ally, the President's counsel, John Dean, had secreted them.) To add to his problems, Hunt was claiming a psychiatric inability to stand trial.

Once, when Glanzer sought to move Silbert's briefcase from under the table, Silbert abruptly protested. Later, when Silbert opened it to search for the statements our clients had made to the FBI and grand jury, I noticed it contained electronics equipment which must have been evidence.

Already, Judge John J. Sirica was pressing Silbert to prove the motive for the burglary. The judge wanted to know the "why" of Watergate. So did the public. So would the jury. But three days before Christmas Silbert was still shopping for a motive.

The day before we met, former CIA agent James McCord had

ordered his lawyer Gerald Alch, not to say in his defense that he had been on a CIA assignment. That same day the prosecutors had come up with a witness to tie the conspiracy case together. He was Thomas J. Gregory, a former Brigham Young University student who sought college credits and earned money for his service as a spy in the Muskie and then the McGovern campaign organizations. He had obtained his spy job through the Howard Hughes organization's P.R. man, Robert Bennett, who headed up the CIA cover-firm where Hunt and other former CIA men worked. Later, the deeply religious, ever-helpful Bennett would swear that within three weeks of the arrests he had told Silbert "fully and completely all our [the public relations firm's] arrangements with the CIA." Bennett would swear he had told Silbert he intended to lie about them to the newspapers but, if asked under oath, he "would answer truthfully." He would say that Silbert had "agreed that there was no purpose in exposing the arrangement. This had no bearing whatsoever on the Watergate break-in. Consequently he did not ask those questions under oath." On July 10, 1972 (twenty-three days after the Watergate burglary), Bennett told his CIA case officer about that conversation with Silbert.

Of course, at lunch Silbert told me nothing about Bennett. But what he did say almost floored me. He wanted to use the Democrats' conversations to prove that blackmail was indeed the motive for the Watergate burglary. Exasperated and angry, he looked across the table at me and blurted out, "Hunt was trying to blackmail Spencer and I'm going to prove it!" We stared at him for a moment, but remained silent. We quickly moved to another subject, but my mind remained fixed on Silbert's sentence. Blackmail? Blackmail of Spencer Oliver as a motive for the Watergate crimes?

Oliver was an unlikely target for blackmail. He was not rich, and for President he favored his friend, former North Carolina Governor Terry Sanford. He was no threat to Nixon. So that blurted-out remark provided me with an early, rare insight into the Watergate case and the vulnerability of Richard Nixon, and another reason to be thankful for Hope Eastman. Later, when Silbert would not be able to recall his words—"Hunt was trying to blackmail Spencer and I'm going to prove it!"—Hope would recall them.

The day after our lunch with Silbert, the moving van from Atlanta arrived. While I read the yard-high stack of newspaper-clipping files obtained from the Democratic National Committee, Camille directed the placement of furniture.

Camille drove us to Birmingham for Christmas. I read. From 5:00 A.M. until late Christmas morning, I read. The next day Camille drove us to our other home in Destin, Florida. I reread the files.

Then I telephoned the victims of the crime to tell them the case was fixed. Probably by Nixon, though I didn't know how he had fixed it. But that didn't matter. The case was fixed! I told my clients that the misguided Justice Department would prove the Cuban-Americans were misguided anti-Castroists who needed money. To all of them he would attribute misguided Republican loyalty. But to Hunt, or Hunt and Liddy, they would ascribe an overriding *personal* criminal motive—blackmail and big money.

That blackmail motive, embroidered with bits and pieces of information acquired from the FBI's investigation of the Democrats and from Baldwin's "memory" of the conversations, might be made believable. If the defendants didn't fight to prove their innocence, the Justice Department would present that motive to the judge and jury and, through them, to the nation's gullible press. Gossip is the poetry of politics, and if the press became absorbed by Baldwin's rendition of the Democrats' conversations, some people would be led to believe that the motive was blackmail. If ultimate blame belonged with Hunt and Liddy, if Nixon's campaign cash had been squandered for his employees' personal ends, then Nixon really was the number-one innocent victim of the Watergate crime.

The legal remedy I proposed was an unprecedented longshot: to enter the conspiracy case by filing a motion to suppress the conversations. At our luncheon, the prosecutors had insisted that third parties couldn't intervene in criminal cases. Under existing law they might be right. Besides, I warned my clients, there would be speculation about their motives for "covering up" purely personal as well as political conversations. And the speculation would be far worse than anything any of them might have said. The prosecutors had assured me that they wouldn't allow Baldwin to go into details. And, aside from the possible effect of the blackmail motive on the public perception of Watergate, my clients could be better off personally if they relied upon the prosecutors to ask questions which elicited only vague, undetailed answers such as, "the conversations were personal," "they involved business," "they discussed politics." But when I asked my clients, "Should I file?" their answers ranged from "Yes" to "Hell, yes!"

15

I didn't know my way to the courthouse, but the taxicab driver did. All I knew about "Maximum John," a.k.a John J. Sirica, was what I had heard from Washington liberals. According to them he wore a black hat with his black robes. He gave stiff sentences. He was all bad. But lawyers tend to confuse friendship and philosophy with character. To too many of my friends, "He's a good guy" means "He's a good man"; "He's a conservative" means "He's a bad man."

On Wednesday afternoon, January 3, 1973, I found the clerk's office. A woman stamped "filed" on my motion to suppress any mention by Baldwin, during the Watergate Seven trial, of the content of the conversations. Then she disappeared. Then she reappeared to say she could not accept the papers without Sirica's consent. Upstairs an employee took the papers into the judge. Soon a short, stocky, shirt-sleeved man—about George Wallace's size—emerged to say sternly, "I'll not allow this to be filed."

The motion was in proper form, but with the trial scheduled to begin in five days, I had come too late.

At four the next morning I finished the appeal papers. Before I left the office to file them, Sirica's law clerk telephoned to tell me that Sirica had changed his mind and wanted me to come to his chambers.

Now Sirica was cordial. We chatted about Birmingham, where he and his friend Jack Dempsey had participated in a World War II bond drive. He accepted my motion and set it for an immediate hearing.

In the courtroom, like an expectant but detached fight fan awaiting the main event, Sirica surveyed the scene. I was still an outsider—for this was a criminal trial, not a tag match, and the judge was supposed to be the only "third man" in the ring.

When I told Sirica that the prosecutors desired to prove "the motive in this case was blackmail, not politics," Sirica bounced. The half-filled courtroom came alive.

"You say that the motive the government expects to show is blackmail?" Sirica asked.

"Yes," I replied.

"That is the first time I heard that," said the judge.

Actually, it was the second time in ten minutes that he had heard that, for McCord's lawyer, Gerald Alch, had told him "hypothetically" that was what the prosecution might do.

Silbert then argued that the public interest was "paramount . . . far outweigh[ing] their right to privacy. . . ." He said he needed the conversations to corroborate Baldwin's testimony, to prove that Baldwin overheard them, and to prove motive. Silbert told Sirica he would not go into "specific details" and would "strenuously object" to improper cross-examination.

Instead of convincing Sirica of the law, I intrigued him.

"Why did they go in there?" he asked rhetorically. "What was the motive? What were they seeking? What did they hear? Was it solely for political espionage, was it for other purposes?"

I told Sirica that the prosecutors "asked me if I have any

information about anybody higher up anyplace* who committed any offense or got the information or anything. . . . And I now do have some information I think they could use. . . ."

Sirica moved forward over the bench. "Let me understand what your statement means. Repeat that again."

"I have been advised . . . that a man named Harry Flem[m]-ing spoke on this telephone, that Harry Flem[m]ing was a Republican official in the . . . Committee to Re-elect the President, and that he has been advised by other ranking Republicans that his job was altered after these wiretaps."

"Now that would show a political use rather than blackmail as a use!"

Sirica suggested that the prosecutors call me to testify before the grand jury if that was their desire.† But Silbert took issue with my having said he had asked me for any information we had about "higher-ups." As he recalled it, he had asked for "information" about "a higher-up or lower-down or a middle-of-the-roader . . . anybody. . . ."

In the hallway, James McCord introduced himself to Hope Eastman. "I want Mr. Morgan to know that we never intended to harm Mr. Oliver. I'm terribly sorry that this is happening to him."

I knew what was scheduled to happen in Sirica's courtroom.

---

*We asked Sirica to haul eighteen Nixon men into court so they could be asked under oath whether they had seen "logs, notes, transcriptions . . . or other memoranda" or heard "tapes or other sound recordings" of the wire-tapped conversations or knew who had. We didn't have the Justice Department or the FBI, but walking-around sense and the ability to read newspapers provided us with the names of those who ought to be asked questions. Later fourteen of the eighteen witnesses we sought appeared before the Watergate Committee. Included were: John Caulfield, Charles W. Colson, John W. Dean III, L. Patrick Gray III, Richard G. Kleindienst, Frederick LaRue, Clark MacGregor, Jeb Stuart Magruder, Robert C. Mardian, John N. Mitchell, Robert Odle, Herbert L. Porter, Hugh W. Sloan, Jr., and Maurice W. Stans.

†It wasn't and they didn't. Nor did they call Flemming. It was not that Flemming had done anything wrong. Like Oliver he was a victim. Months

But I wasn't able to convince Sirica. He ruled that the conversations were admissible evidence. But at least he had heard me say that the Justice Department intended to show the motive was "blackmail, not politics." At least he had heard me say that "in intelligence, in law, in politics there [are] . . . stories we call cover stories."

~~~~~~~~

In his opening statement to the jury Silbert said the Committee to Re-Elect the President had been "concerned about demonstrations by extremist groups . . . against the surrogate candidates who served as Nixon's stand-ins in the primary states." So the committee had turned to George Gordon Liddy for help. "He was to . . . develop an intelligence operation by which he could find out in advance whether there were planned demonstrations in . . . cities such as Manchester, New Hampshire, and Miami, Florida. . . ."

For that, Magruder had "allotted" Liddy $100,000 in $100 bills. "The idea at the time was . . . to develop intelligence at . . . ten different locations using ten different people for ten months. January through the election at a thousand dollars a month, and that is how you get the hundred thousand."

Liddy "was to look into the convention security problem out at San Diego" to "develop information as to how many demonstrators might be expected." For this Magruder provided

---

later, Robert Mardian was to testify that Flemming's job had been changed because of his innocent conversations with Oliver. According to the newspaper accounts, Flemming was not even interviewed until after the appointment of a special prosecutor. He too had been in Key Biscayne at the time of the third Mitchell-Magruder meeting, when authorization of the Watergate wiretap had been made final. Flemming knew of the fact that the meeting had occurred but not what had transpired in it. Frederick LaRue testified that the conspirators had excluded Flemming from the room. Since later indictments were for the cover-up and no one other than the original seven burglars was ever indicted for the burglary itself, Flemming never testified in public.

Liddy with another $150,000 in $100 bills. "[S]o the total amount of money allotted for the different assignments was two hundred fifty thousand dollars. . . ."

"Now the evidence we will produce before you will show that Mr. Liddy . . . received about two hundred thirty-five thousand dollars," said Silbert. But he also said he could account for the expenditure of only fifty thousand.

"What did Mr. [Herbert L.] Porter and Mr. Magruder receive in exchange or in return for that expenditure of funds?" asked Silbert rhetorically. He answered himself, "Some information about an anticipated demonstration in Manchester, New Hampshire, from the left-wing group, . . . a second piece of information about an anticipated demonstration in Miami, Florida, from a right-wing extremist group, [and] . . . instead of the hundred thousand demonstrators they . . . expect[ed] at San Diego they could expect about two hundred fifty thousand." That "caused a good deal of concern" and was a reason for transferring the convention site from San Diego to Miami.*

Silbert concluded his opening statement. Hunt's lawyer, former Justice Department attorney William O. Bittman, rose. "At this time, Your Honor, Mr. Hunt wishes to withdraw his plea of not guilty and enter pleas of guilty to counts one, two, and eight."

"[B]oth the substance and the appearance of justice require that the tendered plea be refused . . ." said Sirica. "Anything further?"

"Yes, Your Honor," Bittman quickly replied. Hunt wanted to plead guilty to all charges. He was willing to leave the next thirty-five years of his life to the tender mercy of a judge known as "Maximum John"!

When Sirica asked Hunt to tell him then and there—in public—how "you got into this conspiracy, what you did. . . ." Bittman interrupted with, "—it was Mr. Silbert's intention to

---

*Silbert covered the "political campaign" motive in a single short paragraph. He took four transcript pages to discuss a possible financial motive.

bring all of these defendants before a grand jury subsequent to their sentencing. . . ."

Silbert suggested that Sirica ask whether Hunt accepted "the essential accuracy of the facts as outlined in the government's opening statement."

"Do you agree with the government's opening statement insofar as your knowledge of the conspiracy?" asked Sirica.

"Yes, Your Honor," answered Hunt.

As the Cuban-Americans considered their future, Hunt was trundled into jail. His bail was set at $100,000.

Within the week, the four Cuban-American defendants fired their lawyer, Henry B. Rothblatt, to acquire the privilege of pleading guilty. Rothblatt understood that good soldiers should follow orders. He also believed that good lawyers can't be good soldiers, so he refused to enter their guilty pleas. I telephoned him in New York.

"Henry, I know what you must be going through and I wanted to congratulate you and wish you well."

"I've waited a long time for a chance to show what being a criminal lawyer is all about," he replied.

The Cuban-Americans' new lawyer, Alvin L. Newmeyer, eighty-nine, entered their bargained plea. Again Sirica rejected the deal. So the defendants entered guilty pleas to all charges. By then, assistant prosecutor Glanzer was concerned about "certain innuendos and insinuations" which had appeared in the newspapers, so Sirica questioned the four hapless loyal "lower-downs" who stood before him.

> JUDGE SIRICA: [I]s anyone at this time or anytime paying anything to the four of you defendants?
> THE DEFENDANTS: [In chorus.] No one.
> . . . .
> THE COURT: Has anyone assured you if you go to jail, either one of you or the four of you, if you go to jail your families will be taken care of?
> THE DEFENDANTS: [In chorus.] No one.

THE COURT: Was there any statement made to you by Mr. Barker or anybody, Mr. Hunt or anybody else, that you would be taken care of if you got in trouble or anything like that?
THE DEFENDANTS: [*In chorus.*] No, sir.
THE COURT: You deny that?
THE DEFENDANTS: [*In chorus*] Yes, sir.

Asked by Sirica who mailed him $25,000, Barker replied, "For a definite fact I cannot state who sent that money."
"Didn't you think it was strange that amount of money coming through the mail without being registered or anything?"
"No, I don't think it is strange, Your Honor. Like I said, I have previously . . . been involved in other operations which took the strangeness out of that. . . ."
The four patriots were sent off to jail. By entering guilty pleas they and Hunt had waived their rights not to testify against McCord and Liddy. Not one of them was called to testify at the trial.
Like the victims of the crime, these "lower-downs" were expendable. Somehow I had stepped backward into Lowndes County justice, and I heard myself humming: "It's the same the whole world over, it's a low down crying shame; it's the rich what gets the glory, it's the poor what gets the blame."

From his line-of-sight listening post in the Howard Johnson Motel directly across the street from the Watergate office building, Alfred Baldwin had typed up and transmitted the fruits of the wiretap up the line of command. (He said his tape recorder hadn't worked. To this day, neither the tapes of the Democrats' conversations nor Baldwin's notes on them, which were said to have been destroyed with the files of the project, code-named "Gemstone File," have been discovered. Thus it was Baldwin's memory which contained the only evidence of the Democrats' conversations.) Soon after nightwatchman Frank Wills telephoned the police, Baldwin watched the arrest of the burglars. Then he fled into the dark morning. During the first week in

July 1972, his lawyers made their secret, unwritten deal with the prosecutors not to prosecute Baldwin if he told "the whole truth."

On the night of September 28, *Los Angeles Times* reporter Jack Nelson, Baldwin, and one of Baldwin's attorneys, Robert Mirto, had secretly met in Mirto's West Haven, Connecticut, home.

As Nelson asked Baldwin for "the whole truth," a tape recorder captured Baldwin's answers. The next day Nelson continued the interview.

At 4:20 A.M., on Wednesday, October 4, 1972, Nelson filed his story on Baldwin.

Later that morning Nelson's breakfast was interrupted by a telephone call from one of Baldwin's attorneys, John Cassidento. "I know this is going to break your heart but Earl Silbert just called and threatened that if we go ahead with the story, Al may be indicted. I don't think you can use the story, and I'm really mad."

Prosecutor Silbert and defendant Hunt's attorney, William O. Bittman (a partner in Hogan and Hartson, the respected Washington firm which also represented Howard Hughes's interests), tried to stop publication of Nelson's interview. They provided Judge John J. Sirica with an "agreed-to" order which barred "witnesses and potential witnesses and alleged victims" from pretrial discussion of the case. Sirica signed it and prosecutor Seymour Glanzer telephoned Cassidento and read it to him.

If the interview were published, Nelson and the *Los Angeles Times* could be convicted, validly, of contempt of court. Nationwide, newspapers (and George McGovern) attacked the order as violative of the First Amendment.

By the next day (October 6), when Sirica withdrew and modified the order, the *Los Angeles Times* had published the interview.

But Silbert did not prosecute. According to Nelson he did predict that the tape recordings of the interview would be subpoenaed, and defense lawyer Bittman did subpoena them.

Baldwin released the newspaper from its pledge of confidentiality and the tapes were delivered to Sirica, who ordered the court reporter to transcribe them.

Later, when a few of Nixon's White House tapes were transcribed and published, the public and the press would be intrigued by them. But very few of those tapes were produced, and they provided only partial—and sometimes wrong—answers.

In a world of listening devices—ranging from office dictating machines to the National Security Agency's satellite and undersea installations which scan and computers which store billions of conversations and provide Intelligence with instant access to words uttered in Alabama and Albania, Taiwan and Tashkent—Nixon's men had entered the Watergate complex to acquire tapes. The White House tapes would entangle the Western world's most powerful man. But even today, it is unrevealed, still unnoticed tapes which contain the untold story of Watergate. And it was the little-known transcript of the taped Nelson-Baldwin interview which would provide me with a fighting chance to find the truth and the Justice Department a forfeited chance to tell it.

~~~~~~~~

On Tuesday afternoon, January 16, 1973, Sirica summoned us to the bench. He told us he had received an order from the court of appeals. Without precedent they had ruled that I had the right to participate in the trial. Prior to the admission of any testimony about the Democrats' conversations, they required that Sirica halt the trial, hold a separate closed hearing, and rule on the admissibility of the conversations. After that, we had the immediate right to return to the appellate court. Sirica was to keep the transcript of the hearing secret.

Four days had passed since I told the three appellate court judges that Silbert had said: "Hunt was trying to blackmail Spencer and I'm going to prove it!"

In rebuttal Silbert had disclaimed, "I must disagree with Mr. Morgan as to the conclusion he draws." Hope Eastman sat beside me at counsel table. When she said I had repeated Silbert's words exactly, I returned to the rostrum and told the judges: "I find no attempt at blackmail. *The only purpose I can find for it is it looks mighty good! Mr. Hunt went off on his own adventure, and nobody else knew anything about it!* [Emphasis added]"

Baldwin would soon testify, so McCord's and Liddy's attorneys were entitled to review the 161-page transcript of the *Los Angeles Times* – Baldwin interview. Sirica provided me with a copy of the document. The next morning, at a 9:30 bench conference which the press couldn't hear, Glanzer, Silbert's associate, told Sirica: "Incidentally, Your Honor, there are a few typos where it says CIA. It should be CRP. . . . I sat down with Mr. Baldwin last night after court, and we went over this. . . ."

Silbert added that the prosecutors had "review[ed] the content of the transcript of the tapes as Your Honor provided them . . . yesterday, and . . . there is nothing in those tapes . . . the government was not aware of . . . long before the return of the indictment. . . .

"Now all matters in there . . . have been fully investigated by the government. . . ."

~~~~~~~~~

I was seated in the back row of Sirica's courtroom. Because the appeals court had seemed reluctant to interrupt an ongoing trial, I tried to be invisible. The jury had no idea why I was there. They had seen me at the bench, but as far as they were concerned I could have been Maurice Stans.

Baldwin was on the stand. Glanzer had promised me that prior to asking any questions about the contents of the conversations they would ask Sirica to close the hearing. I tensed when Glanzer asked Baldwin: "From your monitoring of the telephone were you able to identify some of the individuals who used the phone besides Mr. Oliver?"

"That is correct," Baldwin answered.

I thought I heard Glanzer ask Baldwin, "Can you tell us who those individuals were?"

Like a Perry Mason witness, I vaulted out of my pew, charged up the center aisle, and burst through the low-swinging door. Glanzer must have heard me. He turned and stepped back as I reached the podium.

Baldwin, the wiretapper, had seen me coming. Baldwin, the "lawyer," played by the rules. He didn't answer the question.

> MR. MORGAN: Your Honor, at this point I would like to interpose an objection. That is, contents under the statute—
> THE COURT: You mean disclosing the individuals is disclosing the content of the conversation?
> MR. SILBERT: Your Honor, I was going to approach the bench after he identified who it was he overheard.
> MR. MORGAN: The identity is specifically covered.

At the bench Glanzer was contrite. "Your Honor, I want to apologize," he said. "I thought I could go into the identity and was going to stop as I told Your Honor."

Behind the locked doors of his courtroom, Sirica listened. Again he ruled that Baldwin's recollections of the conversations could be introduced into evidence. By then I had carefully read the transcript, so I was astounded when Silbert went on record. "As Mr. Glanzer explained to you at the bench earlier this morning, the language CIA in the transcript was a misprint, and should have been CRP, Committee to Re-Elect the President."

That night I carefully reread the transcript. Despite Silbert and Glanzer's representations, on not one of its 161 pages could I find the abbreviation "CRP." Whenever the Committee to Re-Elect the President was referred to, either its full name or the words "the Committee" were used.

Baldwin was quoted as saying, Jim McCord "talked CIA-style, he was that type, you know." Walking-around sense told me that neither Baldwin nor anyone else ever said that anyone "talked CRP-style."

"CIA" had to be "CIA." The words in the transcript, "They do not have the authority to order legal wiretap," were followed by:

A. The CIA can.

Q. The CIA doesn't do it with any legal authority. The CIA has a sort of illegal clandestine—

A. —no, no, the CIA can do an operation like that. . . . Don't forget, . . . if they are considered a subversive group they didn't need a warrant to go in.

Elsewhere Baldwin said, "[L]ater on I delivered that particular capsule."

Q. To the FBI?

A. CIA.

Another sentence ended, "there is a very strong feeling on the part of the U.S. attorneys that there was a good possibility that this might have been CIA."

Again, "another possibility . . . CIA . . . I wouldn't rule that out."

Q. Did you ever think the CIA might be involved?—What authority does the CIA have?

A. Security of the country—national security. You better look into that. Don't forget, the Supreme Court had not ruled. . . . Don't forget, it wasn't . . . till after the 17th . . . that from now on even though you are dealing with subversives, . . . you need a warrant.

Q. But it gets back to the Attorney General, though, [it] has to be authorized by the Attorney General.

A. Not if it is CIA. How does the CIA fit under that subversive role? Does the CIA have to go to the Attorney General?

. . . .

When you are in national security you are in a field—

. . . .

A. That is what [Baldwin's attorney] John [Cassidento] was saying, it was a CIA operation. . . .

Sirica had ruled that Baldwin's recollections of the conversations were admissible. On Thursday, January 18, while I was

waiting to argue in the court of appeals, I went to Sirica's chambers to listen to the rest of the tapes. I was dog-tired. Between
two and six that morning I had written still another brief for the
appellate court, citing the *Los Angeles Times* transcript pages
where "CIA" appeared.

Directed to a nearby room where Baldwin and Glanzer were
listening to the tapes, I sat down directly across the table and
thumbed through my copy of the transcript. When the tape
reached page 64, a distinct, clearly audible voice said, "C-I-A."

Baldwin quickly turned and protested that this was not his
voice.

That afternoon, David L. Bazelon, chief judge of the court of
appeals for the District of Columbia Circuit, presided. While
Silbert argued his need to introduce the conversations into evidence, Bazelon casually asked, "Is the government interested in
whether this information would be used to compromise these
people?" He added, "That is a euphemism for blackmail."

Silbert replied that the conversations were "highly relevant"
in laying "a factual foundation so that we can suggest that is what
they were interested in. . . ."

"Why don't you indict them for it?" Bazelon snapped.

"We believe this information goes to the motive and intent,"
Silbert replied.

Bazelon speculated.

"Do you want to show how dirty this thing was? You're talking
about morality.

"You're saying that the jury won't think it's a crime just to
intercept a message? . . ."

Bazelon mused that Silbert might be right.

The next morning there was a flurry of activity in Sirica's
courtroom. He summoned us to the bench to tell us that by two
to one the court of appeals had ruled that the conversations were
"not required to prove the charge for which the defendants are
on trial." Their very disclosure "would frustrate the purpose of
Congress in making wiretapping a crime."

We had won. So had truth. The Republican rendition of the

Democrats' conversations was out. So was blackmail. I still half expected Silbert or Glanzer to tell Sirica of their CIA-CRP mistake. Instead, Glanzer told him, "[E]xcept for some so far unimportant details, the transcription is substantially accurate." Perhaps "CIA" and "CRP" were the then "unimportant details." Later Silbert would say that he had relied upon Glanzer and Baldwin. Glanzer would agree. Not so, Baldwin would reply, and the tapes and transcript did speak for themselves even if quietly and in secret.

Because my legal obligation was to cover up, I was trapped. My immediate job was to protect the conversations—to keep the transcript secret, whether it said "CIA" or "CRP"—and not to solve the Watergate case.

The transcripts and tapes were sealed and secret *at my own request*. To challenge the prosecutors' credibility would have risked disclosure of the transcript. But my knowledge and their statements would fuel my drive against the CIA and the Justice Department during the next few years. While many of those who might have been allies and friends would wonder at the intensity and persistence of my probing, I would remember Sirica's suggestion that Friday, January 19, be used to listen to the tapes. I would remember the following Monday, when Baldwin again took the stand and testified that he, Glanzer, and prosecutor Campbell had rereviewed the tapes. I would remember that the prosecutors never corrected the record and that for the rest of the trial, and perhaps forever, "CIA" would remain "CRP."

16

Twenty years had passed since Senator Joseph R. McCarthy's investigations. Many congressional liberals who remembered that pain had forgotten its cause. Now they feared *all* investigations, *all* exposure, *all* publicity—not merely investigations into First Amendment–protected political rights. In the Watergate case, conduct, not associations and beliefs, was at issue. So was fear.

In "company town" Birmingham, we chose sides. In Washington, there were no sides. The blandest led the bland and the word *controversial* was as frightening as the word *partisan*. Washington was worse than a company town. It was a gigantic firm of 18,000 lawyers, only 700 of whom were said to have trial experience. The President and his attorney general and courtly, gracious, bright insiders like Clark Clifford, Abe Fortas, and Tommy ("the Cork") Corcoran were senior partners. They were the models for young lawyers who worked overtime to achieve "effectiveness" so they too could charge high fees for helping the very rich do legally that which they ought not be allowed to do at all.

Their conversations were feasts of Frankfurterisms, and in my first month in Washington I concluded that if Moses had been a Harvard Law School graduate with two years of Washington law practice, he would have written into the Ten Commandments three exceptions and a savings clause.

I wasn't used to this. In the South, lawyers may be less than totally candid with their wives, their children, the whole world—but not with each other. And never with the court. The few who are, are well known. There is a practical reason for peer-group truthfulness. Cases, pleas, and fees are settled, bargained, and shared with a handshake and the spoken word.

On January 22, 1973, two weeks into the Watergate Seven trial, Hope Eastman and I went to lunch at Washington's Democratic Club with Jerome F. Zeifman, a bespectacled, slightly overweight man in his fifties who served as the House Judiciary Committee's general counsel.

Zeifman had spent years in Washington, but a belief in democracy still lurked within him. First we talked about the general, amorphous, endemic, popular corruption of the Justice Department. Then we talked about Nixon. Too polite to ask if I had lost my mind, Zeifman listened as I asked him to move against the most senior law-firm partner in the Western world. I told Zeifman that, based upon the trial, I believed that Nixon could be impeached; that the House could be forced to act in self-defense; that the people could make them move; and sooner or later congressional cowardice might do Nixon in.

That night during dinner in their Capitol Hill town house, Zeifman told his wife, Donna Le Rew, of our strange conversation. When she asked, "Well, Jerry, what do you think the chances of that happening are?" He replied, "One in a hundred." Then he paused. "Those are good odds. Those are great odds!" The next morning when he drove his new boss, Peter W. Rodino, Jr., the recently selected chairman of the House Judiciary Committee, to work, Jerry Zeifman went to work. That was the first mile in the drive toward impeachment.

〰〰〰〰〰

At 2:30 on the afternoon of Tuesday, January 23, Jeb Stuart Magruder sauntered into Judge Sirica's courtroom, exuding confidence. He was one of those whom the Justice Department's Henry Petersen would term, "persons of high position . . . great notoriety or prestige. . . ."

The inauguration was over, and Nixon was in. Now Jeb Magruder, Nixon's 1973 Inaugural Committee chairman, faced his most important task. Because the cover-up had worked, and Nixon was in, the bland, charming young Magruder had to make the indictment believable. As the Clifford Irving of the Watergate case, he had carefully provided H. R. Haldeman with a preview of his testimony. That was Magruder's way of letting Haldeman know that he knew Haldeman "knew," thereby acquiring job security.

During a trial recess, McCord's and Liddy's lawyers had told me to stick around to watch Magruder perjure himself. They knew what was coming, not because they were involved in wrongdoing, but because they had access to a transcript of Magruder's grand jury testimony.

By 3:05 P.M. Magruder had echoed Silbert's opening statement to the jury, which had echoed Magruder's testimony to the grand jury—the Committee to Re-Elect the President had hired the defendants to protect the stand-in candidates, they had learned that demonstrations might occur in San Diego, they had switched the convention site to Miami; the defendants were on their own. Finished, Magruder confidently strode from the courthouse. Now he really had a "call" on the Administration. The new job he sought was executive director of the American Revolution Bicentennial Administration.

Fifty-five minutes after Magruder left the stand, I sat waiting in Senator Sam J. Ervin's office, munching on North Carolina peanuts. If a Senate select committee to investigate Watergate was organized, Ervin would chair it.

In early October 1972, Spencer Oliver had written Ervin and

asked him to undertake that task. Among Democrats, Ervin was an almost unanimous choice. Other lawyers in Congress overlooked more than they oversaw. One reason was their discomfort when questioning witnesses. They didn't know how to cross-examine. They prepared inadequately, so witnesses almost always knew more than they did, and staff aides got no chance to interrogate witnesses. Even if they had, most of them wouldn't have known how to ask follow-up questions—the ones which were not written down on the typed lists which the aides prepared and to which the senators secretly referred.

Before entering politics Ervin had tried lawsuits—as had other great lawyer investigators in the Senate's past. Their political careers (and their self-confidence) had been built upon their ability to acquire facts which others didn't want them to know. Books lined the walls of Ervin's office. They were stacked, open, everywhere—on the floor and on his desk, on chairs and on the windowsill.

First Ervin spoke softly and reverently about the law. Then he questioned me, but not about the Watergate case. He had followed the Levy court-martial. I brought him up to date.

Then Ervin asked me about the Watergate investigation. I told him we wanted four lines of inquiry. One was the money flow—where it came from and where it went. Secondly we wanted him to track the conversations.* The third simple trail we wanted Ervin to follow was that of "prankster" Donald Segretti. He couldn't personally have known political operatives willing to work with him in each state. Someone had provided him with local allies. We wanted the committee to find that someone.

Then I turned to the most important area of investigation—

---

*Records develop lives of their own. Men believe the potential benefits of damaging documentary evidence outweigh its risks. Good investigators always chart the flow of documents. They know that the simplest lines of inquiry usually are the most productive. So they list every assistant, every secretary, every janitor who surrounds a suspect and they methodically question each of them.

the Justice Department. For up that trail was John Mitchell and the nation's chief law enforcement officer—the President of the United States.

~~~~~~~~~

The case in Sirica's courtroom was moving to the jury. Among Silbert's final witnesses were my clients. Sirica sustained my objections to some questions, but agreed with the prosecutors when they denied they were seeking to skirt the court of appeal's order.

During the cross-examination of Oliver, it was Liddy's lawyer who, knowing the answer (and out of courtesy), asked, "Have you ever been the object of blackmail?"

"No, sir," the answer rang out.

The prosecution rested.

With Baldwin's recollection of the conversations excluded from evidence, Silbert emphasized money in his final argument to the jury, and through them to the press and the world. Liddy was the "leader of the conspirators." "[H]e wasn't content to follow out what he was supposed to do. He had to divert it. He had to turn it."

Seventeen days had passed since I told the court of appeals that Silbert would argue, "Mr. Hunt went off on his own adventure, and nobody else knew anything about it!" Now Silbert argued that "McCord and Liddy were off on an enterprise of their own. Diverting that money for their own uses."*

The case went to the jury.

That evening Camille was driving us up Capitol Hill on Independence Avenue. I was lost in thought.

Suddenly I exclaimed, "He'll resign!"

"Who?" asked a startled Camille.

---

*He covered other motives briefly. But in his argument of forty transcript pages he made it clear that money was Liddy's motive and that he was "[t]he boss . . . the man in charge, the money man, the supervisor, the organizer, the administrator . . . [who] wasn't content to follow out what he was supposed to do. He had to divert it. He had to turn it."

"Nixon! No, he can't resign. He hasn't got anybody to make a deal with. We will impeach him!"

The next morning the Watergate jury stayed out for ninety minutes and found McCord and Liddy guilty. It was then, with all doubts behind me, that I began work on the *People* v. *Richard M. Nixon.*

∽∽∽∽∽∽∽

I searched, but could find no way to say "Impeach Richard Nixon" without using the word *impeach,* a word of "extremists," of "little old ladies in tennis shoes," John Birchers, and other "right-wing nuts."

Articulate liberals had defended Chief Justice Warren (and liberal Justice Douglas) by degrading the impeachment process. It was out of style since "the excesses of Reconstruction," and most constitutional law professors tried not to use the word at all. Lawyers and nonlawyers alike associated the word with bad times brought about by unforgiving, and therefore mean, bad men.

The trial of President Andrew Johnson was one "excess" cited to generations of schoolchildren, even by John F. Kennedy in his *Profiles in Courage.* A century after Reconciliation, we faced a political conspiracy called "benign neglect," and "The Southern Strategy."

Washington is a writhing pit of conspiracy. Running from senators to mail-room clerks, thousands of conspiracies are simultaneously under way. Most are against the people's interests. "Fixers' " lives revolve around how to "get to" one official or another, and literally tens of thousands of Washington's leading citizens are "fixers." Thousands of others (and sometimes the same people) work for the secret agencies. Their American way of life involves "cover" and "national security secrets" and, as the Cuban-American Barker said, that takes the "strangeness" out of otherwise strange things. So it is with Washington, and so it was with Watergate. With so many local lives conspiratorially lived, the word *conspiracy* was as threatening and as out of style as the word *impeachment.*

In self-defense many liberals rejected the very concept of conspiracy. During the McCarthy era they had been accused of being members of the "Communist Conspiracy"; in the South, they had been proclaimed part of the "Jewish-Communist-Integrationist Conspiracy"; criminal conspiracy charges were usually aimed at dissenters; and, for two thousand years, Jews had been accused of conspiring to kill Christ. But those who rejected the concept refused to understand the nature of government, why politicians whisper, the reasons for the Bill of Rights, and the essential truth about Washington and the Watergate case.

There was no single conspiracy, no one cover-up. There were scores of cover-ups which spun within Nixon's universe like minor galaxies of countervailing satellites or Biblical wheels within wheels. As the nation's chief law enforcement officer—the person in whose hands the Constitution placed the law enforcement power—Nixon policed their perimeter and sat at their core. He could pluck out whole circles of conspirators and send them spinning into public exposure and from there into oblivion or jail.*

His best weapon was the law itself. Its secret places—the locked-door grand jury rooms, judges' chambers, and Justice Department offices—worked for him naturally.

The conspiracies to cover up fed upon the appearance of prosecutorial power. The conspirators, bound together in fear and in hope, knew that ultimately Nixon had the power to decide who would be prosecuted for perjury, so their memories faded to meet his favor. He could prosecute. He could fire prosecutors. He could pardon, parole, and pay off.

The criminal process had kept pretrial, preelection publicity down, so the cover-up had worked. But after the election, Nixon had another problem.

The Justice Department was stuck with the indictment

---

*The Constitution requires that the President "take Care that the Laws be faithfully executed. . . ." He also can "grant Reprieves and Pardons. . . ."

brought into Sirica's courtroom. Despite allusions to personal motives of the burglars and emphasis upon Liddy as the "boss" and the "money man," the argument ("[They] were off on an enterprise of their own. Diverting that money for their own uses.") fell flat. So, even though the cover-up had worked, there was an aftermath. From February 1, 1973, to March 19, 1973, the enterprise was in its quiescent, "keep-the-lid-on" phase. Then, after March 20, 1973, there came a "scramble period" of forty-one day-long "points in time."

~~~~~~~~

On March 10, the Association of State Democratic Chairmen met at Caesar's Palace in Las Vegas. My clients Spencer Oliver and Bob Vance had invited me to speak to the association about the Justice Department's handling of their case and about the coming investigations of Watergate.

Some state chairmen and vice-chairmen are cynical political hacks. They all mind and mend the party structure during nonelection years when reformers do something else. Some do work solely from loyalty to a senator or governor, but others are equally dedicated to democracy. All are intrigued by the political process. They enjoy its camaraderie and lore. Because they come in out of the rain, they knew that the Watergate defendants had not gone off "on an enterprise of their own."

So in that city, where vice is virtue and Howard Hughes's interests preside, where Mormons work at helping conventioneers play, where Mafia men applaud tinsel-garbed showgirls, and where Hunt had sought to steal Hughes's documents from the local newspaper publisher's safe, the state chairmen met my projection of Richard Nixon's inevitable departure with thunderous applause. In a few months they would be the first and only Democratic party organization to endorse impeachment.

They understood the simple strategy. The only thing required was the education of the people. The people had to understand the impeachment process and the facts of the case. I presumed

Nixon guilty. Except in judicial trials, it is inherently antidemocratic to presume innocence for political job-holders.* Democracy requires that they, like trustees, bear the burden of proving to the people that they have properly discharged their legal duties. As the people learned the law and the facts, Nixon would be forced to exercise his options. When pushed, he would always exercise the least bad available option. Only he knew what he had done, so only he knew what his options were. It didn't matter which option he exercised. Because each of them was bad, inexorable pressure from the people would force him, step by step, option by option, to lose. Finally, his limited choices exhausted, he would leave office.

If innocent, Nixon had the means to convince the people. He had unlimited access to newspapers, television, and radio. He had unlimited funds, free lawyers, and tens of thousands of federal investigators. He could even testify in his own behalf.

Sam Ervin had told me of a conversation with Senatory Joseph McCarthy. As they walked down a Senate corridor, McCarthy had asked the recently arrived North Carolinian whether he thought he should testify before the Senate committee which was investigating his misconduct.

"Senator, if people were saying about me what they're saying about you," Ervin responded, "I'd testify. If I were in Virginia and the Potomac were a solid sheet of flames and I had the chance to testify about those charges under oath, I'd swim that river of flames to testify."

*In a criminal prosecution, Nixon would be entitled to the same rights as other citizens, including a presumption of innocence. But neither House impeachment nor Senate trial are criminal proceedings. The only political prosecution authorized by the Constitution is impeachment, and the President is entitled to fewer rights than the lowliest citizen charged with a commonplace crime. After impeachment, trial, and conviction, the Constitution denies him the right to plead that he has already been tried (double jeopardy) as a defense to a later criminal charge. In impeachment, he has no right to a jury and, if convicted, he cannot be pardoned; of course the only penalty exacted of him is the loss of the right to a public job.

On March 20, 1973, Sirica received James McCord's now famous letter. Immediately the Watergate case entered its "scramble period." Newspapers scrambled for stories, fixers scrambled to stay out of jail, and those within the Justice Department scrambled for their jobs. It was then that most of the press entered the story. And it was upon the events of March 20 to April 30, 1973, that they focused and stayed.

Whatever Nixon and the secret government really had in mind was to be found, like worms under stepping stones, at earlier points in time. But now columnist Jack Anderson and *New York Times* reporter Seymour M. Hersh acquired "informed sources" within the Justice Department. After that, they dominated the story.

Hersh would never intentionally reveal a source, but he shouted at some of them on the telephone. Everyone within earshot heard him plead, threaten, and cajole. So each morning I read *The New York Times* to learn the plans of Nixon's Justice Department. On Camille's birthday, Thursday, April 19, Sy Hersh gave me a present. He wrote, "The overall thrust of the government's continuing grand jury inquiry is known to have shifted from an investigation into the original break-in . . . to the possibility that administration officials were involved in obstruction of justice—that is, interfering with the Justice Department's inquiry."

On Wednesday, May 2, Hersh detailed their case. An indictment would be drawn against Haldeman, Ehrlichman, Mitchell, Magruder, Dean, LaRue, and, perhaps, four others. "[I]nvestigators said, everyone involved in the operation repeatedly lied . . . to President Nixon."

I stopped reading.

"Well, I'll be damned!" I said to Camille. "The entire administration was off on an enterprise of its own."

Hersh went on. " 'We don't know whether Nixon to this day knows what really happened,' the investigator added. 'He really thinks they're clean.' "

Hersh's sources said that the "overall effect of the initial cover-up was so complete . . . that the prosecutors ignored a number of vital clues. . . ." Hersh added, "The prosecutors, as had been their practice, refused to discuss grand jury matters with a reporter."

So the uninvestigated Justice Department was moving against the President's men—but not against the President. A deal between the Justice Department and the Senate's leadership had excluded that Department from the scrutiny of the Watergate Committee. That deal and Justice Department power might allow the nation's chief law enforcement officer to stay in office.

"Like hell!" I slammed the paper down.

17

Glisteningly attired Robert S. Strauss, the well-connected Dallas lawyer who succeeded Lawrence O'Brien as national chairman, wanted the Watergate civil lawsuit behind him, more money in the Democratic National Committee's bank account, and, above all else, party harmony.

He and Spencer Oliver had never mixed well. Strauss rose to the top and brought a new lawyer, Sheldon S. Cohen, with him to the national committee.

Oliver had a separate legal claim. His association telephone was the only one on which conversations had actually been overheard, so only Oliver and the association really had a claim for wiretap-based damages. Already too busy with other aspects of the Watergate investigation, I declined to handle these civil cases. Other lawyers undertook them. (And several years later recovered more than $200,000 in addition to that received by the national committee.) But my obligation to protect the privacy of the Democrats' conversations continued, and so did my personal relationship with the association and with Oliver. Working together, we discovered lawyers scrambling to settle the national committee's civil case.

On April 12 I met former Nixon aide Charles Colson's pudgy law partner and counsel, David Shapiro, in the swank offices being constructed to house the law firm of Colson and Shapiro.

I was intrigued by the nimble-minded, sure-footed Shapiro. He wanted the ACLU to join Colson in a federal court motion against prejudicial publicity. From our New York office he had procured a draft statement which set forth an ACLU position (that had never been issued) to coincide with Colson's.

When Colson left the White House he toted with him a $100,000 yearly retainer from the Teamsters' Union. Other law-firm power was bound to flow from the White House connection. Colson himself was no legal slouch, and though he had not yet found God, he had found a bright, hard-working law partner.

Shapiro was "promoting" me. I knew it and he knew I knew it. Despite that, his technique was remarkable. Occasionally I threw a name into the conversation. When Shapiro mentioned that Strauss was a "good negotiator," a bell rang and I catalogued that for reference. (Before the week was out I was to learn that Shapiro and Strauss, both excellent lawyers, had been associated in a lawsuit totally unrelated to the Watergate case. They had shared hundreds of thousands of dollars in legal fees.)

A telephone call from a newspaper reporter came in. Shapiro took it, standing up. After a series of jocular, fencing remarks, he hung up and said, "He wanted to know why Haldeman and Ehrlichman won't take Colson's calls at the White House."

"David," I slowly responded, "I think I would rather have a partner under indictment than a partner who couldn't get a call through to the White House."

Shapiro leaned forward, confidence and trust-me cordiality oozing from his words. He laughed and spoke softly. "They'll take his calls. They know who set it up. In the next few days the White House will come out with it; don't worry. In the next few days, the truth will come out."

I knew Colson was still "in" at the White House. If the "truth" was about to "come out" (regardless of Shapiro's belief that they had the right person) that meant Nixon thought he had a fall guy. I telephoned Oliver and Vance to tell them that Nixon intended to have someone (it turned out to be Magruder) plead guilty and publicly name a scapegoat. After that they could return the investigation to the secrecy of the grand jury room.

To really "get Watergate behind us" Nixon had to settle the pending civil lawsuits. With the Justice Department "on top of the case," and the civil cases out of the way, the pressure for appointment of a special prosecutor might subside.

But as Nixon set out to reap the harvest of Magruder's disclosures, Dean and Mitchell refused to be chopped down. Simultaneously Oliver and I went to Jules Witcover of the *Washington Post* with the story that secret negotiations to end the committee's civil damage suit were under way.

Yes, said the Democratic National Committee's new lawyer, Sheldon Cohen, "we have had chats" with Stans's lawyer. Stans had scheduled a meeting to discuss a settlement of another civil lawsuit—an action by Common Cause to discover the sources of Nixon's campaign finances—but Witcover's article would lift the cover of secrecy from both settlement negotiations and end them.

In the White House press room Nixon issued a "major development" statement and announced that "no individual holding, in the past or at present, a position of major importance . . . should be given immunity from prosecution."

By ordering no immunity from prosecution, Nixon cut the odds that Dean or other higher-ups (except Magruder, who was expected to incriminate Mitchell, not Haldeman) would turn state's evidence. Dean was angling for a deal. Nixon's statement was one of his ways of saying no deal. Many thought that his phrase meant "no one will escape judgment through political influence." It took me a couple of days of patient conversation to exorcise that fallacy from the mind of *New York Times* reporter Anthony Ripley. After his article explaining the use of "immunity" appeared, others began to interpret Nixon's remark correctly.

Nixon also said White House staff members would appear "voluntarily," take the oath, and "answer fully." Deprived of their Fifth Amendment right not to testify, and required to go before the Ervin committee without immunity, Nixon's men were certain to produce a passel of perjury. Nixon, who had provided the setting for the Chambers-Hiss perjury confrontation, was going to provide the most massive record of perjured testimony in history.

After my Las Vegas speech to the Democratic chairmen, I crisscrossed the country proposing impeachment to audiences in small and medium-sized cities such as Allentown, Shreveport, St. Louis, Newark, and East Orange. That taught me how many people believed that "impeach" meant "remove from office." I began to explain the process in detail and repeat it: "the House *charges*, the Senate *tries*, the House *impeaches*, the Senate *tries.*"

In Boston, on April 28, I spoke to the Massachusetts Democratic Party's executive committee. Four days later, in Boulder, Colorado, the reaction of a law school audience was precisely the same. Even though Nixon's April 30 speech intervened, the people had good sense, and they didn't believe him.

On the evening of April 30, my presentation at the University of Kansas in Lawrence was delayed while we watched Nixon address the nation. Before each of his speeches, commentators speculated on whether this would be The Speech by which Nixon would resurrect his poor little dog, Checkers, and himself. Their constant expectation led me to understand that Washington-based commentators—like Nixon—had little faith in the good sense of the people.

I sat in the rear of the large student lounge. When Nixon appeared on television, flanked by a bust of Abraham Lincoln, the flag, and a family photograph, an embarrassed giggle ran through the crowd. When he began to talk "from my heart" there was scattered laughter. "I was determined . . . that the truth be fully brought out no matter who was involved" brought groans. At "There can be no whitewash at the White House" they roared with laughter. No chill of fear ran through Lawrence, Kansas, when Nixon uttered the phrase which he had designed to threaten Washington politicians. There are "exactly one thousand three hundred and sixty-one days remaining in my term," he said in a not-so-subtle aside to those who might get out of line. "God bless America and God bless each and every one of you" brought hoots and howls of anger and disgust.

I laughed with them. I went into the auditorium, untroubled by Nixon's remark that Attorney General Kleindienst had "no personal involvement whatever in this matter. . . . ." I was troubled by one word Nixon had used—"supervising."

What had he meant when he'd used that word "supervising"? "Special prosecutor" was a phrase I understood, but what was a "special *supervising* prosecutor?" I had just watched Nixon name Elliot L. Richardson as his new attorney general. I had heard him authorize Richardson "to name a special *supervising* prosecutor for matters arising out of the case." Could that mean that Nixon intended that the special prosecutor merely *supervise* the original prosecutors and that they were to remain in the case?

≈≈≈≈≈≈≈

Sam Ervin convened the Senate's Committee on the Judiciary at 10:40 A.M. on Tuesday, May 15. He nodded and smiled. The cool, patrician Elliot Richardson struggled to smile back.

While serving Nixon in the departments of State; Health, Education and Welfare; and Defense (with the Court of St. James's, the Department of Commerce, and, perhaps, the presidency on the horizon), "Honest El the Hair Splitter" had found reams of reasons to rationally subordinate his personal beliefs to Nixon's. He was painstakingly patient and, as a former Frankfurter law clerk, a master of Frankfurterisms. With Nixon's other two scramble-period appointees—J. Fred Buzhardt, and General Alexander M. Haig—Richardson shared a near-reverence for "national security."

As Sam Ervin led Richardson into the paths of Watergate, it became "perfectly clear" that Nixon's nominee for attorney general felt the Senate confirmation process was an imposition on

his valuable time. Condescension and carefully stated exceptions, splendidly enunciated in that slightly pained Harvard Law
School style, surrounded every commitment.

Richardson reeked of well-modulated reasonableness. To
"Stick 'em up" he might have responded, "Thank you very
much, I need the exercise."

Richardson advised Ervin, as though Ervin were the ninny,
that Petersen held "a kind of supervisory role." Archibald Cox
would replace Petersen, and he, Richardson, had "no reason to
believe that the special prosecutor would displace any U.S. attorneys on his staff." That decision would be up to Cox. "He
might or might not . . . decide . . . to continue to work with . . .
attorneys . . . who are acting now."

Well rested, Camille unsuccessfully fought against falling
asleep in the hearing room. I told her that Nixon might have
solved the problem of sleepless nights by affording us the substitute of Richardson's hypnotic testimony for a sound-of-the-sea
cassette.

Ervin stayed awake by asking questions. Would Richardson
stop the work of the original prosecutors? How would the special
prosecutor be "independent if he is required to prosecute indictments drawn by somebody other than himself?"

Richardson patiently reminded Ervin that "a great many
things are in process. . . ."

Ervin protested that if the special prosecutor began work with
indictments drawn by the original prosecutors and decided to
repudiate their work, it would be embarrassing.

"This could happen," said Richardson. But since he was not
directly involved in the Watergate investigations, Richardson
certainly would not order the original prosecutors to slow down.

To Richardson's comment that the special prosecutor might
not "displace" the original prosecutors, Ervin was incredulous.
"Well, if he should decide not to do that, I see no value in
appointing a special prosecutor."

But the special prosecutor "would assume overall responsibility," Richardson explained.

Ervin retorted, unsatisfied, "If he is going to retain the present personnel . . . you might as well not appoint the special prosecutor."

Richardson said he did "not assume that the U.S. Attorney was assigned the task by the administration. He was the U.S. Attorney who happened to be there."

"The U.S. Attorney and his assistants hold office at the pleasure of the President," Ervin harrumphed.

"That is true," Richardson replied. "I simply am not in a position to prejudge. . . ."

Richardson droned on. Ervin shook his head, waited a few moments, and left the room.

Whether Richardson, a "man of the world," knew it or not, he was to be a respected, but sleepy, sentinel behind whose honesty and skill Nixon could hide. To prosecute Nixon the country needed a man who understood the laws of the street. It got men of the classroom, more at home in the salons of Cambridge than the saloons of South Boston.

In the Justice Department, the largest law firm of all, the better dreams of a thousand prosecutors died while organized crime grew. The Tax Division helped make the tax system so complicated that the H & R Block Company wound up listed on the New York Stock Exchange. As the understaffed Antitrust Division's career lawyers watched great wealth conglomerate, those in the Civil Rights Division watched Deep South poor people starve. Survival became their life's work. "Deference" became "prosecutorial discretion." The four forbidden words were "no," "now," and "I quit," and lawyers learned that if they stayed out of trouble their salaries were assured for as long as the grass grows, the river flows, and the Internal Revenue Service collects.

Stamped-out in Cambridge and New Haven, look-alike, think-alike sets of political lawyers regularly replaced each other in the Justice Department, so there was a naturalness to Richardson's selection of Harvard law professor (and Kennedy Justice Department solicitor general) Archibald Cox to be special supervising prosecutor. Like a wisp of fog, the Kennedy-led opposition to Richardson's nomination lifted and disappeared.

Cox loves the law, respects the Justice Department, practices Frankfurterism, reveres our national security, and adopts "presumptions of regularity." These and elitism are an honest lawyer's convenient, crippling disabilities.*

Cox was no trial lawyer. He had no choice but to "supervise" the prosecution. And he described his duty in the language of public relations. He wanted to "restore confidence in the honor, integrity, and decency of government." That approach was not much different from that of Jeb Magruder, who, on the morning of the Watergate arrests, turned to former Assistant Attorney General Robert Mardian and said he had a slight p.r. problem— "a p.r. problem that requires a lawyer."

When Cox sought to delay the Senate Watergate Committee's hearings until the prosecutions were over, Ervin scoffed. "The American people are entitled to find out what actually happened without having to wait while justice travels on leaded feet."

Cox's first private act was even more revealing. Once on the telephone, another time face to face, I had urged him to "hire a new, non–Justice Department staff." But the Harvard professor was an alumnus of the Justice Department. He would not, *could not*, investigate it. On his first day in office, the original prosecutors, their press release prepared, had met with him privately and threatened to resign. Cox—a Harvard man (like Silbert), unfamiliar with the case, indulgent of lawyers, and a presumer of regularity—feared an end to "continuity" in the prosecution, the very continuity his appointment was designed to end.

At his urging the original prosecutors decided not to resign. Instead they set aside their press release and joined the special supervising prosecutor's staff.

---

*Elitism anesthetizes the sense of right and wrong. Perhaps because its aptitude-testing admission standards were so high, the Harvard Law School taught no legal ethics course.

Following an initial outcry over the loss of daytime television programs, the audience for the Watergate Committee's hearings steadily grew, as did our sorrow and our pride.

My mother, seventy-three, watched Sam as did other "elderly," retired Americans. To them "honor," "truth," and "patriotism" were a common heritage.

To the nation, Watergate was a revelation. To Washington, Watergate was a challenge. The city's leaders were uncomfortable with it, as were other buyers and sellers of "public relations." As Nixon's standards were mirrored in the reflecting pool of television, Maurice Stans's phrase, "I don't want to know and you don't want to know," took on added meaning. That was officialdom's unofficial motto, yet even the officials became fascinated by what they saw of their own standards and by what they learned about themselves.

By midsummer I had an abiding respect for Ervin. Beyond issues there is "upbringing," and even though I believed he was wrong on many issues, he spoke for the basic values rejected by so many of those with whom I agreed.

My father had died in February at the age of eighty-four. Now I heard Ervin saying to me what my father had said to me and his father to him and so on back through time.

Southerners understood how deeply Ervin felt when he said, "[T]he Watergate tragedy is the greatest tragedy this country has ever suffered. I used to think that the Civil War was our country's greatest tragedy, but . . . there were some redeeming features in the Civil War . . . some spirit of sacrifice and heroism . . . on both sides. I see no redeeming features in Watergate."

But John J. Sirica and Sam J. Ervin *were* the "redeeming features."

I remembered the question Justice Hugo Black had asked me from the bench during the 1966 Georgia election case. As I attacked the constitutionality of the state's 142-year-old election law, the old man asked ever so softly, "There's nothing wrong with its age, is there?"

Now, as then, the answer had to be no. Reporters Bob

Woodward and Carl Bernstein were young. So was Frank Wills. But most young liberals were not working to save the nation. The judge, sixty-nine, and the senator, seventy-six, were.

As young-to-middle-aged Nixon men spoke into our living rooms I heard from their liberal Washington counterparts the common refrain: "I'm for impeachment, but the people aren't."

"Ain't you a people?" became my standard response.

They "knew." Congress "knew." Washington's judges, reporters, editorial writers, commentators, and lawyers "knew." So, as a way out, they refused to trust the people.

Nixon knew they would do that. When it came to trusting the people, many liberals and Nixon had a lot in common.

They also shared a liking for Earl Silbert. He is bright. A fine prep school, Phi Beta Kappa at Harvard, *cum laude* at Harvard Law School, and more than a decade of Justice Department experience mark him as honest, intelligent and competent. But as Woodward and Bernstein would write in *All the President's Men*, Silbert's opening statement "didn't make sense."

The keys to Nixon campaign disaster had been in Silbert's hands. With the grand jury in session prior to the election, reports milling around, the power to subpoena witnesses and investigate through the FBI, Silbert had been the second most powerful man in Washington. The most powerful man in Washington had the right to fire Silbert. Nixon hadn't done that. Nixon could have acceded to the Democrats' demands and replaced Silbert with a *very* special prosecutor, a seemingly independent "esteemed member of the bar," upon whose "good judgment" and "sound discretion" Nixon could have relied. He hadn't done that.

Woodward and Bernstein would write that "the prosecutors had not thrown the case." I could agree with that, but Silbert had told me that the blackmail of one of my clients was a motive for the Watergate burglary; he had told the jury that the burglars were on a gambit of their own; he and his assistant, the widely known, widely liked, and highly respected Seymour Glanzer, had told Judge Sirica that the initials "CIA" were a typographical error and should be "CRP"; in his May 22, 1973, speech Nixon persisted in referring to Cox as *supervisory*; so, if Nixon wanted Silbert in, I wanted Silbert out.

After Cox asked the original prosecutors to stay on, I worked day and night on an analysis of their prosecution. As Ervin had said to the Senate when debating the establishment of the Watergate Committee, the resolution was not "broad enough to . . . question whether investigations . . . were properly conducted." There would be no "investigation of . . . the prosecution of crimes." On the evening of June 18, 1973, for the ACLU and for the Association of State Democratic Chairmen, I transmitted to Cox the 106-page "Report to the Special Prosecutor on Certain Aspects of the Watergate Affair."

Three days later, for the ACLU only, I moved to set aside the convictions of the original seven Watergate defendants, including those who had fought to plead guilty. We charged that the trial was a "sham." Five convictions "appear to have been purchased or coerced and, in any event, were accepted as a result of false representations. . . ."

The convictions of McCord and Liddy were "tainted by the perjured testimony of at least two witnesses. . . ." The law had been enforced unequally. Higher-ups were free and lower-downs were in jail. "The integrity of the judicial process . . . is at issue; its vindication demands that the results of that trial . . . be set aside." *

The next morning, when the ACLU's board chairman, Ed-

---

*Four months after I filed the motion to set aside the original convictions, Barker and Martinez sought to withdraw their guilty pleas. On October 16, 1973, they swore that Hunt had told them prior to the day Richard E. Helms resigned as Director of Central Intelligence that Helms would be forced to resign. They said Hunt had told them that he worked for a national security agency "that had greater jurisdiction than both the FBI and the CIA."

On November 8, the *Washington Post* reported an apparent conflict between Helms's testimony (to the Watergate Committee and elsewhere) and a memorandum which Helms had written eleven days after the Watergate arrests.

ward J. Ennis, read about my motion in *The New York Times*, he fired off an "outraged protest" which was followed by a salvo of memoranda to the organization's executive committee. Ennis contended that I should be ordered to withdraw the documents from Sirica's court as "not authorized." He claimed that they set forth views which had not been considered by the ACLU's board of directors. That was true. The "views" in legal papers were rarely presented to the ACLU board. Ennis also wrote that the executive director, Aryeh Neier, didn't have a copy of the motion yet and "apparently just received the report after it was filed." That was untrue. I had obtained authorization from Neier. On the report he had even made editorial suggestions. So had a lawyer from the special prosecutor's office.

Inside the ACLU's governing structures there were law firm partners whose clients included the nation's largest defense contractors. To them neither the draft nor the Vietnam War had seemed like "civil liberties issues." They strongly favored "far-out" cases—one involving a transvestite's right to play guitar on top of the New York State Capitol would have been perfect. At law firm meetings, "crazy" cases caused titters, not conflicts with major paying clients.

In the Levy case, Ennis had come south to show "support." I had listened to his "suggestions" and in turn suggested that he head north. In response to Ennis's memoranda, one member of the ACLU board (and a Washington law firm) referred to my "well-known proclivity for independent action," as if that pro-

---

According to the memorandum, Helms wanted the FBI to limit its investigation to "personalities already arrested or directly under suspicion" and to "desist from expanding this investigation into other areas which may well, eventually, run afoul of our operations." The conviction of the Cubans for civil rights violations in the Ellsberg burglary case was reversed on May 17, 1976. By then the Justice Department had decided not to prosecute Helms on an alleged CIA burglary in northern Virginia. A judge on the court of appeals wrote, "Of one thing I am certain: In 1971 there was not in the United States of America one Fourth Amendment for Richard Helms and another for Bernard Barker and Eugenio Martinez."

254   CHARLES MORGAN, JR.

clivity wasn't essential when representing a client. Once I have
entered a case, my duty runs to the client, not to the ACLU or
anyone else in the world. But in this case the ACLU was my
client. It had the right to change, modify, refine, or alter the
stand I had taken. It could limit its position to those defendants
who joined with us, as McCord had done. If I didn't like the new
position I could recuse myself. But the ACLU could not slide
around a confrontation and base withdrawal of the motion on "a
lack of authorization."

To me Ennis was just one more pragmatist from the Manhattan Stockade, but his background was so markedly different from
mine that he may have expected me to back down. He had spent
the first thirteen years of his law practice within the Justice
Department. As an insider, he opposed the World War II incar-
ceration of the Japanese. When he lost, he administered the
Justice Department's part of the lock-up.

Later, with the cold war raging, Ennis publicly supported the
Emergency Detention Provisions of the McCarran Act, as did
many of his cold-war liberal friends, including Joseph L. Rauh,
Jr. They contended that fewer people would be jailed if Congress authorized the detention camps than would be jailed without them. Without the camps, they reasoned, during a war with
Communists, martial law might be declared.

By July 20, when the ACLU executive committee met, Sirica
had declined to accept our motion to set aside the convictions.
One week after *The New York Times* report which outraged
Ennis, Cox thanked the original prosecutors for their "invalu-
able" help and accepted their resignations. He did say that his
"judgment might have varied from" theirs. But whatever their
differences, Cox wrote, "none of us has seen anything to show
that you did not pursue your professional duties according to
your honest judgment and in complete good faith."

Inside the ACLU, Ennis developed no vocal support. The
executive committee decided I was "not clearly wrong." On
September 28, the eve of the full ACLU board's vote on impeachment, I was declared not wrong at all. The executive

committee corrected its minutes and deleted the word *clearly*. The sentence I wanted to remain, remains. It reads as though I had been off on an enterprise of my own. "The chairman . . . also suggested the question of authority in respect of other staff activities, such as Mr. Morgan's speech before the Maine Bar Association strongly criticizing the President for Watergate."

Later I learned that Silbert had provided Cox with a detailed eighty-four-page "status report" which included, in Silbert's words, "a comprehensive theory of prosecution, the potential defendants, with areas of investigation obviously left to be done at that time." Later still, Silbert told the Senate Committee on the Judiciary they would be "astounded at that particular [still secret] document. . . ."

I believe Silbert. Cox did rely upon Silbert's "theory of prosecution." Cox did build his entire case upon that foundation. Leon Jaworski built upon Cox's foundation. And the House Judiciary Committee built upon Jaworski's. I believe the case is off-center and that it remains unsolved, with questions unasked and Nixon untried. That is what I feared would happen when, during the scramble period, I read Sy Hersh's *New York Times* report that "everyone involved . . . repeatedly lied . . . to President Nixon."

White southern representatives preferred to believe that Nixon was an "aberration." Few approved of his conduct. But their districts were democracy's aberrations—traps of history where law and politics served the harsh racial and economic order. That, the lore of Reconstruction, and Nixon's Southern Strategy, undercut their desire to lead.

I knew the Voting Rights Act would "free" many of them. When finally confronted, they would act upon the better beliefs which they, like Sam Ervin, had learned from their parents and their Bibles. I also knew that Nixon, unlike Wallace and the rest of us, never really understood the politics of race.

By now Nixon's Southern Strategy had begun to work against

him. His uncomprehending men saw black, unsmiling faces on grand juries and on the House Judiciary Committee. Back home, in the Newark of House Judiciary Committee Chairman Peter Rodino, and in other congressional districts, benignly neglected, seemingly impassive, unbelieving blacks were laughing at the lies of Nixon and his men.

In May 1972, before the Watergate arrests, Detroit's black congressman, John Conyers, had introduced resolutions to impeach the President for his usurpation of the Congress's war power. Those were the first such resolutions in 104 years.*

A year later, on May 23 and 24, 1973 (before it was known that the White House tapes existed and almost five months before Cox was fired), several of us began meeting with House members in Conyers's office. We had mixed motives. I had moved to Washington because of the Southern Strategy and Nixon's capture of the courts. To others Nixon's continued prosecution of the war was his highest crime. But we were equally offended by unequal justice. And our common task was to break down House resistance to the impeachment process.

Majority Leader Thomas P. ("Tip") O'Neill's Cambridge district housed many of Harvard's white, liberal intellectuals. Later when Massachusetts's ACLU leaders met with O'Neill he would tell them what he had last done—deftly and quietly—to impeach Nixon. They would tell me that when "the time came" O'Neill would be with them. But that time was to come much later. Now not even the ACLU, let alone O'Neill, favored impeachment, and the nation needed leadership, not a clock.

Every movement must have a forerunner. Massachusetts provided two judiciary committee members, Robert F. Drinan and Harold D. Donohue. The latter was programmed to follow the Democratic party line. O'Neill would help to draw it.

But it was Drinan, the Jesuit priest, who would run ahead of

---

*The other black representatives, California's Ronald V. Dellums and New York's Shirley Chisholm, cosponsored these resolutions, as did two New York whites, William Fitts Ryan and Bella Abzug.

the pack. We had met during the civil rights movement. I knew that Nixon's Southern Strategy ran through South Boston and cut across Drinan's heart. As did the war. There was a religious base to his beliefs. Secure in them, he cast aside fear of embarrassment. On July 31, he introduced the simply worded House Resolution 513: "Resolved that Richard M. Nixon, President of the United States, is impeached of high crimes and misdemeanors."

The next day provided a feast of chuckles. President Nixon toasted Japanese Premier Kakevi Tanaka (who himself would be charged with corruption and jailed two years later), "Let others spend their time dealing with the murky, small unimportant, vicious little things. We . . . will spend our time building a better world."

That night I had dinner at the Maryland residence of Daniel Pollitt, the University of North Carolina's brilliant constitutional law professor. During summers, Pollitt worked with Joe Rauh's Washington law firm or for his old friend, Representative Frank Thompson, Jr., of New Jersey. As Thompson, former chairman of the liberal Democratic Study Group, drove me to Pollitt's house, I urged him to assume leadership of the impeachment movement. He replied that leadership against Nixon was a job for the conservatives. Thompson wanted to disbar him!

I patiently, if laughingly, explained that neither of us was on the Grievance Committee of any California bar association. All Thompson had to do was accept his own responsibility. Watergate nightwatchman Frank Wills hadn't asked, "If I telephone the police what effect will it have on the value of the dollar?" Wills had done his own job. He called the police.

"You are the police, Thompy! You are the police!"

I might as well have urged Thompson to lead a movement to stamp out violets, New Jersey's state flower.

Most of Thompson's companions with near-"perfect" liberal voting records—Representative Robert W. Kastenmeier of Wisconsin, for example—were desperately uninterested. Impeachment proceedings were supposed to commence in the House, but Kastenmeier and company were happy to let the Senate's

Watergate Committee do their job while they stood by as silent and watchful as the nearby statue of the Great Compromiser, Henry Clay.

One day John Conyers returned to his office from an interlude on the House floor. "This is a great job," an unnamed statesman had said to him, "except sometimes you have to vote."

They called themselves judges and jurors and grand jurors, which, under the Constitution, they were not. They relied upon what I came to term "Perry Mason law." They would act after Nixon stood up in the hearing room and, complete with sobs, confessed.

One night Pollitt told me that even Washington's liberal leader, Joe Rauh, was not yet prepared to come out for impeachment.

While the liberals looked to the conservatives, the conservatives looked for a place to hide. Their leader and the keeper of their collective conscience was Senator Barry Goldwater. Carefully tracked by columnists, commentators, and congressmen, Goldwater did occasionally utter an elliptical phrase. But the Arizonan was loyal and Nixon was his man. Nixon had appointed Goldwater's 1964 campaigners Kleindienst, Mardian, and Rehnquist (and Dean Burch of the Federal Communications Commission) to high office. Besides, there was Republican fear of Nixon's strength within the party. Some conservatives told me that Nixon in office until 1976 meant Ronald Reagan would have a chance at the Republican nomination. Nixon out meant Vice President Ford in, and for Reagan that meant trouble.

So throughout the impeachment drive, while the liberals were bad, the conservatives were worse. Their values were at stake, as was their future. Yet their leading journals, *National Review* and *Human Events*, continued to courageously campaign against those dirty, lying, cheating welfare mothers.

For Nixon, they joined Goldwater, Nelson Rockefeller, Nebraska's law-and-order-senators, Carl Curtis and Roman L. Hruska, and California's Reagan in the refrain: "*They* all do it, *they're* all the same."

But Sam Ervin didn't, and wasn't.

18

During my years with the ACLU I watched "strategic think-ing" beguile the minds of otherwise brilliant lawyers who, when they could not predict an outcome, feared it and found rational reasons to counsel "no action" rather than risk defeat.

Looking back it is easy to understand how the ACLU came to its conclusions. We all learn to use convenient analogies in self-defense. As a student leader speaking to incoming freshmen at the University of Alabama, shortly before the Supreme Court's 1954 school desegregation decision, I equated, and then con-demned, dictators—"Communist or Nazi or Fascist." After say-ing that, I felt free to attack the "tactics of leaders of the Ku Klux Klan. . . ." But I went no further.

"Did there come a time . . ." is a lawyer's way of asking "whether." After the witness answers yes the lawyer comes right out with what he wants to know and asks, "When?"

I don't know when personal prosperity, pragmatism, and sen-sitivity to "Communist" charges fatally undermined liberalism. I believe that the tragedy occurred at 2:40 A.M., Wednesday, May 8, 1940. I know that after the vote on Elizabeth Gurley Flynn, the ACLU began to dodge "forty-acres-and-a-mule" economic questions, and the phrase "not a civil liberties issue" became an exclusionary rule. Perhaps that was an inevitable result of the 1886 to 1901 counterrevolution.* Perhaps the dream began to come apart in Eden. But by the time I reached my early twenties, Jim Folsom was referring to most upper-class, stylishly comfortable liberals as "parlor pinks." His friend (and my candidate) George Hawkins agreed. So did George Wallace. But as far as fearfulness was concerned, the color pink seemed a bit generous. Folsom believed liberals and Dixiecrats were similar. Of the latter he said, "Boy, they'll sleep with 'em at night, but they won't let 'em sit down with 'em at breakfast. That's the difference between them and us."

There were other differences. I was a Democrat, not a Red. Weaned on the work ethic, I even favored economic incentives and the private ownership of property. But I wanted everyone to own some property, no one to inherit too much, and an economic floor under all God's children as a birthright.

There was nothing "subversive" about Miss Flynn. A founding member of the ACLU, she was proud of her beliefs and her political affiliation. She broadcast them far and wide. In 1939, with full knowledge of her Communist party membership, the ACLU voters *unanimously* reelected her to their board.

In 1940 she was fifty. By then her glistening black hair was turning gray, but she was still described by her contemporaries as strikingly beautiful—and totally committed to the rights of the poor.

---

*In 1886 the Supreme Court defined the Fourteenth Amendment's phrase "no person shall be deprived of life, liberty or property without due process of law or the equal protection of law" to include within the word "person," the word "corporation." Ten years later it ruled that racial segregation was constitutional. The Populist rebellion, Eugene V. Debs's Pullman strike of 1894, and the Democratic nomination of William Jennings Bryan in 1896 frightened the very rich. Two years later the nation went to war against the Spanish, and laid claim to their far-flung island empire which included Cuba.

Restrictions on the right to vote were not confined to the South. In 1900

As the New Deal died, parts of the government became the National Security League. At first these moves were tentative. Then, boldly, the chairman of the House Committee on Un-American Activities (about whom liberals sang "Ol' Martin Dies got swastikas for his eyes. . . .") charged that the ACLU and its founding executive director, Roger Baldwin, were linked to the Communist party.

In October 1939, a fearful ACLU staff lawyer wrote to Morris Ernst, one of the ACLU's general counsels, urging the organization to take "advantage of any opportunity we have of clearing ourselves after the job he [Dies] has done on us."

Ernst put through the "1940 Resolution" which required the ACLU's staff and "governing committees" to defend civil liberties "in all aspects and all places." It forbade election to those who "justify or tolerate the denial of civil liberties by dictatorships abroad." A member of "any political organization which supports totalitarian dictatorships in any country or who, by his public declarations, indicates his support of such a principle," was barred from the ACLU hierarchy. During the ensuing three decades, equal enforcement of that "loyalty oath" would have eliminated members of most Washington and New York corporate law firms and all Democrats and Republicans, for their foreign policy supported "totalitarian dictatorships" abroad. But the resolution was directed at revolution and domestic Reds, not rogues or the rest of us.

Miss Flynn described the ACLU's national committee which ratified the resolution as "a carefully selected list of well-known liberals." In the *Sunday Worker*, March 17, 1940, she wrote,

---

northern state "progressives" attacked electoral corruption by requiring voters to register before election day. That made last-minute decisions to vote impossible. The poorest northern voters were not literate in English. Their states moved to the complicated Australian balloting system where ballots were provided only at the polls and only to those who had preregistered. As Penn Kimball points out in *The Disconnected*, between 1864 and 1900 the *average* presidential turnout was 76.8 percent. After 1900 the percentage steadily declined.

"[T]hey looked like an old men's home out for an airing." She continued, "[T]oday they are no longer heretics, nonconformists, radicals—they are respectable. They cooperate with the Department of Justice; they play with Mr. Dies for a whitewash. . . . They may not know it, but they are fighting for their system, capitalism. They scuttle civil liberties when their security and comfort are menaced. . . ." Two days later, in *New Masses*, she wrote that there had been an "infiltration" of those "out of sympathy with the traditional position of the ACLU. There are so many wealthy people on the board today that I feel I am to be tried by a 'blue ribbon jury.' . . . When labor was weak they could afford to be the benign, detached liberals demanding the rights of labor. . . ."

On the night of Tuesday, May 7, 1940, eight months after Stalin's pact with Hitler had given rise to Jewish fury, that anger, anti-Communism, fear of the right wing, and liberal pragmatism came together at the City Club of New York, 55 West Forty-fourth Street, where the board of directors of the ACLU met to judge their only Communist member and to become the natural, if unacknowledged, parent of cold-war liberalism.

At eight that evening Miss Flynn's "trial" began. At 2:40 the next morning the board was deadlocked. The ACLU's chairman, the Reverend John Hayes Holmes, broke the tie. By a one-vote margin Miss Flynn was expelled.

The membership of the twenty-year-old organization contained an influential part of the nation's articulate intellectual leadership. Then, as now, columnists, editors, and governmental leaders seeking to justify their positions wrote "*even* the ACLU has said." That night the organization stamped the exclusion of Communists from liberal organizations and labor unions as "Intellectually Respectable."

Internally, the decision was disastrous. According to Corliss Lamont, a board member from 1932 to 1954, those in our New York national office who hired staff "checked with J. Edgar Hoover as to whether one individual or another was a member of the Communist party."

In 1952, a conservative, Irving Ferman, was hired to open the ACLU's Washington office which, twenty years later, I would head. Ferman's mandate was to keep the ACLU off government and American Legion subversive lists. A highly skilled lobbyist-lawyer and a believer in equal rights, Ferman succeeded. He had to become friends with the FBI's top men, share drinks with Senator Joseph McCarthy in McCarthy's kitchen, and ask McCarthy not to praise the ACLU, for that would prove embarrassing.

During Ferman's first year in Washington, the ACLU in New York issued a statement saying there was no civil liberties issue involved in the pending execution of alleged atomic spies Julius and Ethel Rosenberg. In thousands of death-penalty cases the ACLU had taken no position at all. But the organization faced the "Rosenberg problem" with more apparent fear than did the Rosenbergs, and they faced death.

After I moved to Washington, Ferman told me of his continued belief in the Rosenbergs' guilt. And of his continued concern about that ACLU proclamation, for he believed President Truman relied on it to refuse to commute the Rosenbergs' death sentence.

In 1964, when I joined the organization, no one mentioned the Rosenbergs or any "1940 Resolution" or any "Miss Flynn." But I had begun to learn that fear governs the lives of almost all liberal bureaucrats. Often more literate and glib than their conservative counterparts, they are also more able to rationalize the vicious infighting which takes place in college English departments and faraway swampy jungles.

～～～～～～

Now, almost thirty-five years after the trial of Elizabeth Gurley Flynn, and twenty years after the execution of the Rosenbergs, Sam Ervin was trying to discover the causes of the Watergate burglary. Yet there was to be no investigation of the Justice Department or—except for Congressman Lucien N. Nedzi's friendly, secret inquiry—of the CIA. So Watergate Committee subpoenas directed at the Hughes organization were vetoed, for the phrase "national security" caused even Ol' Sam to draw back, and bright, shimmering facts skittered away under hiding places which senators and witnesses from the World War II generation called "points in time."

In 1973 the ACLU *was* the liberal community. Nine years had passed since I opened its southern office. Then, ninety percent of its national legal work consisted of sterile, antiseptic, riskless, friend-of-the-court briefs. As we abandoned that approach, underwrote total case expenses, and directly supplied clients with lawyers whose obligations thereupon ran to them rather than the ACLU, we entered uncharted fields and acquired mass membership—250,000 members. Almost all were white, well-educated (more than 62 percent had graduate education) and well-to-do. Almost half were in the professions: journalism, 1 percent; law, 7 percent; medicine, 7 percent; and teaching, 31 percent.

ACLU members ran the Americans for Democratic Action and the American Association of University Professors. And their members ran the ACLU. They wrote editorials, reported news, and otherwise shaped national opinion. They constituted 12.88 percent of the delegates to the 1972 Democratic Convention.

As the membership grew, the board expanded to include people and viewpoints from west and south of the Manhattan Stockade. Now, if they called for impeachment, and the ACLU campaigned for it, the liberals would begin to write, to explain, to turn a cause into a campaign and the campaign into a movement. In the topsy-turvy world of cold-war liberalism, the ACLU set the style. It could even stamp "Intellectually Respectable" across the word *impeachment*.

Together with Arlie Schardt, whom I had hired to assist me in the ACLU's Washington office, I had spoken to affiliate membership gatherings across the country. The ACLU of Southern California came out for impeachment first. Louisiana second. Then came New York and Michigan. Most southern affiliates were with us. Most others were undecided. Chairman Ennis told me he was certain that the board would take no action. Neier doubted that they would, and he took no position.

At first the agenda they prepared included no time for the issue. On September 7 it was amended to include one hour for the debate. On Saturday morning, September 29, the board assembled in the basement of New York's Barbizon-Plaza Hotel and altered the next day's agenda "to make the impeachment of the President the first item of business."

Marvin Schacter, a Los Angeles clothing manufacturer, led the proponents. A short, heavyset man with a trim mustache, Schacter speaks with clipped precision. He charged that during "the past twenty-five to thirty years, we have become accustomed to illegal acts on the part of the government." The ACLU "had not had enough sense of outrage. . . ."

During the six-hour debate, I marveled at Schacter's accuracy. My immediate predecessor in the Washington office, lawyer Lawrence Speiser, told the board he preferred the courts as a forum. For more than a decade he had presented the ACLU's case to the Congress. As the minutes read, "He . . . suggested that Congress is the worst possible forum for our concerns right now."

Monroe Freedman, a law professor also from Washington, felt "we should not express our individual feelings through the institution of the ACLU."

And "David Isbell [a partner in Covington and Burling, Washington's largest law firm], also advocating no action, stated that we should avoid the self-delusion that what we say will come about." He believed that we should condemn Nixon's acts, but not Nixon. "Pragmatically, he noted that there would be a good chance of acquittal, and thereby vindication of the President."

I had five minutes. Most of these people were my friends. But I had to confront them, to bring them face to face with the reality that an untried Nixon in office meant the death of the republic.

I began by reminding them that Presidents are teachers. When Truman played the piano, children learned to play the piano. Eisenhower played golf, so golf became a major sport. Kennedy said, "ask not" and individual citizens tried to "get the country moving again." Nixon was teaching our children to lie and to cheat and to degrade the Constitution. We *all* knew that. We *all* knew that he sought to implicate all of us in that degradation.

I was desperate to help them understand. To see ourselves solely as representatives of the minority was to be blindered by ghetto thinking. There were scores of rational reasons for others not to move. For us, there was none. Our very purpose—the defense of the Constitution—was at stake. Rapidly, my words tumbling over one another, I emphasized the process. We were seeking to have the President tried. We knew what he had done. He had told us.

We should go to the people. The process was political, not narrowly legal. The trial itself would bring the people the facts. The premise of Jeffersonian democracy is that with facts, the people will find their own way.

Nixon's crimes were not petty thefts. They were offenses against the Bill of Rights, the highest of crimes against the people and their Constitutional system.

I turned to what each of them knew. From New York to Neshoba County, Mississippi, we had condemned law enforcement officials. In California and Texas, when deputy sheriffs had deprived Spanish-speaking citizens of their civil rights, we had sued. We had sought the discharge of police chiefs and had spoken out against public officials.

The President was not a helpless criminal defendant; he was the most powerful man in the world, the nation's chief law enforcement officer, "the biggest kid on the block!"

Our duty was clear, if we really believed in applying to the powerful the standards we applied to cops on the beat, deputy sheriffs, and a Black Belt county judge. I bore down.

"In 1971, *in your name*, I prosecuted James Dennis Herndon, the probate judge of Greene County, Alabama, for contempt of a Supreme Court order which assured blacks the equal right to run for office."

Abruptly I sat down. There was dead silence. Then came applause, then thunderous applause, then they rose. And liberalism came alive.

On the shuttle flight to Washington I tumbled into my seat, turned to Camille, and said, "From here on in, it's all downhill."

The vote had been overwhelming—fifty-five to five. Then the five abstained. Arlie Schardt, who had worked as hard as I had, brought from our office our enumeration of Nixon's high crimes. They served as the basis of the ACLU resolution. Now we would begin to distribute political weapons—from learned literature to bumper-stickers and buttons which bore that simple message: IMPEACH NIXON.

As that board moved, the nation took a long step forward. In ten months the resolution of the House Judiciary Committee would parallel the one we wrote on that September Sunday.

And it *was* downhill. During the uphill struggle against segregation, Birmingham's police commissioner, Bull Connor, had said, "Give 'em an inch and they'll take a mile." He was wrong. We tried to take it all.

I pressed for a newspaper advertising campaign. In the liberal world "the *Times*" is more than the medium and the message. It is the gospel. That was the place to begin making "impeachment" respectable. But a full-page in the Sunday *New York Times* cost $12,500, and contributions to "cause" advertisements rarely paid expenses. The ACLU's never had.

Trust the people, I urged. When that plea failed, I went to philanthropist and General Motors heir Stewart P. Mott for underwriting. Then I telephoned Ira Glasser of the New York Civil Liberties Union to tell him that if the ACLU lost money Mott would cover the loss. That argument, "heads we win, tails Mott loses," helped liberals trust the people.

Glasser and I spent hours on the telephone working up the copy. An anonymous volunteer from a Madison Avenue advertising agency handled the layout. Neier edited and Ennis signed.

On Sunday, October 14, the message in white lettering on a soft gray background leaped from a million pages:

WHY IT IS NECESSARY TO IMPEACH PRESIDENT NIXON
AND HOW IT CAN BE DONE.

By nightfall thousands of people had written checks to the ACLU.

On Friday, October 19, we reran the advertisement.* Then we placed it in newspapers across the land. Some did well, some did poorly, but when the books were tallied, they showed that the series which cost $106,793 had brought a return of $138,928. Even the thousands of detailed printed booklets we wrote in the Washington office and distributed to explain the facts and the law to national leaders made money. And that profitmaking, membership-gaining impeachment campaign taught some within the ACLU to trust the people.

More importantly, those advertisements explained the Constitutional remedy. Their timing—twice in *The New York Times* during the week before Cox was fired and once in the *Los Angeles Times* on the day after—was happenstance, one of those gratuitous, unpredictable accidents which occur when you decide to do the simple, right thing, to go forward and let the people be the jury.

In Washington I had given up trying to explain that. I had learned to nod and say thank you to the political people who smiled knowingly and said, "Good timing."

---

*On November 2 we changed the format to "There is only one thing that can stop impeachment now. Your silence." On November 18 we switched to "Congress is responding to your demand for impeachment. Slowly."

19

It took no time at all for Attorney General Reasonable to accept with humility the applause which flowed from Vice President Agnew's *nolo contendere* ("no contest," meaning no trial and no jail) plea. The Constitution drew no distinction between the nation's two top public servants, but Attorney General Elliot Richardson did. He decided that the Justice Department could seek the indictment of the Vice President (for whom Richardson did not work) prior to his impeachment. He simultaneously found that the Justice Department could not seek the indictment of the President (for whom Richardson did work) until after his impeachment.

By October 10, 1973, when the deal was consummated, Agnew was gasping for the breath to say yes. Information surreptitiously released from the Justice Department destroyed his Republican party base and, after weeks of "twisting slowly, slowly in the wind," the copped plea was a comparatively dignified way to leave office.

Overnight, Richardson's Watergate-degraded Justice Department was in high cotton. Maryland's honest young United

States attorney, George Beall, was hailed for nailing the Vice President and Henry Petersen seemed tough and aggressive. Within a few months Petersen and Nixon would proclaim, "I am not a whore," and "I'm not a crook," respectively. And Beall would be criticized for plagiarizing the speech on legal ethics which he delivered to a meeting of the American Bar Association.

To modern lawyers, all settlements seem reasonable. The first thing they learn in law school is fear of jury trials. Because average-citizen juries are "risky" and "unpredictable," students are taught that skilled lawyers settled their cases and unskilled lawyers try theirs. With compromise their redeeming social virtue, lawyers and judges retain discretionary power to make deals and, with it, ultimate control over the justice system. So lawyers, like buyers and sellers of used cars, get and give "good deals," and they coincidentally deprive democratic juries of the right to return verdicts and thereby set community standards. Richardson's phrases of Frankfurterism were new-car—and Rolls-Royce at that. He saved us from a "Constitutional confrontation" and "crisis" (other ways of saying "trial") and he was universally cheered by lawyers, even those who watched him explain the Agnew deal on our office television set.

Later, at a dinner party given by the Richardsons for mutual friends, Camille complimented our brilliant host on the beauty and setting of his home, overlooking rapids on the Potomac's Great Falls. She laughed as he said, yes, and it's only a few minutes from the White House. My mind flashed back twenty years to one of Big Jim Folsom's future highway commissioners and his thirteen-second dance across the room balancing a tray while spreading cream cheese on crackers. "Yessuh, Guvenuh! Yessuh!"

Neither the people nor their Constitution was as precariously fragile as Richardson's hold on power. And Nixon's. Nixon feared Agnew's impeachment would be a prelude to his own, and it was Richardson's fine, rational mind which saved him.

For Nixon, Richardson repurchased the vice-presidency.

Agnew entered his *nolo* plea and was fined $10,000. A Paducah, Kentucky, deputy court clerk contrasted Agnew's treatment with the jail sentence received by an eighteen-year-old girl who had stolen a bottle of cheap perfume and learned that "it's the poor what gets the blame."

And many of my friends hoped that Nixon would replace Agnew with Sir Elliot Richardson. They desperately yearned for a prince to trust—and for a time called Camelot. They got Gomorrah and the tinsel touch of Disneyworld.

⟡⟡⟡⟡⟡⟡

I was in Howard Hughes's Las Vegas for another speech on impeachment. In our Dunes Hotel room Camille and I watched our leaders applaud Mr. President on television. They had been summoned to hear the Western world's prime criminal suspect announce his vice-presidential selection.

I laughed when CBS told us that it had preempted its October 12 "Friday Night Movie," *Dracula.*

"Camille! Stand behind me while I aim a cross at the television set."

Following his presentation of Gerald Ford, Nixon announced that refreshments would be served. In anger I flipped off the set. "Let them eat cake!"

They were so happy. They didn't have to vote on the impeachment of Agnew. And Gerald Ford was the vindication of their values. His virtues, their virtues; his vices, their vices.

By definition these (and all) politicians are "nice guys." Most are hard-working, petty-cash-honest midwives who believe it is their duty to rise above principle, to broker differences and to settle disputes. But I had lost my ability to identify with the members of this new, well-paid political class. They were so desperate to stay in office, to keep the lid on, to fend off the people and to blunt their will, that until the very end of the impeachment process they remained hear-no, see-no, speak-no bystanders.

Some feared Nixon. Because he controlled the Justice Department, he retained "influence" over them. And he simply had to have tape recordings of "leaders" who had spoken to him (and others) privately about "private matters"; tapes which would eventually cause his downfall, but which also would serve to prolong his tenure; tapes, the retention of which Nixon apparently believed afforded him more advantages than risks.

As part of his defense, Nixon invited the worst in each of us into his White House for refreshments, to josh, jostle, wink, and nod in understanding. He saw in everyone what he saw in himself. When the people said to each other, "They all do it," Nixon said to himself, "Them too," and that was his ultimately fatal misjudgment.

~~~~~~~~~~

Remote, courtly, and fuzzy-tweedy like a prep school headmaster, Archie Cox was an unexciting teacher. He was a settler, not a fighter. His years as a labor arbitrator and mediator must have made Nixon feel secure. So when the courts ordered Nixon to produce the tapes of a few of his conversations, Nixon knew that Cox was no Maximum John or Ol' Sam. With Richardson as his broker, Nixon offered to let Mississippi's Senator John C. Stennis review, verify, and report on the tapes. But Cox refused to go along with the "Stennis-listens-you-don't" deal. So Nixon had three available options: defy the court order; appeal to the Supreme Court; or fire the supervising prosecutor.

He couldn't appeal and risk a collision course with the Supreme Court, for if he lost that appeal, defiance meant disaster. And even though Cox's brother Maxwell's New York law firm, Davis and Cox, represented Hughes, Cox's staff was looking into Nixon's sidekick, Bebe Rebozo, who had secreted $100,000 of Hughes's cash in a lock box. And only Bebe and Nixon knew what else was secreted in his mind.

The house in Washington, some property in Destin, four Redskin and eight Alabama season tickets were our appreciating assets. Depreciating assets included one listing La-Z-Boy chair and a wonderful old color television set. To me, television, like McGuffey's Reader, the Blue Back Speller, and McDonald's hamburgers, provides a nation of nomads with a common bond. And football. I had carefully set aside this Saturday, October 20, for Alabama football.

Five years had passed since the Saturday when the Warren Court required Alabama, including Probate Judge Herndon, to put the names of blacks on the state's general election ballot. I had spent the second half of that year's televised Alabama-Tennessee game in the Supreme Court clerk's office. Now Archibald Cox had called a press conference; and so it went with Alabama football.

Cox began to speak. His informality emphasized a quality of bewildered, wistful confusion as though the President's misconduct were unexpected. The dynamic was simple decency. Cox, confronted, had no problem with his "moral compass." He and Nixon were on a collision course. Cox wouldn't resign. If that presented problems for Attorney General Richardson, Richardson would have to speak for himself.

Before Cox finished, Camille noticed tears streaming down my face. Lawyer Cox, like Bernstein, Ervin, Sirica, Wills, and Woodward had done his own job, on his own terms. And the world would orbit around him.

After that press conference, Archibald Cox may have expected the people to return to football. They did. But millions of them also wrote, telephoned, or telegraphed their congressmen, who, like Nixon, were astounded.

In midafternoon Richardson was ordered to fire Cox. Directly confronted by Cox and by Nixon, with opportunities to rationalize stripped away, Richardson said "no," "now," and "I quit."

Next in the Justice Department's chain of command was William D. Ruckelshaus. General Haig delivered the order of their commander in chief. Ruckelshaus responded "no." To "You're fired," he said, "I quit."

Nixon was running short of soldiers when the order ricocheted to the red-bearded, conservative solicitor general, Robert H. Bork.

I had met Bork in the Supreme Court clerk's office on Saturday, August 4, 1973, just before Burt Neuborne of the New York Civil Liberties Union and I were to try to end the bombing in Cambodia in a case to be argued in Justice Marshall's chambers. In the clerk's office I offered to settle. Bork looked at me quizzically. If we agreed to let Nixon bomb and kill anyplace where Bork and I were not, for three days, three hours, and twenty minutes, I said, would Nixon agree to kill no one for at least three years? Bork smiled, rejected that and later offers.

Later, in Howard Levy's case, Bork would argue to the Supreme Court (and beat me five to three) that the charge against Levy—willful disobedience of a lawful command to teach medicine to Special Forces aidmen—was constitutional.

Now, on the night of October 20, 1973, Richardson and Ruckelshaus urged Bork to obey the command which they refused to obey. Bork was consistent. Like a "good soldier" he figured that because Presidents were entitled to give orders, they were entitled to have someone carry them out. That Saturday night, the solicitor general became that "someone." During the war a poster asked WHAT WOULD HAPPEN IF THEY GAVE A WAR AND NOBODY CAME? Now I knew the answer. Bob Bork would come.

Bright, straightforward, and personally kind, Bork, by firing Cox, returned the Justice Department to its commander in chief. That seemed proper to Richardson. It saved the presidency for Nixon and his still-unconfirmed vice-presidential nominee, Gerald Ford. But for the rest of his life the conservative Robert Bork would be remembered as "The Man Who Fired Cox."

The liberal lawyer Elliot Richardson would survive, survive, survive. Even after Richardson was fired he would not criticize Nixon. He rationalized the dismissal of Cox as "understandable, if wrongheaded," and he attributed no "bad faith to the President," who, when Richardson met him in his office to resign, said, "Brezhnev would never understand it if I let Cox defy my instructions."

From Washington and state houses across the land there came hardly a whisper of political leadership. But in Atlanta a governor named Jimmy Carter cut through the silence. Pausing to chat with reporters on his way to church, he said Richard Nixon had "committed an action that warrants impeachment." He casually remarked that "[a] man of integrity can find little hope in the Nixon administration."

Monday, August 6, I met with a group of liberal lobbyists at Ralph Nader's Capitol Hill office. I urged that we press for an immediate vote on impeachment. Under Jefferson's *Manual on Parliamentary Practice and Rules of the House of Representatives*, the House could proceed against Nixon on the basis of "common fame." If the firing of the prosecutor wasn't an "obstruction of justice" then there could be none. Besides, resolutions for impeachment were privileged. Even if defeated they could be reintroduced daily and voted up or down.

But "now is not the time" was the response (as it had been in Birmingham). Wait until Ford's vice-presidential nomination has been confirmed, they urged. Transfer of party control would be "partisan." Besides, House Speaker Carl Albert was in the line of succession and he didn't want to be President.

Albert didn't seem to want to be Speaker, let alone President. He could step down. Before the Senate convicted Nixon there would be plenty of time to select a new Speaker.

But in the end the liberals decided not to push for an immediate vote. I looked around the room, shook my head, felt terribly sorry about these people, and left.

Billions of dollars had been impounded by Nixon. In the South, where more than half of the nation's poor people lived, a partisan but Constitutionally authorized transfer of presidential power would mean that protein-starved, naked little children, black and white, might be able to eat something more nourishing than rational reasons. And these were their lobbyists.

During the next forty-eight hours, twenty-two impeachment resolutions were introduced in the House, but liberals and conservatives alike believed Nixon would "ride it out." The privileged resolutions were routinely assigned to the House Judiciary Committee, which nonpartisanly scheduled them for consideration after the confirmation of Gerald Ford. The under-privileged waited in line behind Nixon's man, not because of the strength of Nixon, but because liberal leaders had forgotten that there are some things worth being partisan about.

~~~~~~~~

Whether you pass by Newark in an automobile, through it on a train, or over it in a airplane, the sensation is despair. From the ground, its dirty acrid air, and from the air, its after-the-bomb-struck ground are reminders of what the "better class" left behind as they moved up and out. In stark contrast to the Watergate apartments which were home sweet home to new-rich Nixonites, Newark was home to Peter Rodino.

In across-the-river Manhattan, politicians played King of the Mountain. Rodino played hard at remaining King of the Garden State's compost heap. Backed by organized labor in a city run by organized life insurance, manufacturing, oil, and crime, he served his people. Increasingly, "his people" were black.

After *The Godfather* won the Academy Award, Italians who broke into politics were no less suspect than Italians who broke into song. So occasionally there were whispers about Rodino's vulnerability to FBI and Justice Department blackmail. Rodino had more luck than Nixon, for those FBI-released transcripts of the New Jersey Mafia leaders' wiretapped conversations (which diverted attention from the King-Ali wiretap) said, "[T]hey ain't going to cross Rodino. I can't stop that boy."

In 1972, Elizabeth Holtzman, thirty, had made "that boy," Rodino, sixty-five, chairman of the House Judiciary Committee. She had defeated predecessor chairman Emanuel Celler in his Brooklyn district. With Celler's ancient, rusty-liberal grip on the committee broken, Rodino released a bit of the chairman's power to restive liberal subcommittee chairmen like California's Don Edwards and Wisconsin's Robert Kastenmeier. They juggled that bit of power as though it were an exquisite but too-hot hors d'oeuvre. Issuing subpoenas and asking embarrassing questions was beyond them, so, by default rather than design, Rodino retained committee control.

But his hometown congressional bailiwick was as insecure as a bicycle parked on a Newark side street. The state's newly elected Democratic leadership, the blacks' desire to have a black majority congressional district, and the disdainful lack of interest in his future displayed by his fellow New Jersey liberals made Rodino's political life uninsurable.

Jerry Zeifman, the committee counsel, had faith in Rodino's political skills. General Rommel, Zeifman told me, favored Germans for orderly warfare. They accepted discipline and were willing to die for an abstract concept. "But," said Zeifman in his special reconstruction of history, "Rommel would rather have had against him an entire German regiment than one ragtag, Italian partisan using a long knife to defend himself, his family, and," Zeifman paused for effect, "his congressional district."

Zeifman was Rodino's employee-lawyer. Lois D'Andre and Francis O'Brien were his employee-confidants. Rodino was as encircled in Washington as he was in the Newark servant quarters where his black constituents and some Italian-Americans lived.

But Rodino was ever so cautious. It took him two months to hire a lawyer. "Why the hell doesn't he move?" I asked one staff member, then another.

"He's going to give you a lawyer for Christmas," came the embarrassed reply. Rodino was trying to find the perfect non-partisan for counsel for the committee. He shopped, delayed, then shopped some more. He favored a New Jersey judge, then an old friend, then another, then Albert Jenner, the Chicago Republican with whom I had served on an American Bar Association section council. Jenner, an excellent trial lawyer, had been a counsel for the Warren Commission. He wound up in the role of minority counsel.

By mid-December, Zeifman was responding to direct inquiries in increasingly elliptical parables. Finally, one evening, I was with Rodino and Zeifman. They asked what I thought of John Doar.

"Hire him!" came my quick reply.

My friend, John Doar, a Republican, had served in the Kennedy Justice Department. He had worked under Eisenhower and Johnson too, but his loyalties ran to Camelot—as did mine.

Doar's special talent is his ability to organize documentary evidence. With enough of that around to convict, let alone impeach Nixon, the House Impeachment Inquiry hired no staff investigators and conducted no *original* inquiry. Like a Florida fisherman searching the coastline of Cuba for a safe haven from an impending storm, Doar approached Nixon's men carefully, as though he understood Haldeman's fearful remark to Dean: "Once the toothpaste is out of the tube, it's going to be very hard to get it back in." Doar knew that to impeach Nixon, all he had to do was organize the readily available evidence and lay it before the committee. So organized, he would be ready for an immediate Senate trial.

Perhaps Doar really thought he was a nonpartisan, an "open-minded," "judgelike" lawyer. I knew him well enough to leave him alone. I told job applicants that the mention of my name to Doar would do them no good. One of them ignored that advice. Doar shook his head slowly, told her of our friendship. I was "partisan" and that presented him problems, so he declined to hire her. Another applicant, Marilyn Askin, a lawyer whose husband served on the ACLU board, told me, "It was the darndest thing. He wouldn't hire me because of the ACLU, but when I walked through the office the only books I saw on the desks were the impeachment books you published."

Nixon's Southern Strategy had undercut Doar's deepest beliefs. If he wanted to appear disinterested, that was his business. But I laughed aloud as I wondered at the absurd world of "public relations." If Nixon were to appear before the committee, Doar would be in the "nonpartisan" position of Mississippi's former Governor Ross Barnett, who, in 1962, had cast himself as the state university's registrar. After the Justice Department flew James Meredith to Jackson it was John Doar and James Joseph Patrick McShane, the nation's chief marshal, who escorted the university's first black student-to-be through a hostile mass of "Dixie" singers to register. Barnett, dressed in a severely sincere black suit, sat waiting for them at the end of an upstairs hallway in "The New L. P. Woolfolk Downtown State Office Building." The elevator doors opened and out they came. Doar, six feet three inches tall, looking like a young John Wayne, white; McShane, five feet eleven inches tall, looking like an ex-New York cop and prizefighter (both of which he had been), white; and between them James Meredith, five feet seven inches tall, black. They marched. Down the hallway lined with cameras, bright lights, and newsmen sat a seemingly disinterested, fair-minded, decorously polite, Ol' Ross the Registrar. As they stood in front of him, the governor, half rising from his straight-backed chair, smiled and said, "Uh-huh, and now just which one of you gentlemen is James H. Meredith?"

∽∽∽∽∽∽∽

During the Christmas recess of Congress, Arlie Schardt dutifully notified our local affiliates to make certain "our home folks" got in touch with their congressmen, most of whom were ambassadors to their districts, not representatives from them. Washington was "home." And, no matter how overwhelming the sentiment against Nixon, it was hard to hear "homefolks" while humming "Hail to the Head Coach."

Burns W. Roper provided them with a political hearing aid.

Roper Reports is a private survey service, paid for by fifty, mostly corporate, subscribers. Conducted ten times a year, it cost me slightly less than the $5,000 that liberal philanthropist Stewart Mott contributed for it, but it was more help than a year of living-color deathly commentary from CBS's Eric Sevareid. Roper found out that 4 out of 5 (79 percent) of the 2,020 he surveyed believed that one or more of thirteen charges against Nixon was serious and that Nixon might bear responsibility for them. Tampering with the justice system caused the most concern. Contrary to common Washington beliefs, financial finagling—income taxes and the mispayment of public funds for Nixon's San Clemente and Key Biscayne castles—ran second.

Only 52 percent "guessed" right when they were asked to

explain the impeachment process. That figure included two-thirds of the college graduates polled. When Roper's interviewers explained that after the House impeached Nixon, he would be tried by the Senate, 44 percent of the people said they wanted Nixon impeached; 45 percent did not. But of that 45 percent *more than half* were opposed to impeachment because they felt it "would be too destructive to the country."

Blacks overwhelmingly favored bringing Nixon to trial. Next came blue-collar workers. Often looked down on by better-educated liberals, the "hardhats" hadn't been educated away from the rights and wrongs they had learned as children. They had voted Nixon in. Now they were ready to try him.

The message to us was clear: emphasize the obstruction of justice; explain the impeachment process; and stress impeachment as the nation's only way out and therefore its least destructive course.

I provided the *Roper Reports* results to Bill Kovach of *The New York Times*. They appeared on page one, Sunday, January 6, 1974. That story explained the case to representatives who needed an interpreter to understand the millions of messages they had received, thousands of which remained in unopened mail sacks.

In March, Roper reported that 61 percent of the people understood the impeachment process. As their understanding went up, Nixon's chances went down. For the first time a clear majority (53 percent) favored impeachment. Those who feared that impeachment would be "too destructive to the country" dropped to 18 percent.

For representatives who feared or favored Nixon, the results were ominous. Few voters said they would vote for a representative because he favored Nixon. But one out of every four (24 percent) said they would vote against a representative who voted against impeachment.

Still I kept hearing Washington's liberals say, "The people are so apathetic. Why aren't *they* out there marching?" And with good sense mistaken for apathy, columnists and commentators worked overtime to soothe and explain away the politicians' uneasy fears. No matter the facts, television seemed to homogenize Washington's leaders into a blandness which even the Founders might not have survived.

Two centuries after *Common Sense,* had Tom Paine been the regular commentator on the "CBS Evening News" he might have said, "Although these are the times that try the souls of a large number of men, a recent survey conducted by Kings Research Associates demonstrates that not more than 66.6 percent of men believe that they have souls. Of these men who believe they have souls, only 34.3 percent of them believe that their souls presently are being tried." Or as an NBC stand-in for Brinkley, Paine might have told us, "Valley Forge is not in fact a place from which only summer soldiers and sunshine patriots flee. A number of others have left perhaps because this has been, in fact, the coldest winter with the heaviest snowfall recorded in thirty-four years. Indeed, General Washington himself hoped for a little sunshine. The previous record low for Valley Forge was . . ."

Northwest of Valley Forge and west of Newark there was Grand Rapids, Michigan, the home of Gerald Ford, fine furniture, members of the conservative Dutch Reformed Church, an ACLU chapter, and a persistent political loser named Richard F. Vander Veen, who believed in himself and the people.

On January 18, I was in Grand Rapids to speak to local ACLU members. Vander Veen, the Democratic candidate for Ford's vacated House seat, was in the audience. For sixty years that district's congressional seat had been filled by a Republican. Before the meeting several ACLU members insisted that Vander Veen had no chance. People often say their side will lose to deaden the pain of defeat. Some love to lose, for losing is one way to remain not responsible. I bore down on Watergate and impeachment and how badly Grand Rapids needed a President and what kind of a campaign I thought would win. That night Vander Veen told me the campaign I described was to be his campaign—"a referendum on the moral bankruptcy of Richard Nixon."

In other districts the Democrats seemed uncomfortable with

Watergate. They played it down or avoided it, believing they would benefit from it naturally. Democrat John P. Murtha ran in Pennsylvania. Washington-based "experts" advised Murtha to change his slogan. He did. The "One Honest Man Can Make a Difference" sign came down. "Come Back Home—Vote Democratic" went up. Murtha eked in by 220 votes.

Monday, February 18, was election day in Grand Rapids. I telephoned Vander Veen. "*The New York Times* says you've got a chance. I still think you'll win."

"I'll win," he said. He told me of a weekend Bingo game. Total strangers had put down their cards and rushed across the room to shake his hand and pledge support.

On Tuesday, Vander Veen drew a winning card, and the next morning *The New York Times* headlined the warning to Congress. MICHIGAN DEMOCRAT WINS IN VOTING FOR FORD'S SEAT. The day after that the headline read: LOSS OF FORD SEAT SHAKES G.O.P.; DEMOCRATS PREDICT SWEEP IN FALL.

20

From the very beginning, I had known that the Justice Department would be Nixon's final line of defense. Under the "take care" clause of the Constitution ("[H]e shall take Care that the Laws be faithfully executed") he really was the nation's chief law enforcement officer. Those who wrote the Constitution had too much sense to expect a President to prosecute himself, so they provided for impeachment by the House of Representatives and, thereafter, trial by the Senate. That meant that as long as the House failed to act, Nixon remained in ultimate charge. Sam Ervin said the situation was "calculated to pollute justice" and "to make justice weep." The prosecution was "in the hands of men who held office at the pleasure of the President. . . ." The defense was in the hands of men paid from the President's funds.

In late November or early December 1973, five months after Special Prosecutor Cox accepted Silbert's resignation from his staff, Silbert's immediate superior in the Justice Department, United States Attorney Harold H. Titus, told the President of his intention to resign. That was not made public. When Titus left office on December 31, at midnight, Nixon made no move to fill the vacancy, so the district judges, Sirica included, were required by law to fill it. They immediately (and unanimously) promoted the number-two man in the office—Silbert. After that Nixon nominated Silbert to be United States Attorney. In any city but Washington, the promotion by the suspect of the prosecutor whom he had fooled would have been a thigh-slapper. The Washington reaction ranged from unconcern to outright applause.

Hearings are almost never held on nominees for United States Attorney. But the Watergate case and the fact that Silbert had been in charge of it made hearings on his nomination inevitable. With impeachment facing him, Nixon should have been avoiding every risk of a second front. Despite the influence of the Committee on the Judiciary's chairman, Senator James O. Eastland of Mississippi, it was there that FBI Director Patrick Gray's nomination had "twisted slowly, slowly in the wind," as had the nomination of Attorney General Richardson until Nixon quieted Kennedy by authorizing the appointment of Cox. It was there that Kleindienst had been caught lying under oath. And sufficient facts had been developed there to defeat Nixon's Supreme Court nominees Clement P. Haynesworth and G. Harrold Carswell. So, despite Eastland's power, and assuming Silbert's total honesty, there were risks inherent in the nomination.

The Watergate prosecution aside, Silbert had political assets. His co-authorship of Nixon's hard-line, law and order District of Columbia crime bill had cost him nothing. He marshaled the immediate, unqualified support of Washington's top liberals. He even had the endorsement of their leader, Joe Rauh. (Silbert and Rauh's son, Carl, had served together under Kleindienst when Kleindienst served Mitchell as deputy attorney general, and later Silbert made young Rauh his principal assistant.)

By the time of the hearings on Silbert's nomination, the House was moving inexorably toward impeachment. The one charge I was certain they would bring against Nixon was obstruction of justice. While others were working on the prosecution of Nixon, I went to work against Nixon's defense. From the begin-

ning he had contended that the culprits were off on an enter-
prise of their own. That would be Nixon's defense in the Senate.
He had to contend, "I am the nation's chief enforcement officer.
My Justice Department pursuant to my instructions broke the
Watergate case wide open."

Those who worked on the case would adopt the same line not
because they were conspiring with Nixon, but because it was in
their own interests.

On the night of Monday, April 29, 1974, Nixon shelved the
bust of Abraham Lincoln which previously served as his television prop. Instead, he displayed an encyclopedia-high stack of
edited transcripts of White House conversations which, when
printed, would make up a single paperback volume.

On television Nixon told us that due to Kleindienst's "close
personal ties" to Mitchell, Nixon and Kleindienst had originally
agreed to place Petersen "in complete charge of the investigation." Nixon insisted, "From the time Mr. Petersen took charge
[April 15, 1973], the case was solidly within the criminal justice
system, pursued personally by the nation's top professional prosecutor with the active personal assistance of the President of
the United States."

With the active personal assistance of his Harvard classmates,
with Democrat Joe Rauh, the Republicans, and the Nixon Justice Department behind him, Silbert's Senate confirmation
seemed certain. And I knew that Senate approval of the prosecutor could be interpreted as approval of the prosecution. After
that the Senate would hardly be able to find Nixon, who had
promoted Silbert, guilty of obstructing Silbert's prosecution.

In my office I kept a few reminders of where and what I came
from: photographs of my clients from the civil rights and antiwar
movements; bound records and briefs from Supreme Court
cases; the newspaper headline from South Africa which preceded my speeches there for a bill of rights and integration; a
1962 editorial from the *Birmingham Post-Herald* which refers to

the one-person, one-vote case and is entitled, IT CAN BE DONE; a small piece of window glass from the wreckage of Birmingham's bombed-out Sixteenth Street Baptist Church; and, directly above my desk, a Ben Shahn lithograph which bears the names of those killed in the civil rights movement.

It was in this setting that I read a letter from Aryeh Neier, the ACLU's executive director, instructing me not to testify at Silbert's confirmation hearings. The ACLU is nonpartisan. Neier said he believed that I was so closely identified with the ACLU that my personal position would be publicly perceived to be that of the ACLU.

I telephoned Neier. He said no one had asked him to take his position. I told him that if I did testify I would resign. I understood that the ACLU takes no stand on nominees or candidates for public office. But I did take such stands. It was I who would speak, not the ACLU. And I would specifically spell that out. Neier clarified and toned down, but stuck with his order in a second letter. If I disagreed, he suggested I appeal his decision to the ACLU board. I did. I beat him fifty-eight to two. But I told Neier that I didn't intend to do that again. To me it seemed passing strange that an employee of a free-speech organization would have to ask permission to speak freely. The next time I received such foolish instructions I *would* resign.

〰〰〰〰〰〰〰

On Tuesday morning, April 30, Sam Ervin huffed into the hearing room. "I want to make a statement that is not in writing. . . . [B]efore the committee takes action on this particular nomination . . . [it] should conduct an in-depth investigation into how the Watergate affair was handled by the Department of Justice and by the nominee and other legal officers of the government."

The old man seemed angry. "[T]his country is supposed to stand for . . . the equality of all people before the law." Then he ticked off areas of unequal treatment, leads not followed, and the prosecution's reliance upon Magruder's perjured testimony.

Ervin added that he knew "nothing derogatory" about Silbert personally. But the Watergate Committee "did not investigate the handling of the investigation."

Then Ervin questioned my client, Bob Vance, the president of the Association of State Democratic Chairmen. I testified next. I told the committee about the trial, Silbert's remarks to me, and the importance of his nomination. I told them that Nixon could use their confirmation of the Justice Department prosecutor as his defense for an obstruction of justice charge. If they confirmed the prosecutor of the case, they implicitly endorsed his prosecution. I added that "last night Mr. Nixon said, 'My defense is the Department of Justice. . . . I ordered Jeb Magruder to go to the prosecutor. I ordered him to go over to the grand jury. I took care of it with my Justice Department. . . . [a]nd these other people, . . . all of them were off on an enterprise of their own.' "

Back in the office I opened the transcripts of Nixon's tape-recorded conversations. I was uneasy about them. For sixteen months I had relied upon a few facts and walking-around sense. These transcripts could prove me wrong. If they did, apologies would be in order.

The first thing I read was lawyer James St. Clair's analysis of a Kleindienst-Nixon meeting on April 15, 1973. St. Clair wrote, "The President expressed confidence in Silbert doing a thorough job." And he opposed appointment of a special prosecutor, for that would have been an admission of fault by "our whole system of justice." St. Clair concluded that Nixon "conferred with the . . . assistant attorney general in charge of the Criminal Division of the Department of Justice and cooperated fully to bring the matter expeditiously before the grand jury."

Nixon had known his conversations were being tape-recorded, so he had tried to remain conversationally neutral while Haldeman and Ehrlichman warred against Mitchell and Dean. But Nixon's "huhs, uhs, whos, whats," and "[expletives deleted]" merely cut the presidency down to size. Loyalties shifted but, from the transcripts, one central theme emerged—

each person was angling for Nixon's ultimate favor and he was as trapped by them as they were by him. They intended that their lies free Nixon and themselves. Instead, they snarled his options. Any move might expose other crimes. Yet they all needed a higher-up, a "candidate or a body," a man to confess that he had gone "off on an enterprise of his own" so a "limited hangout" and "containment" could work. Nixon temporized. Finally pressure moved him to provide a scapegoat to be led from the White House to the courthouse. Haldeman and Ehrlichman must have breathed a sigh of relief as John Mitchell won the nomination.

〰〰〰〰〰

With his flat, believable voice, unflappable manner, neat appearance, understanding of the Justice Department, knowledge of the immunity laws, and memory of every fact which he desired to remember, John Wesley Dean III emerged as the best and the brightest of the Nixon administration.

Only he knew when the "jig was up," for he had built the jig. In the nether world of secret government, supreme "intelligence" means supreme power. When no one wants to know, facts are deadly weapons. On the tapes Dean told Nixon that Petersen made sure "that the investigation was narrowed down to a very, very fine criminal thing which was a break for us." The narrowness of the investigation made it easy not to "know," and those who "didn't know" could not cover up.

But there were facts everywhere, stacked like cordwood across clearly marked trails. In time Petersen was to say he had walked through a minefield and come out clean, but those were facts, not mines.

As Dean entered Nixon's Oval Office on March 21, 1973, he must have hoped that mutual knowledge would tie them inextricably together. After their meeting Nixon would "know"; and Nixon would know that Dean knew he (Nixon) "knew." Instead, as Dean left the Oval Office, his fear was fueled by Haldeman and Ehrlichman, who had told him of their plan to have Mitchell step forward to shoulder the blame. And Dean, in his own words, had a "father-son relationship" with Mitchell.

Around 1:00 A.M., Sunday, April 15, Dean's lawyer telephoned him. "[T]he attorney general had called Mr. Petersen . . . and wanted a full report on everything that was going on before the grand jury and where the grand jury was headed." Silbert had violated his prosecutor's secrecy agreement with Dean and had reported Dean's information to his Justice Department superiors. They were to meet at 2:00 A.M. and Kleindienst had been summoned to the President's office to discuss the matter.

Dean had been part of John Mitchell's Justice Department. He knew it well. He knew Petersen's every sidestep, Kleindienst's every friendship, almost every order Silbert followed; and they knew Dean knew.* Back in the Oval Office, the straight-faced young lawyer had said to his client, the President, "I will tell you the person that I feel we could use . . . [to] counsel on this, because he understands the criminal process better than anyone over here does."

"Petersen?" Nixon interrupted.

"Petersen," Dean replied.

The best way for Dean to rid himself of blame for the cover-up was to spread the guilt. So, while Haldeman and Ehrlichman (and their temporary ally, Colson) plotted to blame the burglary on Dean and Mitchell, Dean, the Justice Department's "unofficial liaison" with the White House, began dealing with the prosecutors.

Even though they agreed that the facts he provided them would not be used against him, Dean was very careful. He knew

---

*From Kleindienst's small staff Dean had gone to the White House. There, in Petersen's words, he had been "kind of an unofficial liaison with the Justice Department. . . ." Petersen knew Dean well and their "relationships were good." Silbert's and Dean's offices in the Justice Department had been near each other, but Silbert testified that while he had seen Dean in Kleindienst's office, he "worked in a different section and had never worked with him on any common matter." Silbert knew him to say "hello" to but they never "socialized" and he did not consider Dean "a personal friend so that . . . didn't really pose an obstacle of any kind."

the immunity statutes. He had written them. Executive clemency and money might be enough for Hunt, but not for lawyer Dean. He not only wanted to come clean, he wanted to come out clean, and to do that he needed total immunity from prosecution.

By Saturday, April 14, Magruder had moved against Mitchell. Nixon had asked Ehrlichman to perform the distasteful task of giving Mitchell, "the Big Enchilada," the news that he was about to be served up to the prosecutors and the people. And only Nixon and Mitchell know whether Nixon had privately advised his dear friend, Mitchell, of what his response to Ehrlichman should be.

Mitchell said no. Dean moved quickly. One of his lawyers was former Justice Department attorney Charles Shaffer. For twelve days he and Dean had been talking with the prosecutors. Dean, still angling for Nixon's favor, concealed these meetings from his client by, as Dean said, "avoiding conversations with Mitchell, Ehrlichman, and Haldeman as much as I could."

He maneuvered Ehrlichman away from Silbert, telling him that if he went to Silbert directly, the prosecutor would waltz him into the grand jury room. In the transcripts Haldeman seemed totally unaware of what Dean was doing to him. He told Nixon that Dean did not think he was "a target . . . and, if he's not, that means they are just not going to be targeting on the White House." But Dean knew about Magruder and Haldeman. He knew about Ehrlichman, Egil Krogh, Jr., the CIA, and Hunt's and Liddy's burglaries of Ellsberg's psychiatrist. When Dean told Ehrlichman that Haldeman was on the prosecutor's list of those targeted for indictment, that disturbed Ehrlichman. When Dean told Ehrlichman that Ehrlichman was on that list too, that disturbed Ehrlichman no end.

At 6:00 P.M. that same Saturday, Attorney General Kleindienst donned his tuxedo for the White House Correspondents Dinner. The telephone rang. The caller, Ehrlichman, promptly reminded him that they would soon see *Washington Post* reporters "Bernstein and what's his name get their awards."

Ehrlichman's fear was concealed in the meanness of his words. This would be the two men's last conversation. Ehrlichman termed Kleindienst his "favorite law enforcement officer." He brought him "bad news." Magruder had been to the prosecutors. He had implicated Kleindienst's benefactor, Mitchell, in the burglary. Kleindienst's friends, Dean, LaRue, and Mardian, also would be charged.

Kleindienst anxiously asked, "But Mitchell denied it?"

Dean, the seeker of immunity and Nixon's favor, an angler who provided bits and pieces of information to the Justice Department while he held back the big news about Nixon's guilt—until Nixon made up his mind about immunizing Dean—reacted with triumph not anger to the news that the prosecutors had advised their superiors of their conversations with him.* He told his lawyer, "We certainly have gotten the message through to Haldeman and Ehrlichman that they have problems and that the cover-up may begin to unravel at last."

Dean said he "realized that they had gotten the attorney general late at night to get a briefing from the prosecutors, and that is when things really started moving. That is when the activities began to occur."

While Dean was pondering the steps of unravelment, Richard Kleindienst, fifty, waited in his spacious home in suburban Mc-Lean, Virginia, to meet with three of his Justice Department colleagues—Petersen, Titus, and Silbert. "Jovial," "blunt-spoken," "shoots-from-the-hip" were some of the words reporters used to describe Kleindienst, but "successful" was the best of all.

He had come a long way from Winslow, Arizona, where his

---

*This was Dean's testimony to the Watergate Committee. Three years later, in his book, *Blind Ambition,* Dean recounted it with different emphasis. He wrote that he "felt a chill, said 'Goddammit Charlie, they promised us.' " He told of desperately urging his lawyer, Charles Shaffer, to try to dissuade the prosecutors from their course—for a few days.

father had been a railroad brakeman. When Kleindienst's Phi Beta Kappa certificate from Harvard had come home in the mail, his father, who did not understand Latin, had thrown it away. Young Kleindienst had to retrieve that certificate from the trash. Now he had to retrieve his reputation.

If what Ehrlichman had said about Mitchell was true, Kleindienst would have to recuse himself from the Watergate case. Worse than that, if Nixon refused to appoint a special prosecutor, Kleindienst might have to resign. That would look terrible. And there was another more practical fear. While it was rumored that John B. Connally's law firm had offered Kleindienst a small fortune to join them, he needed money. One night at a dinner party he had told me how hard it was for him to live on his $60,000 yearly salary. To others he had put it more precisely, saying that he could live without a job for "about thirty days."

That damned Ehrlichman!

To Ehrlichman and his allies, Haldeman and Colson, Kleindienst owed nothing. But what about LaRue and Mitchell? What about Kleindienst's former Justice Department aides, Dean and Mardian? Especially Mardian. Two months after the arrests of the Watergate burglars, Kleindienst had revealed the closeness of their relationship. He had said, "There are two people I can tell you knew nothing about it: Dick Kleindienst and Bob Mardian." To make certain he would know nothing about "it," Kleindienst had left everything to Petersen and Gray. On the day after the arrests, he had sent Liddy packing from the Burning Tree Country Club, but on this, the worst morning of his life, Kleindienst could not send away the friends who were knocking at his door.

Of course only Kleindienst, Petersen, Titus, and Silbert know what they thought and said when they met early that Sunday morning, but their meeting had to be not unlike that of a troubled law partnership. As they looked at the empty chair, they must have felt sadness and fear and anger that the absent Dean's acts might reflect against them. And a lying Dean was as dangerous to these four men as a truth-telling Dean was to Nixon.

From the Watergate arrests through the first trial they had worked with Dean. Silbert had provided Petersen with "oral reports on a daily basis." Petersen had even reported grand jury information to Dean. Dean had been their primary source of information about the contents of Hunt's White House safe. He had "helped" in their negotiations with the CIA. Dean had sat through every FBI witness-interview at the White House and had arranged for some witnesses to give statements at the Justice Department rather than in the grand jury room. Silbert and Dean had served on Kleindienst's staff and Kleindienst had talked with Dean repeatedly.

The fourth man, Silbert's immediate superior, the relatively unknown United States Attorney Titus, had made arrangements with Silbert for the Committee to Re-Elect the President's lawyer, Kenneth Wells Parkinson, to sit in on FBI witness-interviews at that committee. He had conferred with Silbert about the case. And Titus, a bachelor in his fifties, was the godfather of presidential secretary Rose Mary Woods's nephew. He was also her sometimes escort and longtime friend. He understood the appearance of that relationship and later said that after the burglary he "purposely" had not seen her.

Now these four lawyers had to set things right. To do that they had to remain in the case. Recusal could be misinterpreted as an admission of wrongdoing. McCord had skirted them and gone directly to Sirica. But Magruder, LaRue, and Dean had come to them and they might be believed if they stayed in the case and really solved it.

Lawyers cannot prosecute cases in which they are witnesses. These men had been in charge of the justice that had been obstructed, so they *were* witnesses. Their information was the information relied upon by Dean in the preelection, pretrial cover-up.

The only time Dean had not ostensibly worked on the side of the Justice Department was after the first trial—after Silbert had told me "Hunt was trying to blackmail Spencer and I'm going to prove it"; after the CIA-CRP mis-statements after Silbert's argument that they "were off on an enterprise of their own, diverting that money for their own uses." But if the case centered on the obstruction of justice which occurred *after* the first trial, they need not testify. After the delivery of McCord's letter to Sirica on March 20, 1973, Dean had not tried to appear to be their "co-counsel." He had revealed his role as a lawbreaker and had become their informer.

Four days after these men met at Kleindienst's home, Sy Hersh was to write in *The New York Times* that "the overall thrust" of the prosecution had "shifted" from the burglary to "obstruction of justice—that is, interfering with the Justice Department's inquiry." Two weeks later, on May 2, 1973, he would write that "every one involved in the operation repeatedly lied . . . to President Nixon."

But at sunrise on that April 15 Sunday morning, after Petersen, Titus, and Silbert had left his home, Richard Kleindienst, Attorney General of the United States, understood a few things Sy Hersh might never understand. Sleepy-eyed, Kleindienst shaved, dressed, and screwed up his courage. That day he would scramble to retrieve his reputation and his career. He would meet with the President, as would Petersen. They would lay out for Nixon plans grounded in loyalty to him while adversary to *almost* anyone else close to him—Mitchell, Haldeman, and, of course, that damned Ehrlichman.

Kleindienst had used his wife's stationery to take "copious notes" during his early-morning conversation with Petersen, Titus, and Silbert. He carried them to the White House for his meeting with Nixon. After that, he was unable to "find" those notes. He said he was in a state of shock "from April 15 to April 29 and I don't know what happened to them. . . ." At 1:12 P.M. Kleindienst and Nixon met. At 2:22 P.M. the recording machine ran out of tape. Later that day, Nixon held at least ten other conversations with Kleindienst and Petersen, which, according to Nixon's lawyers, were not recorded. But the edited transcript of the conversation which was recorded disclosed part of the Justice Department's strategy.

"[T]hat was all after the election that that happened, huh?" Nixon asked Kleindienst.

"I don't know, but that happened after the conviction—after Liddy's conviction," the attorney general replied.

They continued.

> P.   Oh, in other words, the obstruction they are talking about is what happened after the conviction?
> K.   Yes sir.
> P.   Rather than before the conviction.
> K.   Yes sir.

Kleindienst told Nixon that during the summer of 1972 "the conduct of everybody over here, Mr. President—really created great suspicions in the mind of Silbert and Petersen, you know." Then he suggested the name of a special *supervisory* prosecutor.

Nixon replied, "I can get that down, but I'm going to get that U.S. attorney in one way or another."

Kleindienst said, "The special prosecutor would not try the case, Mr. President. What he would do is substitute himself for the attorney general. Silbert would try the case."

I found no "expletives deleted" around Silbert's name in the transcripts.

~~~~~~~

There was another winding trail in the transcripts that was of special interest to me.

My overriding aim was to destroy Nixon's "Justice Department defense" to an obstruction-of-justice charge. To this end, Daniel Ellsberg and I had been trying to fit together the connecting parts of the two most widely publicized prosecutions of Nixon's Justice Department.

Years had passed since I first met an attractive young woman and the thin, intensely serious young man with penetrating blue eyes and curly brown hair who awaited me on a between-floors stairwell landing at the Columbia University Law School. That was on Saturday, June 13, 1970. I had been attending an antiwar lawyers' meeting and it had just adjourned.

The waiting man had "a hypothetical question." Assuming our

government was committing war crimes in Southeast Asia, and a hypothetical person possessed highly secret hypothetical government documents which proved these crimes to be a matter of policy, what penalty would the hypothetical person face for revealing them?

I laughed. "Ten years to life, if it's peacetime; death if we're at war."

The man smiled grimly. He was the "hypothetical person"—Daniel J. Ellsberg. He would marry the nearby woman—Patricia Marx.

That was six weeks after the United States' "incursion" into Cambodia.

Daniel Ellsberg understood that the escalation policy required that Nixon lie to us while he told the Russians and the Chinese our plans in Vietnam—*in advance.* Our "national security" required that the American people not know his intentions ever—or, at least, not until after the next election. Ellsberg had lectured to Dr. Henry Kissinger's seminars. He understood the fear and fury hidden within the jovial, dumpy Harvard professor. But Ellsberg's computerlike ability to recall facts and his Marinelike patriotism made him an adequate adversary to the chairman of the National Security Council.

In 1967, soon after the Levy war crimes defense, the Pentagon had begun to compile its top-secret study of the Vietnam War. In August and September 1970, Ellsberg went to Nixon's home in San Clemente to urge Kissinger to read and learn from the Pentagon Papers. And that was the end of that.

Ellsberg gave the papers to Senator J. William Fulbright. He gave some of them to Senator Charles McC. Mathias, Jr. He offered them to Senator McGovern. And that was the end of that.

His search for official action ended, Ellsberg gave them to the people.

Almost two years passed before the Watergate burglary. Within a month of the arrests, the prosecutors knew that six of the seven defendants had once been employed by the CIA. The seventh man, Liddy, had an intelligence background with the FBI.

The prosecutors even knew that Hunt was "a consultant on the declassification of the Pentagon Papers"; that the sign on their Executive Office Building door read PLUMBERS; and that Hunt's "responsibility was to investigate the Ellsberg leak. . . . [H]e was concentrating . . . on Ellsberg." *

Even though the transcripts of Nixon's tape-recorded conversations included nothing definitive, Dean's remark to Nixon "Within the files . . ." had to be a reference to the files of the Justice Department.

"Oh, I thought of it. The picture!" the President had replied to Dean, as though they were playing "Twenty Questions."

"Yes, sir," said Dean. "That is not all that buried . . . there is no telling when it is going to pop up."

"The picture" had to be one of the Justice Department's ten CIA-provided Xerox copies of CIA-developed casing photographs of the office of Dr. Lewis J. Fielding, Ellsberg's psychiatrist, taken by former CIA agent Hunt with his CIA-provided camera.†

By January 3, 1973, the day I first went to Sirica's chambers to file my motion to suppress the illegally intercepted telephone conversations, Petersen had all of the Xeroxed pictures, including those of the inside of the psychiatrist's office. He had reproductions of Hunt and Liddy's CIA-provided "pocket litter" (false identification cards which set forth their aliases, "Edward J. Hamilton" and "George Leonard"). He had memoranda which set forth the name, address, and automobile license-plate identification of Dr. Fielding. He had pictures of Liddy, of Fielding's

---

*Later Silbert would testify that he knew "nothing" about the Ellsberg case except that Ellsberg "was charged with . . . stealing or leaking the Pentagon Papers."

†On March 13, 1973, Dean told Nixon that "it wouldn't take a very sharp investigator very long because you've got pictures in the CIA files that they had to turn over to [unintelligible]". Dean told the Senate Watergate Committee

automobile clearly showing those license plates, and of Fielding's prominently identified reserved parking space, and pictures of the exterior of Fielding's office building with his address shown, and pictures of the exterior and interior of Fielding's office.

And Silbert would testify that they "spent an inordinate amount of time" during the summer of 1972 trying to find out what Hunt and Liddy had been doing in their travels.

To the Watergate Committee Petersen said they "really did not make the connection. We hadn't found anything . . . to arouse our suspicions. . . . [W]e might have checked the name [Fielding]. We did not. Strangely enough, I didn't. I don't know why. It just did not seem to be any way related to Watergate.

"I did not know anything about the Ellsberg case. . . ."

On Monday, April 16, 1973, the day after the prosecutors were told of the Ellsberg burglary by Dean's lawyer, Silbert wrote a brief memorandum to Petersen about it.* On April 17, Petersen received that message. He scrawled upon it, "Kevin, check this out. Let me know what this is about." Then he bucked it to the Justice Department's Kevin Morony.

Morony replied that neither he nor the FBI knew about the burglary. Petersen asked if there was a psychiatrist involved in the case. Yes. Ellsberg's psychiatrist was named Lewis J. Fielding and he had been interviewed by the FBI.

"Well, that clicked," Petersen told the committee. "Fielding," the name on the CIA-provided Xerox copies of Hunt's

---

that any investigator "worth his salt" was capable of linking the Xerox copies of photographs with the Fielding office burglary. Ehrlichman swore that Dean told him that Silbert and Petersen understood the meaning of the "casing" photographs by the fall of 1972. Ehrlichman added that his testimony was based upon hearsay from Dean. Ehrlichman was unwilling to vouch for Dean's credibility. So am I. The prosecutors and Petersen deny that they had any such understanding.

*In Blind Ambition, Dean recounts the story differently from the prosecutors. He says he told the prosecutors. They say Dean's lawyer told them.

casing photographs, "clicked" and "led us to the photographs and we made the connection."

Later in the day Nixon asked Petersen, "What's new?"

When Petersen told him of the burglary, Nixon said, "I know about that. This is a national security matter. You stay out of that. Your mandate is to investigate Watergate."

Petersen telephoned Silbert. "The President said stay out of it, Earl, and that is it." And that was "it."

Five days later, a mine went off. Wisconsin Congressman Henry S. Reuss charged, "Exchanging Mr. Petersen for Mr. Dean as chief investigator does not remove a fox from guarding the hen house; it simply changes foxes."

Whether Petersen was foxy or fooled, hounds were sniffing at his heels and columnist Jack Anderson was publishing excerpts of secret transcripts from the Watergate grand jury. On the morning of April 25, another mine went off near Petersen. Acting FBI Director Pat Gray and Senator Lowell P. Weicker, Jr., met in Gray's office and Gray revealed that he had burned some of the documents removed from Hunt's White House safe. Now Petersen had to be frightened.

That morning, Petersen said he told Kleindienst, "Look, you are out of Watergate but you are not out of Ellsberg. I need some help." Kleindienst enlisted. They went to see Nixon and received permission to disclose the burglary to Judge Matthew Byrne, who was presiding over Ellsberg's trial in Los Angeles.

By the time the President next met with Petersen, Nixon had heard that the newspapers were reporting how a lawyer for Dean had told the prosecutors that if they insisted on going after him, "Dean . . . would be tying in the President, not in the Watergate, but in other areas." Dean the angler had become Dean the snake.

Petersen told the President, "[W]hat those areas are, we don't know. . . . Silbert said, 'Stop.' So, he didn't let them go on. He said, 'Why get into that?' "

Dean had urged Nixon to accept Petersen as his lawyer. Petersen had resisted Nixon when the President wanted to withhold immunity from Dean. But allegiance shifted. Now Petersen explained to Nixon why disclosure of the burglary in the Ellsberg case had been important. Now Dean could not use that secret for leverage against them. By April 27, Dean was desperate. And Petersen told Nixon, "Well, if I sound like a devil's advocate—I am. I have been saying to the prosecutors—how in the hell can I immunize John Dean?"

Petersen stressed his understanding of Dean's threat and explained what had happened to it. "They [Dean's lawyer had] said, 'tying in the President' not in the Watergate but in other areas and the prosecutor [had] said: 'Stop! We don't want to get in this. We don't want to discuss this.' "

~~~~~~~~

Senator John V. Tunney was a member of the committee which would pass on Earl Silbert's nomination as United States Attorney. Many Golden State liberals resented Tunney. They said he was a "lightweight." After he defeated the incumbent Republican movie star, song-and-dance man George Murphy, there were few, if any, Senate votes upon which he could be faulted. So liberal critics chorused, "He isn't smart enough," which is what I had heard them say about Sirica.

I went to Tunney. He seemed smart to me. It was the prosecution of Daniel Ellsberg, the brilliant number-one hero of Tunney's liberal critics, which most interested him. At breakfast in his apartment, on Monday, June 24, 1974, the senator questioned me carefully. He had been thoroughly lobbied by Silbert's friends, local bar association and liberal leaders, and fellow senators. That day it would be his turn to ask questions. Henry Petersen would be the next witness. I told Tunney what I knew.

Later that day, surrounded by friends and Justice Department lawyers, a relaxed Petersen faced Tunney in the hearing room.

First Tunney read Petersen the news conference remarks of Nixon's lawyer. Then Tunney said, "Mr. St. Clair is asserting that the President as the chief law enforcement official in the country has the overall responsibility for directing the Department of Justice and criminal investigations. . . . Would you not agree that this is what the thrust and purport of that statement is?"

Petersen replied, "If the President is responsible for the abuses of . . . subordinates, *. . .* he is also entitled to the benefit of other subordinates in the administration who are said to have done a credible job. . . ."

Tunney leaned forward. "[I]f Mr. Silbert is confirmed, are we in effect saying as a senate that we are satisfied with the investigation . . . and that inasmuch as the President is the chief law enforcement officer we are satisfied with the part that he played?"

Petersen astounded everyone. He rocked backward, started forward, half rose from his seat and exclaimed:

> You are to be commended, Senator. You are the first guy who has stated it. That is a gut, tough, tough, question, but you are right.
> . . . .
> As John Kennedy said, the lowest point in hell is reserved for the neutral. You all have a tough, tough decision to make.
> . . . .
> I think that inference may be drawn. I do not think it is necessarily a valid inference, any more than it is an invalid inference. . . .
> SENATOR TUNNEY: That is the problem that we face here in this committee, the problem that I face.
> MR. PETERSEN: I can appreciate your predicament, Senator. I really do not envy any of you who may have larger responsibilities in this matter. . . .
> SENATOR TUNNEY: . . . . If Mr. Silbert is confirmed, you do not think that . . . fact . . . has any bearing upon the President's conduct of his office during the period . . . of the investigation of the Watergate?
> MR. PETERSEN: I do not know because as far as I have been able to ascertain, the President was not directly involved either affirmatively or negatively in the conduct of the investigation. . . .

And so it was John Tunney, "lightweight," who demolished Richard Nixon's defense. In executive session Tunney pushed for a negative vote on the nomination of Silbert. Senator Roman Hruska, the ranking Republican, asked the committee to simply let it lie, and it was still lying there when Nixon left office.

Eventually, after Gerald Ford assumed the office Nixon had left, Silbert was renominated and approved. But again he would have to testify about the Pentagon Papers case.

~~~~~~~~

Secluded and unnoticed on a steep hillside near Mill Valley, California, behind a gate and at the end of a narrow driveway, stood the beautiful home rented by Daniel and Patricia Ellsberg. I arrived there in December 1974. By then their house had been burglarized once—as far as they knew. The burglar had taken some files. General Haig, who presumably knew about such things, had blamed words missing from Nixon tapes on a "sinister force." In Ellsberg's case the "sinister force" seemed to be ever-present.

It had been almost three years since the CIA had constructed its psychological profile of Ellsberg, and simultaneously Hunt and Liddy's Cubans had broken into Ellsberg's psychiatrist's office. The CIA's retiree-burglars had been provided with their camera and other equipment by the CIA, and that burglary and the CIA did seem logically related.

Before he dismissed the charges against Ellsberg, Judge Matthew Byrne had furnished him with copies of the documents which Dean had taken from Hunt's White House safe soon after the Watergate burglary. They had not been placed in evidence in any trial or hearing, but since the end of June 1972, they had been in the possession of the Justice Department's Watergate case prosecutors!

At our December 1974 meeting in Mill Valley, Ellsberg gave me the documents.

Included was a two-inch-high stack of news articles related to the Ellsberg case. The one on top was headlined: ELLSBERG FACES 115 YEARS. On others, Hunt had underlined references to psychiatry.

Hunt's twenty-eight-page typewritten chronology of Ellsberg's life contained references to analysts and psychiatrists.
One read, "December 29, 1970—January 5, 1971—Mr. & Mrs.
Ellsberg arrive at Bel Air Hotel, Los Angeles. . . . Jan.
5—Ellsberg checks into Bel Air. Telephone records for these
rooms reflect numerous calls including: Lewis Fielding, psychiatrist . . ."!

And there were FBI reports of interviews. One of them was
about a "Dr. Lewis J. Fielding"! Another reported an FBI attempt to interview "Fielding"!

That "clicked" with me. Petersen had testified to the Watergate Committee that on April 18, 1973, he had obtained the
name "Fielding," and that had "clicked" and led them to the
Xerox copies of photographs and disclosure of the burglary of the
psychiatrist's office.

Yet twenty-two months after the Justice Department acquired
the documents with Fielding's name on them, Glanzer of the
Justice Department did not know they had them. That was his
testimony to the Committee on the Judiciary on May 20, 1975,
after Ford had renominated Silbert to be United States
Attorney.

Questioned by Tunney at the same hearings, Silbert testified,
"I never knew who Dr. Fielding was, or heard the name, until
late April of 1973, so I made absolutely no association or connection with Dr. Fielding."*

But what bowled Tunney over was Silbert's testimony about
the Xerox copies of Hunt's casing photographs. "I do not recall
seeing those pictures," said Silbert.

Thirteen months had passed since Silbert had last testified, on
April 23, 1974, about the Xerox copies of Hunt's casing photographs. Then he had said the CIA had provided him with its
"packet of materials" in December 1972. That was when he

---

*He explained that the third prosecutor, Donald Campbell, had been in
charge of the contents of Hunt's safe. Later, in an affidavit, Campbell agreed.

learned for "the first time" that the CIA was the source of Hunt and Liddy's "phony identifications." Asked if there were "photos of Liddy in front of the office of . . . Fielding, and other photos . . . in California . . ." Silbert said yes. He didn't notice the "Fielding" aspect of the photographs. But "I remember pouring [*sic*] over these photos with Mr. Petersen. . . ." When they couldn't figure them out, Silbert said, he "took the whole packet," including the "photographs back and showed them to Mr. Glanzer and Mr. Campbell and again we went over them and tried to figure out what was going on."

On Wednesday, June 26, 1974, Petersen had testified that the Xeroxes had been "made available to Mr. Silbert."

Then Tunney had asked about the photograph which clearly depicted the inside of an office. "That did not mean anything to you?"

> MR. PETERSEN: Right.
> SENATOR TUNNEY: The third one, it looks like there is a couch, a chair. That did not mean anything?
> MR. PETERSEN: No.
> SENATOR TUNNEY: The next one is a picture of a man, biting a cigar, near a stationery store of some kind. Is that Mr. Liddy?
> MR. PETERSEN: Yes. . . .
> SENATOR TUNNEY: The next one is an address: 11928. It says "The Brentwood." And that address did not mean anything to you?
> MR. PETERSEN: No. . . .
> SENATOR TUNNEY: The next picture is of two cars; above one it says "Reserved for Dr. Fielding," and one says, "Reserved for Dr. Rothenberg." That did not mean anything?
> MR. PETERSEN: No. We did not relate any of that.

Eleven months passed. Now, on May 20, 1975, Tunney asked Silbert, "Does one of those photographs indicate a ransacking? Or a burglary having taken place?"

"I do not recall seeing those pictures," said Silbert. He recalled having seen only two of them—the one of Liddy and of the automobile which displayed Dr. Fielding's license plates. He insisted he had not seen "any photographs of the interior of a building indicating that a ransacking had occurred."

Petersen and Silbert both testified that even if they had investigated they would have ended up in a blind alley. A California ne'er-do-well had confessed to the burglary.

But Tunney had investigated that too. Soon after his "confessions," the jailed Californian had "recanted."

Tunney asked: "An investigation would not have indicated that there was a burglary?"

MR. SILBERT: No . . . Or . . . if it had revealed it, it would have indicated that the case was closed and confessed to by a narcotics addict.

SENATOR TUNNEY: Yes, but you were investigating burglars. . . .

MR. SILBERT: No. We were not investigating burglaries. We were investigating the responsibility for the Watergate break-in.

SENATOR TUNNEY: That is a burglary, was it not?

MR. SILBERT: That is true, but that doesn't mean, Senator, that because they burgled, or engaged in that one particular enterprise, that they somehow wound up in a psychiatrist's office. That is a preposterous non-sequitur.

SENATOR TUNNEY: It just happens to be the fact, though, does it not?

MR. SILBERT: That's right. It happens to be the fact.

The Committee on the Judiciary voted not to recall Petersen regarding his and Silbert's apparently contradictory testimony about the photographs. After that, the committee and the Senate overwhelmingly approved Silbert's nomination. He now serves as United States Attorney for the District of Columbia and he seems to be doing a fine job. Two lawyers worked with him in the Watergate case. Donald Campbell now serves as Silbert's assistant. Seymour Glanzer entered private law practice (in Charles Colson's former law firm).

Their Justice Department superiors also did well. Henry

Petersen retired and entered private practice, as did former Attorney General Richard Kleindienst. Kleindienst received a federal judge's general commendation along with a $100 fine for lying under oath to the Senate's Committee on the Judiciary. He then represented Algeria for a yearly retainer of $100,000 plus expenses. And for the five hours he spent rearranging the Teamsters' Union's insurance, he is said to have received $250,000.

Glanzer found it "ironic" that the Pentagon Papers case was "tied into" the Watergate case. To Silbert that was "a preposterous non-sequitur." But it is casual, seemingly irrational, unrelated, and minor events which weave the fabric of history. That is where legal education fails us. It provides us with ways to distinguish and thereby close our minds to what Tom Paine called "laws of nature and common sense."

21

On the way in from Dulles International Airport, my taxicab driver missed the turnoff. As we meandered down winding, narrow, wooded roads in the early evening, the driver repeatedly apologized. He even threatened to turn his meter off. Before grace overcame greed, we arrived at the palatial Mc-Lean, Virginia, home of Washington-based, private investigator Richard L. Bast.

I had been out of town when Bast telephoned me at the suggestion of a mutual acquaintance, his attorney, Philip J. Hirschkop, and said, "I have talked to Colson. I have three hours and thirteen minutes of notes you might be interested in." I arrived at dusk, Wednesday, June 19, 1974.

Bast's businesses included investments. He lived more like a king than a cop. We sat beside his large backyard swimming pool. Behind us was a steep, wooded hillside surrounded by a high, sloping retaining wall of railroad ties.

Bast's first conversation with Charles W. Colson had taken place here on May 13, 1974. The top Nixon aide was facing trial, as were Ehrlichman, Haldeman, Mardian, and Mitchell. Colson sought to hire Bast to investigate CIA-Watergate relationships, so he may not have known that Bast was tape-recording him. Eighteen days later they met for the second and final time. By then Colson had pleaded guilty and his only fear about repetition of his remarks was his fear of the sentencing judge.

He also had pleaded that he was a "born-again Christian." Had he continued to act tough and smart, Washington's smart-set liberals might have believed him. But when Colson said he found God, he lost them.

In sharp contrast with well-manicured suburban tranquility, two police dogs roamed nearby. A revolver rested two feet away. I felt as though the clock had spun back fifteen years to Birmingham.

The tape turned slowly. That caricaturist who depicted the White House as a giant tape recorder missed the point. The whole world was a listening device, and now the captured voice of Charles Colson cut through the night.

"The Hughes Tool Company, . . . the Hughes interests, Summa Corporation, . . . is the biggest single contractor, of the CIA.

"The guy who handles all of the work . . . CIA-Hughes is a guy by the name of Maheu."

The "Hughes interests" were those of Howard R. The Maheu was Robert A. He had been ousted from the management of the billionaire's Las Vegas interests by early 1971.

The tape rolled on.

COLSON: Okay . . . Howard Hughes fires Maheu. Maheu had . . . Larry O'Brien on a hundred-thousand-dollar-a-year retainer.

BAST: Yes.

COLSON: So Maheu and O'Brien are fired. Hughes then hires the Mullen Company for his chief PR counsel in Washington. There is some indication in the file that the Hughes Company was put together with Mullen by the CIA.

Okay, one of the things— Now we know that Maheu and Hughes are on the outs and Hughes was very worried about Maheu, presumably also worried about O'Brien. We know that

Maheu was the chief contact between the CIA and the Hughes Tool Company.

As I listened to Colson, then rewound and played the tapes back again and again, the three hours and thirteen minutes of "notes" stretched into six hours, then nine. Despite a light rain, the stars shone brightly. Later I would learn that we and the Russians had slipped strange objects under the seas and had invaded the sky with 2,000 working satellites. Now I heard Colson term Hughes "the biggest single contractor of the CIA." He continued: "They do a lot of their contract-out work like . . . satellites, this new Global Marine, this Glomar Express, this new oceanographic vehicle is CIA." Colson also spoke of Charles G. Rebozo, a.k.a. "Bebe," who had received $100,000 in cold, hard cash from Hughes. Neither he nor Nixon had reported or paid income taxes on that money. Rebozo said he had kept those hundred-dollar bills in a safe-deposit box. They had remained there for years—untouched.

"You want to know what I really think?" Colson asked.

"I don't know," Bast answered.

"And I'm loyal to the guy."

"Yeah."

COLSON: I think they paid Bebe that dough.

BAST: Who paid Bebe that dough?

COLSON: Hughes.

BAST: Oh, yeah.

COLSON: The hundred thousand dollars.

BAST: Yeah.

COLSON: I think Bebe used that to . . .

BAST: Walking-around money you mean?

COLSON: Yeah, for himself and for the President and for his family and his girls. . . .

BAST: Yeah.

COLSON: And, I think that the President figures, this is my worst suspicion, that if he really blows this, Hughes can blow the whistle on him.

BAST: About that money there?
COLSON: Well, who knows that that is the only hundred thousand dollars.

It was almost daybreak when Bast drove me home to Capitol Hill. Colson's remarks (and his dreary political life) sank in. Sometime after dawn I dropped off to sleep hoping that Colson really had found something decent to believe in on his way to the penitentiary.

He was a kind of "poor devil," for in law and politics Colson had served the very rich. As had Nixon. Nixon had bragged that he had the Justice Department's "Petersen on a short leash." And Nixon had lawyer Colson on another. But what was the length of Nixon's leash? Hughes had paid Nixon's brothers, F. Donald and Edward C., and other family members. And what did Hughes know? What did Hunt know? And Liddy? And the CIA? Another question kept nagging at me. Was there a difference between Hughes and the CIA?

The surprise came to me when, bleary-eyed and unshaven, I awakened with a start. My God! There had been another kind of coup d'etat in the United States! No one had noticed! The government had been overthrown in secret. The President had been captured, not by a mere $100,000, not even by force of arms, but by blackmail!

Now I began to wonder what secret wars were under way within the subterranean government. What men never seen or known were helping us topple Nixon? If Presidents could be bought and sold, and blackmailed by men like Hunt, men within the seamy crevices of the intelligence community, then what about the power of men like Hughes? If there was a Hughes.

Had our "national security system" made blackmail as American as Kansas City beef? At lunch in that Kansas City Beef House, on December 22, 1972, Silbert may have been close to understanding the motive for the Watergate burglary. If only he hadn't focused on lower-down defendants and lower-down victims.

Twelve months later, in December 1973, Senator Howard Baker had come closer. He had remarked, "There are animals crashing around in the forest. I can hear them but I can't see them."

Obviously the CIA had been involved in the Ellsberg case. On July 28, 1972, six weeks after the Watergate burglary and the day before he became the CIA's Watergate-case liaison officer with the Justice Department, the deputy director of Central Intelligence, William E. Colby, had written CIA Director Richard Helms that there was a "possibility" that the photographs which the agency had developed for Hunt "were somehow connected with the Rand Corporation"—the "think-tank" home of the Pentagon Papers. Colby said that the California location and the existence of Xerox establishments in the photographs, plus Hunt's reference to "a highly sensitive mission," had led him to the "possibility" that Hunt had been engaged in an investigation of "the Pentagon Papers leak." Now, months after the Watergate hearings had ended, Senator Baker was trying to prove that the Watergate burglary had been a "setup." Perhaps. But I needed no double- or triple-agent theory to believe that someone within the CIA had helped to pull the rug from under Nixon.

～～～～～～

The lawyers in the House had said they needed "a smoking gun." They had a shooting gallery. They really did believe in "Perry Mason law." They wanted Nixon to sob "I did it! I had to do it. . . !" What House members desperately wanted was for Nixon to impeach himself; to resign; to rise in the rear of the committee room and confess.

Because House members were up for reelection in November, the Democratic leadership scheduled Nixon's fall to meet their fall needs.

On Friday, July 19, 1974, John Doar shucked aside "nonpartisanship" and assumed the role of prosecutor. Then came the hearings.

At last Judiciary Committee Chairman Peter Rodino, speaking from the committee room, said, "We have reached the moment. . . ." Democracy came alive.

And finally, on Monday, August 5, the President of the United States, Commander in Chief of the Western World, loser, trapped by his lies and secrets and the secret agencies which surrounded him, confessed.

It was Sirica who thrust personal responsibility for the tapes upon Nixon's White House lawyers. Once these lawyers "knew," they made Haig, Kissinger, and the other members of the national security establishment "aware" or "witting." Nixon, faced with the option of releasing his lawyers or the transcripts, chose to confess—again.

On the tape of a June 23, 1972, Nixon-Haldeman conversation, the President asked, "Well, can you get it done?"

"I think so," Haldeman replied.

FBI Director Gray hadn't been able to "get it done," so Mitchell proposed, Dean concurred, and Haldeman agreed that Nixon should order CIA Deputy Director Vernon Walters to tell Gray to limit the Watergate investigation.

Nixon said they had "protected [CIA Director] Helms from one hell of a lot of things." But Nixon's primary concern still ran to Hunt.

McCord testified that Hunt had told him he had information which "would be sufficient to impeach the President. . . . [V]ery bad to have this fellow Hunt, ah, he knows too damned much, if he was involved—you happen to know that?" *

Before the Watergate Committee, Helms testified that he had been unconcerned about Haldeman's "incoherent reference to an investigation . . . running into the Bay of Pigs." Despite his "unconcern," it was clear to me that the CIA's men were deft at political infighting and counterplay. In scores of nations, CIA

---

*Before she was killed in an airplane crash, Hunt's wife told McCord of her husband's threat "to blow the White House out of the water."

agents earned their livings just that way. During the early stages of the Watergate cover-ups they had covered for Nixon. Then, suddenly, they pulled back.

Deputy Director Walters had revealed that Director Helms's initial instructions were to "remind Mr. Gray of the [written] agreement between the CIA and FBI, not to interfere with one another's operations." * And Walters had told Gray that a continued FBI investigation "might lead to some projects. . . ."

Nixon's tape was confirmation. Not news. He had told Haldeman, "Of course, this Hunt, that will uncover a lot of things. You open that scab, there's a hell of a lot . . . the whole Bay of Pigs thing . . . just say this is a comedy of errors. . . ."

With that phrase, Nixon had laid down the party line—a comedy of errors. Silbert and Richardson and Petersen and all the rest of them had seen the burglary as "stupid," a "caper," "bizarre," "third-rate."

To Haldeman, Nixon had urged, "This involves these Cubans, Hunt, and a lot of hanky-panky, that we have nothing to do with ourselves." I read Nixon's words remembering Silbert's "Hunt was trying to blackmail Spencer and I'm going to prove it." And "they were off on an enterprise of their own. Diverting that money for their own uses."

Now the national security establishment—Haig, Schlesinger, Kissinger, and others securely anonymous—ordered the armed forces to obey commands only when they were transmitted by the Secretary of Defense.

One after another the politicians fell into line. Speaker Albert

---

*In mid-1975, two years after Walters's testimony, the terms of the "agreement" came to light. Its significance went unnoticed. The formal document was dated March 1, 1954. In it the Justice Department ceded to the CIA the right to investigate crimes committed by CIA personnel. If the Company determined that a prosecution would "require revelation of highly classified information" it did not have to forward the matter to the Justice Department. The CIA had a similar arrangement with the Internal Revenue Service which must have come in handy for corporations which provided CIA agents "cover."

and Chairman Rodino were asked hypothetical questions about whether they would push for an impeachment vote if Nixon resigned. They quickly answered no.

Special Prosecutor Jaworski agreed to let Vice President Ford know when and if he intended to proceed against Nixon. Jerry Ford could be counted on. For more than two decades, when Nixon needed him, Ford had been there. He had helped kill the House Banking and Currency Committee's Watergate investigation in October 1972. Ford "understood," and, in case he forgot, Nixon must have had the former House minority leader's voice on those tape recordings.

On Thursday, August 8, 1974, Nixon spent a final, fitful evening in the White House. To the nation's commentators, this really was "agony." Despite Tom Paine and Proverbs, they had put their trust in princes. Nixon admitted no guilt. He was "conciliatory." Only CBS commentator Roger Mudd seemed to understand that confessed felons are *supposed* to be conciliatory. Some of Nixon's judgments "were wrong." His departure was for the "good of the country." He was a loser, not a "quitter." His "political base" had disappeared.

The next morning, Gerald Rudolph Ford appeared at the door of his Alexandria, Virginia, home dressed in his bathrobe. He picked up the newspaper, waved to the cameras (and to all of us), went into his kitchen, and fixed breakfast. Later he waved, climbed into an automobile, and went to work. Those were the finest moments of his administration.

We watched as hordes of Secret Service men, deferential television and newspaper reporters, generals and house servants, foreign leaders and congressmen, old and new friends, turned good old Jerry into "Mr. President."

To some, Impeachment was "a triumph of the system." But Nixon remained unimpeached and unprosecuted. As the Prince of San Clemente fled Washington, the trucks that had driven up to the White House to transport away his blackmailer's treasure-trove of tapes left empty. During the next two years the thousands of conversations remained in Ford's possession, unsought and unlistened to by the prosecutors, the courts, and the Congress. But even today, lawyers express pride in their justice system, in their special prosecutors, Justice Department, and House Judiciary Committee. And even the judges had suppressed "pretrial," and therefore, *preelection* knowledge of the facts.

A few reporters and Sam Ervin said no, and that is how the national jury learned.

From conservative Ol' Sam, during the summer of 1973, the people learned more about their Constitution than all of their law schools had taught their lawyers during the preceding fifty years. The people learned, but some of their lawyers would never learn. Long after the Ervin hearings, Henry Petersen told the senator, "While . . . everybody is equal before the law . . . not everybody can be treated equally, and that applies to senators and congressmen and government officials. . . . I hope Justice is not blind. I do not apply it blindly. I can tell you."

The Watergate case was a failure of justice. The triumph belongs to the people.

〰〰〰〰〰〰

For one month there was a freshness on the land. We again understood that truthfulness was more important than brilliance. Of Ford, the cynics laughed, "Honest but dumb; can't chew gum and . . ."

But even the cynics seemed proud.

Then Ford pardoned Nixon!

He said he had made no deal.*

---

*Soon Ford admitted he had lied to us "in the national interest" when he told us that he had not known that Nixon was about to resign. I remembered Ford's confirmation hearings. Asked by ranking minority member, doughy, doughty Edward Hutchinson of Michigan, if he would "shade the facts in the national interest" and if it wouldn't be better to remain "comfortably silent,"

A week later, *The New York Times* reported Nixon's remark to White House physician Dr. Walter R. Tkach: "If I go into the hospital, I'll never come out alive."

He placed his life in the hands of his private physician, a personal supporter since the early 1950s. Suffering from phlebitis, Nixon refused to enter a California naval facility where the government would have picked up tens of thousands of dollars of medical bills.

Three months had passed since I heard Charles Colson tell Richard Bast, "You won't believe this . . . people who haven't been in the White House won't believe it, but the President is scared as hell, . . . he's weak and under attack . . . he's frightened. He's afraid to alienate the military and foreign policy establishment."

Ford carefully responded. "[I]f a person can't for national security reasons tell the whole stóry accurately . . . it would be better to withhold the information, but Presidents, secretaries of defense, secretaries of state, and other top officials don't always have that opportunity. . . ." They "may have to make statements that they might have preferred not to make."

So it went with candor. And freshness.

22

It was the desire for national security and the desperate efforts to avoid disclosure which turned ironies and preposterous non-sequiturs into our national reality. So many leads. So few people willing to follow them. So much "national security" to beguile us all. At every stage the CIA and Howard Hughes were common to the case. When you wade through facts rather than tiptoe around them as though they were mines, you stumble over them. If you really want them to, they sometimes sail up to your dock. And that is almost how "one of the nation's best-kept secrets," the Glomar *Explorer*, arrived and offered itself to me as the one certain way to publicly link Hughes to the CIA.

~~~~~~~

Destin is a tiny Florida fishing village which took root in snow-white sand as naturally as the native sea grass, palmetto and yucca plants, hickory, pine, magnolia, and centuries-old, weather-gnarled live oak trees which line the high bluff of East Pass Lagoon. Nearby Choctawhatchee Bay flows into the Gulf of Mexico. For more than 100 miles of the panhandle, East Pass provides the only safe harbor and passageway from the Gulf into the Intra-Coastal Waterway.

The beach glistens in the sun, the clear water turns exquisite shades of green and blue, and game fish entice swarms of summer visitors from Atlanta, Memphis, and "the Magic City"— Birmingham.

Camille was an infant when she first went there. When I was sixteen, my family brought me. For thirty years Destin changed little. Now condominiums have begun their inevitable rise from the beach and a spot of skyline which mimics Manhattan invites "progress."

In Destin, in early July, I read in the *Pensacola News-Journal* that Exxon's leased ship, the Glomar *Grand Banks,* was to drill the first exploratory well forty miles offshore. I shouted to Camille. Congress fiddles while Nixon gives away the oceans! They belong to all of us! They should set up a public corporation like TVA to own and drill for oil!

"Glomar"—"Glomar?" Where had I heard that word? Glomar? Glomar? Glomar?

Of course. The Colson tape. Bast corroborated. Colson had said, Hughes, "is the biggest single contractor of the CIA. They do a lot of their contract-out work like . . . satellites, this new global marine, this Glomar Express, this new oceanographic vehicle is CIA."

John Crewdson of *The New York Times* checked out the word *Glomar,* an abbreviation for Global Marine, Inc. Its stock was listed on the New York Exchange. Crewdson ran the corporate names through the newspaper's computer. Next he went to the Securities and Exchange Commission. I sent Denise Leary Reston from my office.

Floating in a sea of annual reports, they each found accounts of the Glomar *Explorer*—the "deep sea—mining" part of Global Marine's worldwide, oil-drilling fleet.

One of the men charged with protecting oil and our other vital national interests was William E. Colby, the slight, squint-eyed, bookkeeper type who carried his Princeton education and

Catholic choirboy manner with him to Vietnam and, from there, to the top of the CIA. In South Vietnam he had overseen the Phoenix Program, which tolerated political assassinations. At his confirmation hearings Colby had said he considered "the overthrow of President Diem one of the real disasters that occurred . . . out there." But the real disaster was Colby's Vietnam Phoenix Program, which fingered that tiny nation's "Communist infrastructure"—thousands of talented young leaders—an entire generation of them.

After July 28, 1972, Colby served as Watergate case liaison between the CIA and the Justice Department. A highly skilled pragmatic man of the "real world," he testified that it was his duty to convince Silbert of the "limited nature" of the CIA's involvement in Watergate. Colby said he and Helms were concerned that "too much noise . . . [would be] made about the peripheral details of CIA's activities which in any possible way could be connected with the Watergate."

After the guilty pleas of Hunt and the Cuban-Americans, the CIA's problems disappeared into jail. Later Helms was exiled into the Iranian ambassadorship. His successor at the CIA, James R. Schlesinger, became Secretary of Defense, and the CIA's Watergate case liaison man, Colby, a former ACLU cooperating attorney, ascended into the directorship of Central Intelligence.

He was there when I set out to prove that the "Hughes" interests (and perhaps the entity) and those of the CIA were the same.

~~~~~~~~

If he was alive and sane, Howard R. Hughes was the most secure man in the world—better protected than Henry Kissinger. Transported in the dead of night, slipped through customs, secluded on the top floors of resort hotels, in touch with his closest employees by telephone or scrawled messages on yellow pads, surrounded by a cadre of Mormons and private guards, he seemed impregnable.

Some said he was basket-case crazy—with long hair, long beard, long fingernails, and Kleenex boxes on his feet for shoes.

If he was insane, then we had approached the ultimate national absurdity. We had deliberately placed "Our National Security" in the sharp talons of a stark-raving madman!

When a newspaper reporter told me he had heard that there was a labor dispute on board the Glomar *Explorer*, I sent lawyers Denise Leary Reston and Mary Ellen Gale to the National Labor Relations Board. They were to find the transcript of a hearing involving Global Marine.

The first report came back. "Can't find it."

Second report. "Doesn't exist." (As may have been the case with Hughes.)

Third report. "Found it!" (As was never the case with Hughes.)

From the transcript it appeared that even crew members on the ship's test run knew next to nothing about the ship or what it was designed to do. The 35,000-ton vessel was 618 feet long and 115 feet wide—too wide to pass through the Panama Canal. It had sailed south. Off Nicaragua, where Howard Hughes was said to reside, it dropped anchor. So fearful of earthquakes that he was willing to drop tens of thousands of dollars on a political campaign if LBJ would only end nuclear testing in Nevada, the unfindable Hughes, then allegedly holed up in a Managua hotel, was found by an earthquake in Nicaragua in December 1972. If he still existed and was sane, I wondered, what did he know about nuclear testing and earthquakes which the rest of us didn't know?

Proceeding from disaster to disaster, the Glomar *Explorer* dropped anchor off Valparaiso, Chile. By checking average speed against days in transit, Denise Reston estimated that it could have anchored on the very day that Chile's president, Salvador Allende Gossens, was killed.

There was a "hole" in the ship, termed a "moon pool," and around it there were secret watertight compartments. According to public documents the ship could drill twenty thousand feet beneath the sea; suck matter from the ocean floor; ride out the fiercest storms by using its marine hydraulic system; drill through a thousand feet into the core of the earth; cut through ice floes, and . . .

Gene Roberts, of the *Philadelphia Inquirer*, produced articles about the ship's construction at the Sun Shipyard in nearby Chester, Pennsylvania. From Bill Kovach of *The New York Times*, and Les Whitten, Jack Anderson's ace reporter, there came other bits of information. From Jack Nelson at the *Los Angeles Times* came a description of a submersible companion barge the size of a football field, and stories from Honolulu newspapers which told of the ship's tight-lipped 150-man crew-cut crew which had arrived on a hush-hush, Hughes charter flight.

But the Russians had to know what the Glomar *Explorer* was. And what it was up to. Satellites, submarines, and sensors—even fishing vessels—must have told them. As with the plans to escalate the Vietnam War and to bomb Cambodia, only the American people were kept in the dark.

By now the American people did know that the CIA had a secret air force, Special Forces, and secretly recruited mercenary armies. Logically the CIA would have a secret navy. Nixon had placed "oceans policy" under the National Security Council. Our military defenses had silently slipped under seas. And as the domino dictators of Southeast Asia fell, the Maginot Line—minded men of containment were arming the islands of the North Pacific. By now the National Oceanic and Atmospheric Administration (NOAA) had been put in charge of weather, oceanography, and related research. NOAA ran the sea-grants college program. Other "private" research institutions were underwritten by secret funders like the Defense Advance Research Projects Agency, which had developed filmless cameras, laser beams which could turn corners, and computers which could take oral commands and a limited set of orders from electroencephalograph (brain) waves. And the world's number-one "scientific" vessel, the Glomar *Challenger*, had been built with a $90-million National Science Foundation grant.

I learned that "weather war" is the use of short-term

phenomena such as tornadoes, hurricanes, tidal waves, fog, and lightning. And that "climate war"—referrring to long-range weather change, like one degree per year in the average temperature—is the covert alteration of a nation's food supply. Scientific miracles like alternating and direct current, even light switches, did not come to me easily. But I understood how secrecy subverts scientific research, which, to better mankind, must be freely published. For national security, reputable scientists hedged, concealed, and lied. Over the years we had learned, almost too late, that nuclear fallout threatens milk; nuclear waste threatens water; wastewater threatens earthquakes; and fast breeder reactors, and some say, even aerosol sprays, threaten all mankind.

As secret computer networks stored data about the ocean's currents, the wind's speed, the earth's temperature and its tremors, and environmentalists fretted about holes in the ozone layer, 1,000 American objects twirled silently across the sky, listening, looking, sensing, broadcasting, waiting for commands. Few men knew whether there were nuclear warheads within them. And Hughes—a crazy, basket case if there was a Hughes—was one of those men.

On Friday, February 7, 1975, Jack Nelson called me. He told me that they had a source "in Los Angeles who said there was a burglary at Hughes's Summa Corporation's office. Hughes's files were stolen, including the CIA contract on that ship. They say it was after a sunken Russian submarine."

A lawsuit was pending between Robert Maheu and Howard Hughes. Maheu had subpoenaed Hughes's handwritten memoranda. The burglary appeared to have been an inside job. Hughes's employees had covered up. They had lied to the police about the missing items. A Los Angeles state court grand jury was investigating.

Nelson had a copy of my Hughes files. He went to work. At 2:30 P.M., when the *Los Angeles Times* small final edition hit the stands, a double-bannered headline proclaimed: U.S. REPORTED AFTER RUSS SUB.

Later another story came out. Before the 9:30 P.M. deadline for Saturday morning's newspaper, the CIA had reached Franklin D. Murphy, chairman of the board of the Times-Mirror Corporation, one of the nation's most powerful newspaper publishing houses and parent of the *Los Angeles Times*. Murphy had seen no conflict between his publishing position and service on the CIA-overseeing Foreign Intelligence Advisory Board. But he issued no instructions. He suggested that the caller talk to William F. Thomas, the newspaper's top editor.

In the next edition, Nelson's story was moved to page 18. After telephone calls from the CIA to the *Washington Post* and *The New York Times*, the story sank.

Detailed briefings followed. Top CIA personnel explained how a giant claw, used to retrieve submarines, was carried in the submersible football field-sized barge. When it enveloped a sunken submarine, its grip was unbreakable. As the submarine approached the surface, its weight pulled the ship low into the water. If the claw had broken, the *Explorer* would have popped corklike out of the ocean. The crew would have been killed. Later, the CIA explained that the unbreakable claw had not broken. Later still they explained that it had broken. Some said they had gotten the whole submarine. The CIA said two-thirds of it had broken loose. I suggested that Colby be asked if the ship had popped two-thirds of the way out of the water.

Colby did not ask newspapers to kill the story forever. He merely wanted it killed for a little while, until the CIA got its claw on the other two-thirds of the submarine.

Perhaps the Glomar *Explorer*, first presented as a deep sea drilling and mining ship, was really an international harvester of sunken submarines. But cover stories are designed to sound reasonable. To me there were other more logical uses for a $250 million to $550 million ship. The American people would have approved of an expensive vessel to salvage our own sunken submarines, to find out why they sank, to keep the Russians from salvaging them, and to recover our own nuclear warheads and sailors' bodies. That purpose could have been presented openly in a request for appropriations. But I knew that sometimes CIA burglars put things in. They plant them—like forged documents in an office safe or, perhaps, like nuclear missiles in ocean-floor silos, or sensors in the deep seabeds.

We and the Russians have solemnly promised each other not to emplace nuclear warheads in the skies and ocean floors. That makes it almost certain that both nations have placed them there. Perhaps because we pay CIA men to lie to us and to the world, top executives of the nation's mightiest newspapers consider it their patriotic duty to believe them.

Except at the *Philadelphia Inquirer*. There, top editor Gene Roberts assigned Pulitzer Prize winners Donald L. Bartlett and James B. Steele to cover Hughes. They didn't break the Glomar *Explorer* story, but they undertook the most thorough and painstaking search of the subterranean Hughes-government empire, and they are still at work on it.

Elsewhere great reporters had to fight top management. Seymour Hersh had a whiff of the story before the *Los Angeles Times* broke it. He took my files, talked with Colby and others. Then he wrote and filed his story. *The New York Times* typeset and held it. It was fit to print—but not first.

In the middle of this struggle, I flew to New York to meet with the ACLU's executive committee. If I couldn't cause newspapers to publish the story, I expected the ACLU, in defense of a truly free press, to print it *and* the story of the press cover-up. During the meeting a Washington lawyer casually asked me if I had looked into liability under the Espionage Act. Chairman Ennis commented that he hoped everyone's personal life was in good order, that "The CIA can be tough," and "Chuck, you lived in a company town." Later he said, "When you find out who the CIA representative on our board is I hope you'll let me know. " I replied, "I still live in a company town," and "Ed, you'll be the very first to know."

On Monday, March 17, at 5:00 P.M., Colby telephoned Nelson and reported to him on "our conspiracy." He really believed that Nelson wanted the story suppressed. I laughed when I learned that the Director of Central Intelligence didn't even know who his own co-conspirators were.

Colby told Nelson he had "locked up CBS and the Public Broadcasting System." The wire services and networks had agreed "to telephone him first if they ran into any story about the CIA and the oceans." He chuckled and said that with responsible journalists "in tow" the pressure was "on others not to be irresponsible." Then, "if the story spreads to the crazies" they won't be believed. They "lack credibility."

By Tuesday, I had the story caroming around Washington and New York like a runaway billiard ball. I telephoned columnists, reporters, and editors. Higher-ups and lower-downs. I sent packets thick with documents to prove the story to newspaperman after newspaperman. My son, Charles, twenty, had taken one packet to an old friend, the *Washington Post*'s Robert E. L. Baker, by then an executive rather than a reporter. Baker scrawled a note, attached it to the packet, and forwarded it to the appropriate editor. Later a reporter told me he had written, "Any reporter worth his salt will do this story." But none did.

Charles had met great reporters from great newspapers. He understood their love of the truth. He himself wrote well and had a weekly column published in forty student newspapers. Now he was learning that freedom of the press means nothing unless the very wealthy men who own newspapers want to use it, and that when it comes to "national security," newspaper executives, like lawyers, speak reverentially of "responsibility" and "self-restraint."

I left the office as discouraged as I find it possible to get, and angry. I had done almost everything I could do. Still, tomorrow, one more "last" try. . . .

That evening the message came from Les Whitten: Stay off the telephone. Anderson's going to run the Glomar story! Tell no one and stand by. We may need to talk with you. We'll be on the air at nine o'clock.

"One call, Les. To my son. He's back in Tuscaloosa."

At 9:00 P.M. I listened to Anderson's radio bulletin. At 10:00

P.M. he was on television. The next morning the nation really began to learn about the workings of the Intelligence-Industrial Complex. Their attention captured, I could move on. Now others would investigate and write about the link between Hughes, the CIA, and Watergate.

Of course the newspapers which had agreed to suppress the story editorially praised the CIA for doing the job it had been created to do. They attacked Jack Anderson for doing the job that the newspapers had been created to do. As they justified their cover-ups, they ignored the lies which the CIA had told congressmen in order to secretly acquire the funds with which to build the ship. They ignored the special treatment which Hughes had received from the Internal Revenue Service; the failure of the Securities and Exchange Commission to move against Global Marine, Inc., for violation of disclosure laws; the repeated failures of the Justice Department to extradite Hughes, to enforce subpoenas against him, to indict him for crimes, and to prosecute for perjury those who had filed false affidavits of ownership with the coast guard. They ignored the effect of nonenforcement of the law upon the lawmen and the corporate lawyers (introduced as CIA men by an FBI agent) who had induced the tax assessor of Los Angeles County to leave the ship off the tax rolls.

The cold war had turned the beliefs of liberal editors inside out. They never questioned their own values. Instead they righteously condemned the man who published first. As it was with the editors and publishers, and with the men of Watergate, so it was with most of the rest of us. National life was based on the "need to know" principle of World War II security. Bits and pieces, complicated puzzle parts, even the secrets of the universe, when finally fit together, provide simple answers. But they remained scattered. When even good men—scholars, lawyers, judges, editors, and public officials—reached to touch them, something called "national security" caused them to hesitate and draw back.

Well-motivated men like the Cuban-Americans had followed enunciated national policy. As cold-war warriors, these otherwise sane men had carried out insane orders, orders couched in euphemisms which made them easy to take. To them burglaries were "surreptitious entries," and "cover stories" were "cover-ups," which is just another way of saying "lies."

23

Now we know. There is no way for us not to know. What was true in Birmingham is true in Washington—and everywhere else in the world. Governments grow. The ultra-rich get richer. They purchase governments, use them to lock out competitors and, together with bought bureaucracies they cheat the poor.

Our national teachers were Presidents who lied. We liberals lied to ourselves and euphemized. When Richard Nixon lied, we got him. When John Kennedy lied we forgave him. When Lyndon Johnson lied we euphemized him by terming his lies the "credibility gap."

From Vietnam to West Point, the Assassination Generation learned to lie. Children lied to draft boards, cheated in the Boy Scouts, fixed the Soap Box Derby, and termed thefts "rip-offs."

Residence windows are barred like cells. The middle class has fled the streets, to lock themselves in as they lock the underworld out. And the ultra-rich—light years away from poorly lit streets—get richer.

Our worst crimes are committed within the world's bureaucracies in the plush offices of multinational, and therefore by definition, unloyal, companies. Above party, patriotism, and philosophy, the loyalty of millions of organization men runs to those who occupy governmental and private executive suites. From there orders are sent to millions of bright, bland Jeb Magruders who really do believe that our worst crimes are "p.r. problems" which require "the services of a lawyer."

The Bay of Pigs invasion had been that kind of a crime. The CIA censored advance notice of it out of the newspapers. Tad Szulc of *The New York Times* wrote the story. His newspaper altered it and played it down. Later Szulc wrote, "It was like plumping Disneyland in the middle of Times Square and then asking newspapermen to obligingly look the other way." Which they did.

The CIA-backed Cuban Revolutionary Council hired Lem Jones Associates, Inc., 280 Madison Avenue, New York, New York, OR 9-5636, to issue press releases. Our country retained lawyer Adlai E. Stevenson, its ambassador to the United Nations, to tell the world that our airplanes were really Cuban air-force planes stolen by defectors. Of course Castro knew how many airplanes he had. Castro could count. So lawyer Stevenson was mortified to discover that he had been lied to, not by the Cubans, but by his own government.

At the August 28, 1963, march on Washington, Martin King and John Lewis stood together. Martin dreamed "that one day on the red hills of Georgia the sons of former slaves and the sons of former slave owners will be able to sit down together at the table of brotherhood."

But John attacked the indictment of nine SNCC leaders "in Albany, Georgia, not by Dixiecrats but by the federal government. . . ." He called the indictment "part of a conspiracy . . ." and asked, "[W]hich side is the federal government on?"

Three years passed. When John read that "treasonous" Vietnam statement, Julian Bond stood up for it. So did Martin. The lower federal court said it aligned SNCC with blacks "in the Dominican Republic, the Congo, South Africa, Rhodesia. . . ."

Another decade passed. We "learned" of our government's

efforts to kill foreign leaders, including Patrice Lumumba. His crime was described in a September 13, 1960, CIA cable to Leopoldville. LUMUMBA TALENTS AND DYNAMISM APPEAR OVERRIDING . . . IN OTHER WORDS EACH TIME LUMUMBA HAS OPPORTUNITY HAVE LAST WORD HE CAN SWAY EVENTS TO HIS ADVANTAGE.

In our own country, we had subtler ways to take that last word away from men of talent and dynamism.

What had been true in Birmingham was true everyplace else in the world. Like the leading citizens of Birmingham, too many leading liberals "didn't care enough to know."

After Howard Levy wrote to that intelligence sergeant in Vietnam and asked, "[W]ho are you fighting for?" Levy was jailed. That was in 1967. At Levy's trial, Donald Duncan and Robin Moore told us about our "assassination teams." Peter Bourne, and later Tony Herbert, told us how our officials reacted to their reports of war crimes. Two years later, in Muhammad Ali's case, the FBI's wiretap on Martin King was revealed.

In 1975, the leading liberal in the Senate, and its nicest man, Philip Hart of Michigan, returned from the hospital where he had been treated for cancer. As the Select Committee on Intelligence heard testimony about the federal government's war against Martin King, Hart faced the cameras and said: "I have been told for years by, among others, some of my own family that this is exactly what the bureau was doing. . . . I assured them that they were wrong. . . . I did not believe it."

Of the few assassination efforts which they studied, liberal senators expressed gratitude that each attempt had failed. These Keystone Cops adventures were unauthorized "hanky-panky," clearly showing, said the senators, that Americans just weren't good killers.

When liberal Senator Frank Church called the CIA a "rogue elephant," I heard the phrase "off on an enterprise of their own." I sent Church a gift cookbook, *How to Cook a Rogue Elephant and 300 Other Recipes.* He thanked me kindly. But he fretted when he discovered that the Company had enough shellfish toxin to kill 100,000 people. He said that was enough to destroy a whole town. Administered by a special dart gun and unnoticed upon injection, deadly in twenty seconds, and undetectable in an autopsy, it wasn't designed to kill a whole town. It was designed to kill dynamic and talented leaders—one at a time, Senator. One at a time.

More deadly to democracy is public relations. As with Birmingham's leaders, Washington's leaders are concerned about "our image."

After the despised John D. Rockefeller hired public relations man Ivy Lee, the granddaddy of the multinationals was pictured distributing dimes to children. Time turned dimes into dollars, and public relations into a respectable way of life.

After the Sixteenth Street Baptist Church bombing, Birmingham's leaders hired a New York public relations firm. Its owner was quoted as saying to his staff, "If you can sell Birmingham, you can sell anything." He quickly corrected the newspapers. He had said, "If you can sell anything, you can sell Birmingham."

In our society, when the risks of truth are too great, even good men lie. To the charge that he stole, Jim Folsom could afford to tell the voters, "I plead guilty." In 1954 he did just that and swept to victory. But during his second (and final) term (1955–59) he vetoed segregation bills. And, worst luck, he was charged with entertaining Harlem's flashy black congressman, Adam Clayton Powell, at the governor's mansion.

"They say I drank Scotch with him at the governor's mansion." After a pause Big Jim added, "Now ya'll know I don't drink Scotch."

But we all knew he did drink Scotch.

We learned of FBI Director Hoover's May 10, 1962, memorandum which memorialized his meeting with Attorney General Kennedy. "Maheu [Hoover described the Howard Hughes employee as though he were a stranger rather than a former agent of the FBI] had been hired by the CIA to approach

[Mafia leader Sam ("Momo")] Giancana with a proposition of paying some one hundred fifty thousand dollars to hire gunmen to go into Cuba and kill Castro. He further stated that the CIA admitted having assisted Maheu in making [sic] the bugging of Las Vegas."

When the Senate sought Giancana to testify, he was assassinated in the basement of his Chicago home. Soon his Mafia sidekick, John Rosselli, who did testify (in secret), was found inside a fifty-five-gallon drum bobbing in Florida's coastal waters near Key Biscayne.

And so it goes with public relations, elephantine memories, and rogues.

And so it went with Nixon, who believed "they all do it."

To those who had lost faith in democracy (and so many of them said, "They all do it") I could respond, "So what. We've got to start someplace." Perhaps that came from the stark reality of the Deep South during the civil rights and Vietnam War years, but many who agreed with me saw Nixon as an aberration and his impeachment as an ultimate answer. I did not. Nixon was a symptom, less an aberration than a caricature, a false conservative in a world run by liberals who want desperately to lie even to themselves.

〰〰〰〰〰

"How would you control Chuck Morgan?" was the question asked of Aryeh Neier when he negotiated his nomination to become the ACLU's executive director.

"With difficulty," he replied.

No one bothered to ask who wants to. Or why. And the roots of my beliefs are what my parents taught me. Tell the truth. Be your own man. A "proclivity for independent action" is your birthright. And your duty.

In the South we redistributed justice and the vote. But we never moved against great wealth. As Thomas Jefferson knew, no rights can be secure for those whose work depends upon the whims of others. For years the ACLU had retreated from "forty-acres-and-a-mule" questions of economic rights.

It still does not recognize the birthright of every person to food, shelter, clothing, health, and legal care—simply because they are born here; that employees have rights against the "private" corporate governments for which they work; that people should have freedom not to travel, the right not to be forced by economic necessity into a faraway city's suburbs or a big city's slum-ghettoes; that it is people who have a right to the land, not ever-growing corporations; that the First Amendment requires the dismantling of communications conglomerates; that corporations ought not have the same rights as people; that multinationals must obey the people's laws; that dictators and kings and sheikhs and shahs never can be allies of democracy; and that it is the rights of the people of the world and not those of Oil and Steel or the pleasure of the rulers of antidemocratic powers which are our vital national interests. But to secure these rights we must first move against the company cops. And now there came that time. . . .

Assuming the noblest motives, I knew that a struggle against the subterranean government would bring opposition inside the organization. First I set out to alter the ACLU's policies. After that we could go to the people, to teach them the inherent effect of the peacetime spy system on a free society. As Watergate burglar Hunt testified, he spent most of his "adult life abroad involved in activities . . . quite clearly illegal under U.S. law, . . . which were . . . encouraged by our government . . . which . . . trained people extensively for it, paid large sums of money, for just the type of expertise that . . . [he] exercise[d] in behalf of the executive branch of the government."

Sanctioned assassinations, blackmail, bribes, burglaries, and other low crimes abroad lead to that kind of lawlessness at home. But it was sanctioned lying by elected officials which was depriving democratic government of its legitimacy. All other crimes are subordinate to and dependent upon sanctioned lying, for they can only be committed under cover.

Thomas Jefferson believed that to govern themselves the people must have access to the truth. But the very existence of peacetime human spy networks meant that Presidents had to lie to keep them secret. Satellites and submarines had rendered them useless and unreliable absurdities, but the important reason to fire the spies was that their very existence was wrong. Understanding that Russian and Chinese bureaucrats were no less warlike than our own, we had to fire our spies in self-defense. For sanctioned lying and clandestine government had done more to destroy the democracy from within than had domestic and foreign Communists.

The simple answer was to make it a crime for nonelected federal officials to lie to the people. It was a crime for the people to lie to government officials about their income. The ACLU should propose the same sentence for lying to the people.

Aryeh Neier disagreed. His experience differed from mine. In 1967, when secret CIA funding of the National Student Association and other liberal organizations was disclosed, Neier contended that it was not a "civil liberties issue."

He did favor an end to the secret funding of secret wars, mail openings, and the like and, of course, assassinations. He sought to abolish the agencies. But I believe that with the spy system, that is impossible, for the system is inherently corrupt.

The ACLU board referred my proposed policy to a committee. Neier won there seven to four. At its February 1976, meeting the board agreed with me by a vote of thirty-two to eighteen.

On March 4, Neier wrote me that he was still "troubled about your—and our—proposal for a statute against lying by government officials. . . ." He was displeased at "my" and "our" policy favoring the appointment of a special prosecutor to proceed against the criminal misconduct of intelligence agents.

I began to plan the campaign.

While he was still governor of Georgia I had talked with Jimmy Carter about his presidential campaign. Camille and friends of ours, including Peter Bourne, were for him. I was attracted by his decency as governor. He rejected the values of Washington-based blandly "liberal" politicians and secret government. He understood the "Watergate issue." During the primary campaign he alluded to not being from Washington, to not lying, and to not being a lawyer. Those phrases translated into one word—*Watergate!*

And he was a southerner. In 1960 in Alabama I had been chairman of the Kennedy Speakers Campaign. I remembered the concern over Kennedy's Catholicism and his accent. Now I heard from northern liberals the phrases about Carter which I had heard southern white Protestants utter about Kennedy.

One afternoon in the home of a friend on Capitol Hill, a stranger from New York told me he could never vote for a person with a southern accent; he could never vote for a southern governor; he could never . . . I replied, "That's bigotry. . . " I recounted that conversation to friends. Roy Reed of *The New York Times* heard about it. He telephoned to ask if he could quote me. He did so in a *New York Times* article in which I clearly spoke for myself, not the ACLU. I told Reed that northern establishment liberals were opposed to Carter because they didn't have "their hooks in him." They feared loss of "access."

A letter from Neier arrived. He suggested that I be more inhibited in my remarks. I wrote back, no. He wrote asking me what steps I was taking to further separate my already clearly separated views from those of ACLU.

At that board meeting in 1964, Roger Baldwin had commented about having sent a man south who lasted six weeks. That was not my problem. For six hundred weeks—twelve years—I had been an employee of the ACLU. Its members were my friends. I liked them. Camille said it spoke well for them that I had lasted so long. In the civil rights and antiwar movements, the Watergate case and impeachment, I had become deeply involved long before the organization had. Each time the ACLU board and its members had moved with me into swirling uncharted turmoil. And mass membership. Again I could win before the board. But when bureaucratic struggles come too often, you lose time even when you win. And time is all we have.

My thoughts kept returning to the days before the ACLU, to

Birmingham, to all the times when for one "poor devil" or another I ran against the winds of prejudice and bureaucracy, beginning on that lonely, long-ago night when I broke ranks and left behind me the John Dean–Jeb Magruder American Way of Life and military school.

～～～～～

Discussing Nixon's power to deny documents and witnesses to the Watergate Committee, Kleindienst told Dean, "Your boss has got the army."

Haldeman proudly said he "tried to run a tight ship. . . ."

Gray was well prepared to serve on it. He said, "In the navy I was trained in, you said, 'Aye, aye, sir,' when given an order."

Hunt said, "My twenty-six-year record of service to this country predisposed me to accept orders and instructions without question and without debate." He felt "that the country . . . which directed me to carry out the Watergate entry is punishing me for the very thing it trained and directed me to do."

Barker summed it up. "I was not there to think. I was there to follow orders, not to think."

"Why," Nixon asked Dean, "did Petersen play the game so straight with us?" Dean replied, "Because Petersen is a soldier."

Petersen put it differently: "Keep your eye on the mark," he ordered.

As William H. Whyte, Jr., wrote in *The Organization Man,* young men believe that "to make a living these days, you must do what somebody else wants you to do." They rationalize that into "an inherently good proposition." So their world is colored shades-of-gray and the day-to-day fight "lacks heroic cast."

On November 11, 1975, William C. Sullivan, who had headed up the FBI's Domestic Intelligence Division, told a Senate committee of the effect of the cold war. "We never freed ourselves from that psychology we were indoctrinated with, right after Pearl Harbor, you see. . . . It was just like a soldier in the battlefield. . . . We did what we were expected to do. It became a part of our thinking, a part of our personality."

But not of mine.

On April 9, 1976, I wrote Neier, "You ask me what steps I am taking to correct the impression that when I am 'identified' by my employment I 'appear to speak for the organization.' The step I am taking is to resign." *

That day the ACLU board reinstated Elizabeth Gurley Flynn. She had been expelled for thirty-six years. And dead for twelve.

And, so it goes.

〜〜〜〜〜〜

I had been brought up on my father's salary. And, in return for that salary, he (and we) believed in the Company. In Birmingham I had learned that entire cities as well as lives were run by the Company. Then I learned about Alabama, the South, and other underdeveloped nations.

In 1955, when I was twenty-five, I made my first trip to Washington. After that, on every such journey, on the way back to the National Airport and Birmingham, I had my taxicab stop at the Lincoln and Jefferson memorials. I walked up the steps and stood for a few moments drawn by the majesty of memory and dreams of what a people, who knew that there was a difference between right and wrong, might make of this nation and the world. Back then, those monuments gave me the feeling that there really was a United States.

Like Martin King at the Lincoln Memorial, I believed there would be that day "on the red hills of Georgia. . . ." During the 1976 Democratic convention, Martin's father gave the benediction to "children of former slaves . . . slave owners" who nominated a President from Plains, Georgia, just north of "Allbenny," over near Americus where the SNCC kids worked. Then came November, and the black and white voters of the Deep South—even Mississippi—put him over the top.

The souls of those who sang and clapped out freedom's songs

---

*After I resigned, the national constituency of the ACLU elected me to their board. I ran first in a field of twenty-six. Then their board elected me to their executive committee.

during their too-brief lives beckon and say: Find your own answers and move on, move on.

They tell us that which we know. Our government had gone
from the Bay of Pigs to Camranh Bay; from high-flying U-2 spy
airplanes to the bombing of Cambodia; from Disneyland to Disneyworld. There had been no Camelot. Yet, it is we who will
win. There is still time for democrats who remember the simple
lessons taught us by the lives of our friends and the words of our
Founders and our mothers and our fathers. Confront the evil.
Risk truth. Trust the people. Tell them the truth.

Index

339